Flesh Becomes Word

Studies in Violence, Mimesis, and Culture

SERIES EDITOR
William A. Johnsen

The Studies in Violence, Mimesis, and Culture Series examines issues related to the nexus of violence and religion in the genesis and maintenance of culture. It furthers the agenda of the Colloquium on Violence and Religion, an international association that draws inspiration from René Girard's mimetic hypothesis on the relationship between violence and religion, elaborated in a stunning series of books he has written over the last forty years. Readers interested in this area of research can also look to the association's journal, *Contagion: Journal of Violence, Mimesis, and Culture.*

Flesh Becomes Word

A LEXICOGRAPHY OF
THE SCAPEGOAT OR,
THE HISTORY OF AN IDEA

David Dawson

Michigan State University Press · *East Lansing*

Copyright © 2013 by David Dawson

♾ The paper used in this publication meets the minimum requirements of ANSI/NISO Z39.48-1992 (R 1997) (Permanence of Paper).

 Michigan State University Press
East Lansing, Michigan 48823-5245

Printed and bound in the United States of America.

19 18 17 16 15 14 13   1 2 3 4 5 6 7 8 9 10

LIBRARY OF CONGRESS CATALOGING-IN-PUBLICATION DATA
Dawson, David.
Flesh becomes word : a lexicography of the scapegoat or, the history of an idea / David Dawson.
p. cm.—(Studies in violence, mimesis, and culture series)
Includes bibliographical references (p.   ).
ISBN 978-1-60917-349-4 (ebook)—ISBN 978-1-61186-063-4 (pbk. : alk. paper)
1. Scapegoat (The English word) 2. English language—Etymology. 3. English language—Religious aspects. 4. Scapegoat in literature. I. Title.
PE1599.S33D39 2013
422—dc23
2012028339

Book design by Charlie Sharp, Sharp Des!gns, Lansing, Michigan
Cover design by David Drummond, Salamander Design, www.salamanderhill.com.
Cover image of "The Goat" is a relief engraving by Barry Moser from the Pennyroyal Caxton Bible, 1999, page 90, and is used by permission of the artist. All rights reserved.

g green press INITIATIVE Michigan State University Press is a member of the Green Press Initiative and is committed to developing and encouraging ecologically responsible publishing practices. For more information about the Green Press Initiative and the use of recycled paper in book publishing, please visit *www.greenpressinitiative.org*.

Visit Michigan State University Press at *www.msupress.org*

For Clive and Silas

Contents

Preface

For it should be obvious that all that matters to a psychologist of morals is what has really existed and is attested by documents, the endless hieroglyphic record, so difficult to decipher, of our moral past.

—Friedrich Nietzsche, *On the Genealogy of Morals*

There is a not yet conscious knowledge of *what has been*: its advancement has the structure of awakening.

—Walter Benjamin, *The Arcades Project*

New evidence suggests the English word "scapegoat" was a portent of epochal passage in the dawn of the modern age, a sign in whose semantic evolution we may read the demise of religion and the advent of the secular world. By religion we understand an older, collective form of social existence and its metaphysical economy of propitiatory substitutions, something that begins to break up with the emergence of more democratic ideals (personal accountability, equality under the law, etc.) that are today so widely deemed to be self-evident their late historical emergence can pass unnoticed. To define religion in this way is to insist on an anthropological common denominator uniting pagan cult and Christian theology in a millennial process of religious efflorescence and collapse, a process that the history of our word serves to illuminate.

The *OED* tells us the word "scapegoat" was coined by William Tyndale for his 1530 translation of the Bible. It names "one of two goats that was chosen by lot to be sent alive into the wilderness, the sins of the people having been symbolically laid upon it." The Day of Atonement prescriptions in Leviticus 16 that describe the rite say the other goat was to be immolated. What precisely does the Levitical scapegoat signify? The answers proffered during a millennial history of typological interpretation clearly run to extremes. This is probably why the *OED* does not list the word's second denotation—"one who is blamed or punished for the sins of others"—as a figurative deployment of the first. Centuries of sharply divergent readings make it difficult to say precisely what the animal represents, and the Mosaic prescriptions are themselves too laconic, little indicating how the goat whose life is spared becomes a figure of victimization. That said, the word's second denotation obviously originates as a metaphor of some kind. As we shall see, a highly theologized reading of the Levitical scapegoat holds the key. In it the two most ancient and widely attested typological traditions coalesce to produce a new meaning, the one that is in such wide use today. The *OED* dates the earliest use of the scapegoat in this sense to 1824, erroneously, as our evidence will show.

A review of scholarly literature reveals a fair mix of fact and fiction about the word, its history, and meaning that have served to obscure the scapegoat's inaugural role in the making of the modern world. Recent polemic complicates the issue further, exploiting a suppositious history of the scapegoat's linguistic bastardization and increasingly promiscuous usage to pillory certain démodé theories of religion whose reckless comparativism allegedly split the word into competing senses, the second and more popular of which is decried as a source of error and confusion. Bradley McLean records his irritation at the widespread use of a Jewish technical designation to translate the Greek *pharmakos* as follows:

> It is a puzzling fact that this Jewish term has been universally employed for the description of *Greek* expulsion ceremonies. I can find no instance in any book where an author attempts to explain the application of the term 'scapegoat' to non-Jewish rituals. Despite the fact that not one of these Greek rites involves a goat, much less shares any genealogical connection with the Jewish cult, the intended meaning of the term is always taken to be self-evident.[1]

McLean's concerns are scholarly, lexical, and fastidious. He indicts "the practice of classifying a collective group of rituals by the name of one of that group's constituent members" as both "confusing and imprecise, for it presumes common features between the Levitical scapegoat and these other rituals without even specifying them or demonstrating the cogency of the parallel."[2] The term's overgeneralization is blamed on Sir James Frazer's *The Golden Bough* and the "anthropological theory" of René Girard, which, McLean says, decontextualize and compare elements from different religious systems in a "questionable way," without first understanding how they function within those systems.[3] Frazer is at fault because he packed one volume of *The Golden Bough*, entitled *The Scapegoat*, with "countless instances of irrational mass violence against individuals, from all periods of history, and every imaginable country," although the Leviticus scapegoat was no "victim of mob feeling" but carefully selected by the casting of lots.[4] There is here no "spontaneous, uncontrolled, irrational act of mass aggression" but instead a deliberate act "limited in scope for the achievement of a definite end."[5] According to McLean, Frazer's use of the term proved "decisive for general and learned usage alike,"[6] and the scapegoat thereby acquired "connotations which are foreign to its technical meaning."[7] Girard confuses matters further with a "universalist theory" of violence that uses the word to designate a "generative principle" in the foundation of human culture, thus saddling the scapegoat with even more "confused and value oriented connotations."[8]

The anthropologist Mary Douglas is similarly alert to the word's contradictory significations, noting that its "accepted meanings . . . are at variance with the original biblical piece in which the scapegoat figures."[9] As a verb in common usage, "to scapegoat" means to blame or persecute, and this sense has little to do with the Leviticus ritual, which lacks a punitive aspect. Douglas traces these meanings to the rite of the *pharmakos*, which does not involve goats, but to which the term "scapegoat" has been inextricably linked so that "when talking about scapegoats in everyday parlance we are drawing upon Greek rituals to rid the city of scum, discarded elements, useless and dirty people."[10] Frazer and others of his ilk are to blame. Their "indiscriminate comparisons" and "search for parallels" allowed the "Greek idea of riddance or elimination of evil to dominate the discussion."[11] Because the Leviticus rite is far richer in meanings, many of which militate against this "underlying principle," the time has come to restore the rite's polysemy and "honor the Levitical purification ceremony in its full integrity without importing assumptions from other similar seeming purification rites."[12] More importantly, we must ask whether any justification remains for the category "Scapegoat Rites."

Douglas will call Girard to account for deploying the term in its persecutory sense—a meaning "he cannot possibly get . . . from the biblical rite where the goat is not attacked, shamed or harmed"[13]—and for his comparativist approach, which ultimately betrays him by seeming to disclose a single idea underlying all religious phenomena. She summarizes it with evident distaste: "the idea that slaughter, blood and killing have always been the central element in religion, the main form of communication with the gods."[14] Among notable theorists of religion, Girard is closer to Burkert, with whom he shares a taste for the sanguinary and a rather cheerless view of human origins, although both alike succumb to the monomania that claimed Frazer.

> Walter Burkert said, "blood and violence lurk fascinatingly at the heart of religion," and claimed that sacrificial killing underlies the experience of the sacred. About the same time René Girard placed the same emphasis on human cruelty in *Violence and the Sacred.* . . . Yes, we must agree that humans tend to be violent and persecutory, and also that religion tends to be pervasive. We can agree that violence and religion will be likely to coincide in human history. But does that account for the basic experience of the sacred? With as much right others would offer different candidates for a basic religious experience: search for truth, longing for ecstatic union, the idea of an external moral imperative, the desire to make sense of existence, to experience a transcendent reality.[15]

The question is less how compelling Douglas's other candidates may be than whether we ought not consign them all to so much undiscoverable speculation on the meaning of life.[16] Douglas, like McLean, rules out big comparativist theories *in limine*.

If the scapegoat had become a pretext for the airing of more basic grievances over the nature of scholarly inquiry and the relative legitimacy of some questions, a number of which had clearly fallen into disfavor and were no longer deemed worth asking, it seemed wise for the purposes of this study to avoid philosophical disputes and begin instead with the historical record. Our guiding question would be, "How and when did the scapegoat acquire its metaphorical meaning?" A rapid review of the relevant literature reveals three main stages in the term's semantic history: it begins life as a ritual animal, spends sixteen centuries as a Christian typology, and ultimately wanders into the vernacular as an expression whose popularity and breadth of application quickly surpass that of its primary meaning. Both the scapegoat's long prehistory, which begins with the ceremonies of Yom Kippur in Leviticus 16, and its lengthy typological history predating Tyndale's coinage of the word prove indispensable for our examination of the word's metaphorical development. Then there is the question of its earliest metaphorical uses. One dictionary notes that "the history of the biblical scapegoat in English literature following Tyndale's translation is virtually a blank page" and that the word "has almost entirely lost the force of biblical association by the Victorian period" and so "tends merely to indicate a person, group, or thing that bears the blame for others."[17] The time has plainly come to fill in this blank page. The final stage of the scapegoat's lexical history has never been told because the information retrieval capacities needed are too recent. Digital archiving of so much English historical matter allows us to chart the semantic evolution of the word from its origin in Tyndale's sixteenth-century translation through biblical commentaries, sermons, and lectures, to its first metaphorical uses in print. Altogether a picture of the scapegoat's millennial passage from Mosaic ritual to ubiquitous cliché emerges.

How does the goat that got away become a signifier of vicarious punishment? Updating the data allows us break a number of impasses in recent discussion. For example: if use of the metaphor dates no further back than 1824, it is no stretch to conclude that Frazer was its original popularizer. Its deployment as a category heading for *The Golden Bough* at the fin de siècle could then be definitive. As it turns out, the metaphor is alive and circulating in English well before 1824, having become something of a hackneyed expression as early as the 1750s, with its first appearances in print dating to at least a century before that. For much longer than previously believed, the English word named people from every walk of life, victims both religious and otherwise, and a host of inanimate things as well—failed political treaties, leaky ships, fortune itself. There are even a number of "anthropological" references predating Frazer that deliberately compare the Jewish ritual with those of other cultures. Girard himself mentions the Abbé Raynal, who, writing in the eighteenth century, observes that the Indians "have a scape-horse, analogous to the scape-goat of the Jews."[18] As we shall see, the scapegoat's entanglement with *human* religious victims begins even earlier, at least two hundred years before Raynal. Indeed, the first such comparison is in Latin and dates to a century before the English word's earliest figurative use.

The first part of this book addresses the history of the scapegoat with a view to the formation of the English word and its meanings; it answers the question of who is to blame for the scapegoat's present usage. Here we may note that many English words and expressions begin as technical designations to which in time other meanings become attached. After 250 years of popular usage the question of whether the word ought to be used in the way that people use it, of whether it illuminates or confuses the original sense, has long ceased to matter. The late meanings become established conventions, joining a myriad of ungainly enrichments bedecking the mother tongue. Their inclusion is a fait accompli, for better or for worse. The evidence collated below will show that Frazer and Girard are but late inheritors of a common usage that originates centuries before either of them began writing.

This brings us to a second question that needs to be cleanly disentangled from the first—that of the scapegoat's theoretical uses. Big theories of history were undeniably launched in its name, and a corrected philology allows us to rule on them in new ways. Frazer's adaptation of the English word generalizes what he saw as the primary significance of the Israelite ceremony—a paradigm of ritual transference with its operative confusion of material and immaterial burdens—more nearly than it conscripts the extant metaphor, although the latter's popularity meant his title would be instantly recognized. The highly plastic character of the popular expression can only have recommended the word for a book that compiles and purports to essentialize such a bewildering variety of customs. Then too, the poor devils upon whose shoulders the freight of curse was laid were nearly always abused in some manner and variously run out of town so that the idea of transfer and disposal by proxy could be seen to slip quite naturally into that of vicarious punishment—the metaphorical signification, in a word. That is to say, Frazer probably found the bifurcated English expression doubly serviceable.

There can of course be no question that he deploys the "scapegoat" as a signifier of savage ignorance and superstition, of all that has been superseded by the coming of science, whereas Girard will read the historical advent of our metaphor, stripped of ritual associations and designating vicarious and therefore undeserved blame or punishment, as foretokening that precisely which supersedes the generations of religious superstition—not science itself but its precondition, the catalyst of an historically unprecedented postreligious or secular age. The question becomes that of the word's second, metaphorical denotation and the implications of its historical entrance precisely, of its status as a delimiter of worlds.

In this perspective, the old world is that for which the scapegoat is at once a real victim of communal violence and a *structural principle* whose role in the foundation of human culture it takes centuries of demystification to reveal. Situated at the very threshold of hominization, as an occulted driver of human evolution, the victim becomes a major interpretive key for explaining everything from the emergence of sacrificial religion and culture in all its institutional diversity to the otherwise merely fortuitous irony that the scapegoat theorists have themselves become the scapegoats of those decrying a debased and heedless usage of the word. A reciprocal force of social cohesion corresponding to the scapegoat's expulsion is the glue that binds the old religious order, that both constitutes it and allows it to proliferate, though beyond a certain threshold it must gradually begin succumbing to the disabling effects of exposure to scrutiny and doubt, the historical unraveling of its mythic accusations and disclosure of the truth that belies them. It is this process that ushers in the modern age, for which the scapegoat remains perceptually embattled if it is also significantly demystified.

In a sense, the better we understand the phenomenon, the more peripheral and evanescent it becomes. If we live in a world where acts of scapegoating are "increasingly transparent to criticism," this only serves to conceal their constitutive role in earlier societies, which are completely "imprisoned in the illusion of persecution."[19] This illusion "is no simple idea but a full system of representation" whose importance is concealed by the degree to which it has degenerated under more critical attitudes and scientific standards of inquiry.[20] The more demystified we are, the more clearly we see what persecutors are doing, the less we are able to understand what it is like to be imprisoned within the hermetic enclosure of a persecutory viewpoint. "As soon as we begin to study the scapegoat," Girard writes, "we imagine a deliberate manipulation. We think of skillful strategists who are fully aware of the mechanisms of victimization and who knowingly sacrifice innocent victims in full awareness of the cause with Machiavellian ease."[21] We read back upon early persecutors our own awareness of what is really going on, making it nearly impossible to understand how they once thought and acted. Even today to have a scapegoat is precisely not to know it since we see ourselves as confronting only legitimate enemies. Although we live surrounded by scapegoating, we never catch ourselves in the act.

A historical shift in perspective has nevertheless taken place, so that today we compete with one another to discover scapegoats. This represents real progress over the fourteenth century, when "no one decoded the representation of persecution as we do today" and "'scapegoat' had not yet taken on the meaning we give it today."[22] The question of the word's double meaning is therefore of the essence:

> J.-M.O: To my knowledge the word 'scapegoat' has the double semantic sense of ritual institution and unconscious, spontaneous psycho-sociological mechanism only in the languages of those societies that have been part

of the long process of cultural deciphering, in other words, the Western languages from the end of the Middle Ages and many non-Western languages since. The semantic conjunction is really something of a paradox. Ritual and spontaneous behavior are generally thought of as being poles apart. How is it that they have come together in the term 'scapegoat'?

R.G. . . . The merit of this conjunction is that it reveals a very widespread intuition that ethnology and the sciences of man have never officially recognized: there is a relation between the forms of ritual and the universal human tendency to transfer anxiety and conflict on to arbitrary victims. The double meaning of the English term 'scapegoat' is found in the French *bouc émissaire*, the German *Sündenbock*, and in all modern Western languages. Ultimately, everything we say here is an attempt to understand this semantic evolution of the word and evaluate its impact. Our whole hypothesis has existed silently in common language since the emergence of what is called rationalism. Strangely, there has been no work up to this point, as far as I know, concerning this evolution.[23]

In this perspective the historical emergence of the metaphor has the significance of a moon landing—a point of contact at which Girard's historical hypothesis becomes a lexical fact. The metaphor embodies what is hereafter "the most interesting meaning of the expression," identifying as it does "the unconscious mechanism for . . . acts of persecution."[24] The sense that McLean and Douglas so decry is therefore a matter of the highest interest for Girard.[25]

In the metaphor of the scapegoat an occluded principle of structure makes its linguistic debut, but it joins a party already begun in an incomparably misleading way—behind the mask of ritual. The conjunction is of course as deceptive as it will be, finally, revealing. The new sense of the scapegoat as a reflexively selected and merely expedient victim—the hidden truth of religion and, by extension, culture at large—slips unconsciously into the vernacular, disseminating itself universally. Between polarized meanings now joined in a single term the trajectory of a millennial process of demystification stands revealed. Dictionaries give the biblical scapegoat as the literal meaning of the word and the popular expression as derivative, but "I reverse this order," Girard writes. If the scapegoat "can be seen as a symbol for all sacrifices," then "I say the modern meaning is really the meaning of the institution."[26] This idea is susceptible to a test against the record in ways unforeseen in the late 1970s when Girard insisted that "ultimately, everything we say here is an attempt to understand this semantic evolution of the word and evaluate its impact."[27] The scapegoat's evolution can today be scrutinized rather closely. Does the evidence corroborate or explode the theory of its progressive historical revelation?

Since it is already in circulation as early as the 1650s, what *really* drove the historical emergence of the scapegoat as secular metaphor? The initial aim of this monograph was simply to give the scapegoat's history, beginning with the Leviticus ritual and ending with a dozen or more of the English word's earliest metaphorical uses. We guessed the longest portion of this history—the scapegoat's 1,600-year run as an exegetical type—would prove critical for understanding the semantic development of our term, but little expected to find the typological record so marked by formal consistencies and recurring patterns. As a Day of Atonement animal, the scapegoat is quite naturally assimilated to Christian reflection on the meaning of Jesus' atoning death and resurrection, which is itself undergoing a number of changes during this period. The formal distribution of historical scapegoat typologies allows us to trace this theological development as it unfolds from the patristic age through the early modern era, when two robust and fully antithetical traditions in scapegoat interpretation begin converging in new readings whose implications for the fate of the theological enterprise and the making of the modern world exceed the narrowly lexical question. These typologies plainly destine our word to its present meaning and usage, but this is only a part of the story they tell.

If a coherent pattern appears in dozens of scapegoat readings ventured over the centuries, the first metaphorical uses of the word also fall curiously into groups, informal typologies. There are a host of references to kings, some to plagues both actual and figurative, and then there are the references to victims—of religious violence and social oppression. What explains the contents of these pseudotypologies? Tracking the scapegoat through its successive embodiments (ritual animal, symbol, exegetical type, technical designation, cliché), we cover a vast historical expanse where the long contours and semantic thresholds of its itinerary emerge to view. This imposes two objectives on our study, the first of which is simply to adduce the relevant citations and set the lexical record straight. Chapters 1 through 5 of this book treat the scapegoat's prehistory and typological history with this aim in mind. Then, in chapter 6 we turn expressly to the reckoning of implications, situating the amended historical record within the larger context of Frazer's, and then Girard's, theoretical endeavor. Both thinkers venture theories explaining the persistence of the scapegoat as an identifiable pattern in cultural phenomena. Do their theories anticipate or explain formal patterns in the scapegoat's history leading up to the word's first metaphorical uses in print? Even more to the point is the distribution into "pseudotypes" of the first scapegoat metaphors to which we devote the final chapters of this book. How do the scapegoat theories fare against this documentary record?

A grasp of this history will position us to understand the rapid evolution of attitudes toward all forms of punishment by proxy occurring in the early modern period. We witness it from close range in the scapegoat's earliest figurative uses. As it turns out, the English word escapes the orbit of typological exegesis in different semantic configurations, all but one of them opposed to its current sense, so that it is not immediately clear which of several contemporaneous figures will prevail. This begins happening in the early seventeenth century. Once it does, a hundred years pass before the expression stands plainly and without variance for what it does today.

Still, by the time a verbal form of the word like the gerund *scapegoating* appears (not before the 1940s according to the *OED*) a connotative prejudice in favor of the scapegoat and against his accusers has indissociably colored the expression. The scapegoat is clearly an innocent victim, and the pejorative verbal forms put his accusers in a bad light. An article on Boston newspaper reactions to the Cocoanut Grove nightclub fire analyzing the process of fixing blame appears in the *Journal of Abnormal & Social Psychology* in April 1943, employing the verb to designate persecutory thinking and behavior as reflexive, cathartic, and above all, unwarranted. In 1950, Theodore Adorno writes, "Lack of insight into one's own short-comings and the projection of one's own weaknesses and faults onto others . . . probably represents the essential aspect of . . . scapegoating," a definition that captures the blind or delusional character of scapegoat making.[28]

There are a number of roughly analogous expressions in English and other languages that betoken this evolution in basic attitudes. At one time the whipping of a whipping boy for the misdeeds of young English princes, whose royal birth exempted them from punishment, was deemed an acceptable means of negotiating blame, which could in good conscience be transferred onto someone else. Justice demanded that someone pay, even if that person were not precisely at fault. Of course the whipping boy has long ceased to exist as a cultural institution, although it lives on as a common expression, rather like the Mandarin "ti si gui" (替死鬼) or "substitute ghost," an ancient custom permitting death by proxy in cases of capital punishment.[29] The logic of the phrase turns on the belief that to lose one's life is to become a ghost. A person sentenced to die might accordingly contrive for someone to take his place and so escape with his life. Our earliest reference to this practice dates to the Ming Dynasty (1368–1644). Like our "whipping boy," "ti si gui" survives only in the vernacular, with many of the same connotations that attend the English "scapegoat," which is often employed to translate it. As we shall see in the following chapter, the Levitical scapegoat ceremony enacts a ritual transfer and banishment of sin but lacks that clear sense of vicarious punishment which informs these customs and Greek rites like the *pharmakos*. In such rites "the community sacrifices one of its members to save its own skin," as classics scholar Jan Bremmer observes,[30] a sense that only the metaphorical "scapegoat" captures. Bremmer's derogatory appraisal reminds us that in current usage the deflection of blame onto a scapegoat is always *undeserved*, that the punishment he suffers is *justly* owed to others. It is, above all, the implicit judgment that attends the use of "scapegoat" for which we must account in plotting a semantic genealogy. The formal denotation ("one who is blamed or punished for the sins of others") makes no mention of it. The judgment is that precisely which goes without saying. How and when does it crystallize in the word?

CHAPTER 1

Rites of Riddance and Substitution

The Levitical Scapegoat

Tyndale coins the word "scapegoat" for his version of the Bible with the following translation of Leviticus 16:8: "And Aaron cast lottes ouer the .ii gootes: one lotte for the Lorde, and another for a scapegoote."[1] The precise meaning of the Hebrew עֲזָאזֵל or 'aza'zel—which occurs again in verses 10 and 26, but nowhere else in the Bible—has been debated since antiquity and still divides opinion among scholars, a majority of whom favor the proper name of a demon against Tyndale's interpretation, which, like the Septuagint's τῷ ἀποπομπαίῳ—"for the one who bears away evil"—and the Vulgate's caper emissarius (whence the French, bouc émissaire), appears to read 'ez meaning "goat," and 'azal, "to go away," for "the goat that goes" or departs or is removed and so (e)scapes.[2] Toward the end of the nineteenth century, the Committee for the Revision of the Authorized Version advises a return to the name Azazel, and a number of modern translations follow suit. The JPS rendition of Leviticus 16:5–10 runs as follows:

> And [Aaron] shall take of the congregation of the children of Israel two
> he-goats for a sin-offering, and one ram for a burnt-offering.
> And Aaron shall present the bullock of the sin-offering, which is for him-
> self, and make atonement for himself, and for his house.

> And he shall take the two goats, and set them before HaShem at the door of the tent of meeting.
>
> And Aaron shall cast lots upon the two goats: one lot for HaShem, and the other lot for Azazel.
>
> And Aaron shall present the goat upon which the lot fell for HaShem, and offer him for a sin-offering.
>
> But the goat, on which the lot fell for Azazel, shall be set alive before HaShem, to make atonement over him, to send him away for Azazel into the wilderness.

Aaron dispatches the goat "for HaShem" (literally "the Name," a circumlocution for the ineffable name of God), aspersing its blood upon the horns of the altar as well as inside the Tabernacle, while the goat for *Azazel* is "set alive before HaShem," in an official way suggesting to some the legitimization of a more ancient, pagan custom that has found its way into the Yahweh festival.[3] Aaron then lays both hands on the goat's head, confessing the sins of the people over it, after which a man standing ready leads the beast "into the wilderness" (16:21), to "a land of cutting off" (16:22).[4] Having "let go the goat in the wilderness" (16:22), the man "shall wash his clothes and bathe his flesh in water, and afterward he may come into the camp" (16:26). Later tradition includes details of the scapegoat's abuse and killing. The Mishnah Yoma gives the following account:

> 6:4 A. They made a ramp for it, on account of the Babylonians,
>
> B. who would pull out its hair and say, "Take and go, take and go."
>
> C. The eminent people of Jerusalem used to accompany him to the first booth.
>
> D. There were ten booths from Jerusalem to the ravine, a distance of ninety *ris*—
>
> E. seven and a half to a mile.
>
> 6:5 A. At each booth they say to him, "Lo, here is food, here is water."
>
> B. And they accompany him from one booth to the next,
>
> C. except for [the man in] the last [tabernacle] among them,
>
> D. who does not go along with him to the ravine.
>
> E. But he stands from a distance and observes what he does.
>
> 6:6 A. Now what did he do?
>
> B. He divided the crimson thread.
>
> C. Half of it he tied to a rock, and half of it he tied between its horns.
>
> D. He then pushed it over backward, and it rolled down the ravine.

E. And it did not reach halfway down the mountain before it broke into pieces.

F. He came and sat himself down under the last tabernacle until it got dark.⁵

This ceremony bears a number of striking resemblances to Hittite and Mesopotamian expulsion rites that some scholars have used to speculate on the meaning of the Leviticus ceremony, suggesting lines of influence and wondering about pre-Israelite antecedents. Note the correspondence between the Mishnah ceremony and the Hittite ritual of Ashella:

1. Thus (says) Ashella, the man of Hapalla:
2. If in the land or in the army a plague occurs
3. I perform this ritual:
4. I take this: When day becomes night,
5. all whoever are the leaders of the army, each
6. one prepares a ram. If the ram(s) are white
7. or black it does not matter. A cord
8. of white wool, red wool, (and) green wool I wind together. He weaves them (into) one.
9. I bring together one *erimmatu*-bead and one ring of iron and lead.
10. I bind them on the necks and horns of the rams.
11. They bind them (i.e., the rams) before the tents at night.
12. They say the following at that time: "Whatever god is moving about,
13. whatever god has caused this plague, for you, behold, these rams
14. I have tied up. Be herewith appeased!"
15. At morning, I drive them to the open country. With each ram
16. they take a jug of beer, one thick bread, (and) one cup of milk. Before the tent of the king
17. he has a decorated woman sit. He places with the woman one *huppar*-vessel of beer and three thick breads.
18. Then, the leaders of the army place their hands on the rams.
19. Thereupon, they say the following: "Whatever god has caused this plague,
20. now, behold, the rams are standing; they are very fat in liver,
21. heart, and member.
22. Let the flesh of humans be hateful to him. Moreover,
23. be appeased with these rams." The leaders of the army show reverence
24. to the rams, and the king shows reverence to the decorated woman.

25. Then they bring the rams and the woman, the bread, and The beer out through the army.

26. They drive them to the open country. They go and make them run inside the border of the enemy

27. (so that) they do not arrive at any place of ours.

28. Thereupon in this way they say: "Behold, whatever evil of this army

29. Was among men, cattle, sheep, horses, mules,

30. and donkeys, now, behold,

31. these rams and woman have taken it out from the camp.

32. Whoever finds them, may that land receive this evil plague.[6]

The two goats, the twining of horns, and the mention of food and drink have all excited comparison with the Mishnah scapegoat, although as Bremmer observes, the rite of Ashella "is not tied to a specific place in the calendar, but is executed *ad hoc*"[7] to ward off pestilence. It also contains an explicit propitiation of malevolent spirits that the Leviticus and Second Temple ceremony do not. Wright mentions that "the feature of an angry deity who needs appeasement" contrasts sharply with the shadowy figure of Azazel in the Bible"[8] and that, while Aaron transfers the sins of the Israelites onto the head of the scapegoat, there is no real sense of the animal having thus become a substitute. The scapegoat is no more than "a transporter of impurity"[9] and there is nothing to indicate it must suffer in place of the people, something visible in the prayer of the Hittite officers that the deity "be satisfied with the rams instead of their human flesh."[10] The Leviticus scholar Jacob Milgrom observes that "the Bible rejects the idea of substitution, which presupposes demonic attack and the appeasement of threatening demons,"[11] and there is, of course, no mention of any harm coming to the Leviticus scapegoat. If Ashella gives us an exemplary moment of propitiatory substitution in ancient ritual, it is, curiously, this very same meaning with which the scapegoat will one day be identified; in a late and fateful reading of Leviticus 16 the primordial religious instinct recrudesces. Here we note merely that it structures a Hittite ritual dating to the thirteenth century B.C. and that the Leviticus ritual appears to have different aims.

As a chief proponent of the view that Azazel was "a true demon, perhaps a satyr, who ruled in the wilderness," Milgrom is quick to emphasize the evisceration "of his erstwhile demonic powers by the Priestly legislators," leaving "just a name designating the place to which impurities and sins are banished."[12]

First, the goat sent him is not an offering; it is not treated as a sacrifice, requiring slaughter, blood manipulation, and the like, nor does it have the effect of a sacrifice, namely, propitiation, expiation, and so on . . . [Neither can it be] the vicarious substitute for Israel, because there is no indication that it was punished (e.g., put to death) or demonically attacked in Israel's place. Instead of being an offering or a substitute, the goat is simply the vehicle to dispatch Israel's impurities and sins to the wilderness/nether-world. The banishment of evil to an inaccessible place is a form of elimination amply attested in the ancient Near East.[13]

The animal's choice by lot further obviates any sense of the rite as a demonic propitiation by leaving the selection to Yahweh.[14] Like the goat's formal placement "before Yahweh" (16:7), the casting of lots gives "clear evidence of the Priestly efforts to alter what was most likely in its original form a pagan rite."[15] If Azazel is "no longer a personality" in the priestly ritual, the persistence of his name is not surprising, since "demons often survive as figures of speech (e.g., 'gremlins') long after they have ceased to be figures of belief."[16] According to Wright, the placement of two hands on the goat's head is a gesture "designating the focus of ritual action"[17] as opposed to "an identification between the offerer and animal,"[18] which is indicated with just one hand in biblical and Hittite ritual. If by one hand the offerer affirmed that he "was offering himself by means of the victim,"[19] the two-handed gesture "should not even be considered a transfer of sins in the strict sense," as "Aaron never carries or embodies these evils," which cannot, therefore, be "passed from Aaron through his hands to the goat."[20] The two-handed gesture is rather merely indicative; it signifies that this goat "is the recipient of the sins of the people."[21]

A fair number of Midrashic sources read the word "Azazel" as a place-name. The Sifra interprets "a hard to access mountain precipice"[22] and Rashi understands a "precipitous and flinty rock."[23] Rashbam observes that the expression was just another name for "desert." The medieval exegete Ibn Ezra reads the "name of a mountain near Mount Sinai" where the goat was chased and then jettisoned,[24] but alludes to a second interpretation: "Now if you can understand the secret of the word after Azazel, you will know its secret and the secret of its name, since it has parallels in the Scriptures. And I will reveal to you part of the secret by hint: when you will be thirty-three, you will know it."[25] Pinker notes that "to count 33 verses from this verse brings us Leviticus 17:7,"[26] a proscription of sacrifices to satyrs:

What man soever there be of the house of Israel, that killeth an ox, or lamb, or goat, in the camp, or that killeth it without the camp, and hath not brought it unto the door of the tent of meeting, to present it as an offering unto HaShem before the tabernacle of HaShem, blood shall be imputed unto that man; he has shed blood; and that man shall be cut off from among his people. To the end that the children of Israel may bring their sacrifices, which they sacrifice in the open field, even that they may bring them unto HaShem, unto the door of the tent of meeting, unto the priest, and sacrifice them for sacrifices of peace-offerings unto HaShem. And the priest shall dash the blood against the altar of HaShem at the door of the tent of meeting, and make the fat smoke for a sweet savour unto HaShem. *And they shall no more sacrifice their sacrifices unto the satyrs, after whom they go astray.* This shall be a statute for ever unto them throughout their generations (17:3–7; italics added).

Azazel in the Wilderness

The prevailing opinion in the Midrashim going all the way back to the early postbiblical period, is that Azazel is the name of a supernatural entity or demon.[27] I Enoch portrays him as one of "the watchers" or "children of heaven" who descend upon Mount Hermon, having bound themselves by oaths and imprecations to take wives "from the daughters of earth" after whom they lust.[28] This links the account with the story of human corruption in Genesis 6 and the time of the Nephilim.[29]

> And they cohabited with the daughters of the men of the earth, and had intercourse with them, and they were defiled by the females and revealed to them all manner of sins, and taught them to make hate-charms.
> And now behold! the daughters of men brought forth from them sons, giants, bastards; and *much blood was spilled upon the earth*, and the whole earth was filled with wickedness.[30]

These offspring who grew to "3000 cubits" in stature "devoured the entire fruits of men's labour" and soon began to attack "all birds and beasts of the earth and reptiles [that crawl upon the earth], and fish of the sea; and they began to devour their flesh, and they were drinking the blood."[31] The sins of the giants draw an immutable sentence from heaven: God sends word to Noah that "a Deluge is about to come on the whole earth, to destroy all things from the face of the earth."[32] He then orders the archangel Raphael to fetter Azazel "hand and foot" for his crimes,[33] which include the impartation of "mysteries"—knowledge of metalwork and antediluvian fashion design.

> Asael[34] taught men to make swords of iron and breast-plates of bronze and every weapon for war; and he showed them the metals of the earth, how to work gold, to fashion [adornments] and about silver, to make bracelets for women; and he instructed them about antimony, and eye-shadow, and all manner of precious stones and about dyes and varieties of adornments; and the children of men fashioned them for themselves and for their daughters and transgressed; and there arose much impiety on the earth and they committed fornication and went astray and corrupted their ways.[35]

God directs Raphael to "make an opening in the desert...of Dudael and there go and cast him in."[36] He is to "place upon him jagged and rough rocks,"[37] language recalling the cliff from which the Mishnah goat is thrown.[38] "Cover him with darkness and let him abide there for all time," God says, "And on the day of great judgment he will be led off to the blazing fire."[39] Because "the whole earth has been devastated by the works of the teaching of Asael," the archangel is to "record against him all sins" and then "announce the healing of the earth which the watchers have ruined."[40] Another text, the *Apocalypse of Abraham*, depicts the descent of Azazel in the form of a bird who attempts to prevent Abraham from performing a sacrifice undertaken at the behest of an angel:

> And I did everything according to the commandment of the angel, and gave the angels, who had come to us, the divided animals, but the angel took the birds. And I waited for the evening sacrifice. And there flew an unclean bird *down upon the carcasses*, and I drove it away. And the unclean bird spake to me, and said: "What doest thou, Abraham, upon the holy Heights, where no man eateth or drinketh, neither is there upon them (any) food of man, but these consume everything with fire, and (will) burn thee up. Forsake the man, who is with thee, and flee; for if thou ascendest to the Heights they will make an end of thee. And it came to pass when I saw the bird speak, I said to the angel "What is this, my lord?" And he said: This is ungodliness, this is Azazel. And he said to it: "Disgrace upon thee, Azazel! For Abraham's lot is in heaven, but thine upon the earth. Because thou hast chosen and loved this for the dwelling (place) of thine unclean- ness, therefore the eternal mighty Lord made thee a dweller upon the earth

and through thee every evil spirit of lies, and through thee wrath and trials
for the generations of ungodly men.[41]

These accounts point to a widely attested belief in the wilderness as a haunt
of evil spirits.[42] W. F. Albright supposed "that popular fancy identified the
scapegoat with the class of goat demons, giving rise to objectionable ideas
which later ritual eliminated by the expedient of killing the goat."[43] Ida
Zatelli suggests that Azazel was at one time a "Canaanite demon connected
with the chthonian power expressed by goats," noting that the wilderness is
itself "a symbol of the netherworld."[44]

The scapegoat's early Canaanite extraction and later mythologization
may explain the punitive additions to the original rite. Stökl says the scapegoat's abuse on its way from Jerusalem should be read as "ritual anticipation
of the eschatological purification of God's creation from sin," since "the
goat originally sent *to* 'Az'azel was seen as the personification *of* 'Az'azel, the
demonic source of sin."[45] Grabbe suggests that sins loaded onto the scapegoat
as symbol of the archdemon were sent packing, as it were, on the back of
their chief instigator.[46] Either way the animal was driven out as though it
were the Devil himself. Gerstenberger has written that the scapegoat was
killed simply to ensure the "sin-heap" never returned.[47]

Whether practical or symbolic considerations prevailed, there is little
here to suggest the scapegoat's substitutionary death as sin-bearer. If Second
Temple celebrants destroyed the animal as a personification of Azazel, they
would appear to have done so only in the same spirit as others burn effigies or
smash the icons of public figures. The scapegoat does not die in place of those
whose sins are laid upon it.

CHAPTER 2

Ancient Types and Soteriologies

The Blood and Mystery of the Cross

At the threshold of the Christian era, the historical path of the scapegoat divides in two directions: on the one hand, the first Christian Day of Atonement typologies; and on the other, two early conceptions of Christ's saving work that have little if anything to do with the Day of Atonement. One writer notes that "the doctrine of the atonement, the doctrine that God has resolved the problem of human evil by means of the suffering and death of Christ, is the central doctrine of Christianity."[1] Because the scapegoat is a Day of Atonement animal, its interpreters will eventually find ways of using it to comment on this problem and its resolution. This happens at important moments in the long historical evolution of Christian thinking on the subject, although the two things—typologies and soteriologies—run at an oblique angle initially.

The business of rendering Day of Atonement types begins early and persists for centuries, with many different writers venturing typologies of one or both goats. Early interpreters are divided between those who see the scapegoat as a demonic figure and others who see it as divine. Indeed, most readings ventured during the first fifteen centuries of the Christian era tend to run to one extreme or the other, giving rise to fully antipodal scapegoat traditions. In time a "structure" of polarized interpretations stands forth whose collapse at the dawn of the modern age produces the current metaphorical usage.

The Epistle to the Hebrews establishes a decisive connection between the death of Jesus "outside the gate" (13:12) and the burning of slain Day of Atonement animals "outside the camp" (13:3:11). Among these animals is the immolated goat chosen by lot "for Yahweh" whose blood the priest conveys inside the sanctuary "to make atonement" (Lv. 16:16). The New Testament never mentions the scapegoat explicitly, although the text of Leviticus plainly stipulates that it, too, shall be "set before Hashem" to "make atonement over him" (Lv. 16:10). The Hebrew word translated "make atonement"—כָּפַר *Kāphar*—means to wipe out or to cover, though it comes in time to stand for other things too—annulment, purging, and sometimes propitiation or appeasement. The Septuagint renders it with *exilaskomai*—which means "to propitiate" or "appease" in pagan Greek usage—adapting the expression considerably to specify the removal of guilt and defilement. This Greek word does not appear in the New Testament; instead, the verb *hilaskomai* is used, notably in Hebrews, for a description of Christ's high priestly work. The author tells us that Jesus "had to be made like His brethren in every respect, so that He might become a merciful and faithful high priest in the service of God, to make expiation (ἱλάσκεσθαι, *hilaskesthai*) for the sins of the people" (2:17). Taking the merciful initiative, God sends Jesus not merely to expiate sin but to perfect his son "through sufferings" (2:10) and make him a sympathetic intercessor for humankind. The cardinal verse for what we will be calling the *Christus Victor* idea of the atonement comes in Hebrews 2: "Since then the children share in flesh and blood, He Himself likewise also partook of the same, that through death He might render powerless him who had the power of death, that is the devil; and might deliver those who through fear of death were subject to slavery all their lives" (2:14–15). In this glimpse of the drama of salvation, four distinct players appear: God the Father, Jesus the Son, a captive humanity, and the Devil. Death and its enslaving fear are plainly the works of the Devil. Other images of Christ's triumph over the powers of evil appear in Colossians, which records that "He delivered us from the domain of darkness and transferred us to the kingdom of His beloved Son" (1:13) and having "disarmed the rulers and authorities" made "a public display of them, having triumphed over them in him (Christ crucified)" (2:15).

With this image, the author of Colossians adds that Christ nails "the certificate of debt consisting of decrees against us" to his cross (2:14–15).[2] The pecuniary metaphor recalls the Gospel claim that "the Son of Man did not come to be served, but to serve, and to give his life a ransom (λύτρον, *lutron*) for many" (Mark 10:45; Matt. 20:28).[3] The letter to the Ephesians says that "we have redemption (ἀπολύτρωσιν, *apolutrōsin*) through his blood, the forgiveness of our trespasses" (Eph. 1:7), while Peter's first epistle observes that "you were not redeemed (ἐλυτρώθητε, *elutrōthēte*) with perishable things like silver or gold from your futile way of life inherited from your forefathers, but with precious blood, as of a lamb unblemished and spotless, the blood of Christ" (1 Pet. 1:18–19). In these commercial images, the exchange that takes place is mostly unspecified. Who, for instance, are the parties involved in the transaction? To whom is the price of redemption paid? Thus the New Testament witness shows us the soteriological drama in many enigmatic glimpses that invite further questioning. The first rough narratives of salvation in the church fathers take up these questions and might be read as attempts to reconcile two of the New Testament's most persistent soteriological motifs— the liberating exchange whose price is blood, and the victory of Christ over death and the Devil.

Justin Martyr (second century) is the first to articulate the soteriology of *Christus Victor*, or the "classic view," which Gustaf Aulén famously called "the ruling idea of the Atonement for the first thousand years of Christian history."[4] In setting forth the human predicament from which Christ saves us, Justin's *Second Apology* begins, curiously enough, with angels entrusted to care for human beings who instead defile themselves, being "captivated by the love of women."[5] The angels "begat children who are those that are called demons," and it is they who "afterwards subdued the human race to themselves."[6] As in 1 Enoch, the impartation of forbidden knowledge hastens the ruin of humankind "partly by magical writings, and partly by fears and the punishments they occasioned, and partly by teaching them to offer sacrifices, and incense, and libations, of which things they stood in need after they were enslaved by lustful passions."[7] Justin charges the demon spawn with sowing "murders, wars, adulteries, intemperate deeds, and all wickedness" among human beings,[8] depicting Christ as the bringer of enlightenment who frees a benighted people. In other places he writes of the redeemer having become "a partaker of our sufferings [that] He might also bring us healing"[9] and of his "acquiring" enslaved peoples "by the blood and mystery of the cross."[10]

Irenaeus (second century) takes his cue from the biblical account of human sin in the Adam and Eve story in Genesis 3, writing that the Devil "enticed man to transgress his Maker's law, and thereby got him into his power."[11] Christ redeems "those who had been led into captivity . . . through His own blood, giving His soul for our souls, and His flesh for our flesh."[12]

Origen (third century) makes the parties in this saving transaction more explicit: "To whom did he give his soul as a ransom for many? Certainly not to God! Then why not the devil? For he had possession of us until there should be given to him the ransom for us, the soul of Jesus."[13] In similar terms, Gregory of Nyssa (fourth century) observes that "those who have sold their freedom for money" are henceforth the "slaves of their purchasers" so that, just as "it is illegal to use force against a purchaser, though perfectly legal to buy a person out of slavery," so God induces the Enemy to take Christ "as a ransom in exchange for those who were shut up in death's prison."[14]

The cosmic rivalry depicted in these and many other patristic sources is frequently marked by an insistence on God's reclamation of humanity by nonviolent means. Irenaeus offers that

> since the apostasy tyrannized over us unjustly, and, though we were by nature the property of the omnipotent God, alienated us contrary to nature, rendering us its own disciples, the Word of God, powerful in all things, and not defective with regard to His own justice, did righteously turn against that apostasy, and redeem from it His own property, not by violent means, as the apostasy had obtained dominion over us at the beginning, when it insatiably snatched away what was not its own, but by means of persuasion, as became a God of counsel, who does not use violent means to obtain what he desires; so that neither should justice be infringed upon, nor the ancient handiwork of God go to destruction.[15]

Gregory of Nyssa too insists that God's justice is shown "in not using tyrannical power against him who held us in his sway,"[16] since the Devil is he who both "shut his eyes to the good in his envy of man in his happy condition" and "suffered from the disease of the love of rule, that primary and fundamental cause of propension to the bad and the mother, so to speak, of all wickedness that follows."[17] Augustine (fourth to fifth centuries) likewise notes that "the devil was to be overcome, not by the power of God, but by His righteousness."

> For what is more powerful than the Omnipotent? Or what creature is there of which the power can be compared to the power of the Creator? But since the devil, by the fault of his own perversity, was made a lover of power, and a forsaker and assailant of righteousness—for thus also men imitate him so much the more in proportion as they set their hearts on

power, to the neglect or even hatred of righteousness, and as they either rejoice in the attainment of power, or are inflamed by the lust of it,—it pleased God, that in order to rescue man from the grasp of the devil, the devil should be conquered, not by power, but by righteousness; and that so also men, imitating Christ, should seek to conquer the devil by righteousness, not by power.[18]

How precisely does God rescue humanity in Christ? Gregory answers that "a just method of restoration [had to] be devised by him who in his goodness rescued us from bondage," as is evident in "His making the ransoming of the captive a matter of exchange."[19] To this he adds, "[In order] that the exchange for us might be easily accepted by him who sought for it, the divine nature was concealed under the veil of our human nature so that, as with a greedy fish, the hook of divinity might be swallowed along with the bait of flesh."[20] On one hand God's justice demands fair play, on the other he deceives the Devil.[21] The Incarnation is therefore an artifice: "the reason why the Godhead was veiled in flesh [is] that Satan should observe what was familiar and congenial and thus have no fear in approaching the transcendent power. He only noticed the power which shone quietly more and more in his miracles; and what he saw seemed to him an object of desire rather than an object of fear."[22]

"If they had known, they would not have crucified the Lord of glory," says Ambrose, quoting 1 Corinthians 2:7. "Thus he deceived the powers for us: he deceived so that he might conquer. He deceived the Devil . . . so that he should on no occasion admit his own divinity."[23] In this soteriological configuration the Devil, who alone wields the power of death, exchanges his human captives for Jesus, killing him without even realizing that he is divine and immortal. Death cannot hold the redeemer and the Devil forfeits his claim on the human race. Cyril of Alexandria is more picturesque: "the Father gave a ransom for us. . . . One died for all, that we all might live in him: Death devoured the Lamb on behalf of all, and then vomited all in him, and with him. For we were all in Christ, who died and rose again on our account, and on our behalf."[24] The central theme, says Aulén,

> is the idea of the Atonement as a Divine conflict and victory; Christ— *Christus Victor*—fights against and triumphs over the evil powers of the world, the "tyrants" under which mankind is in bondage and suffering, and in Him God reconciles the world to Himself. . . . The background of the idea is dualistic; God is pictured as in Christ carrying through a victorious

conflict against powers of evil which are hostile to His will. This constitutes Atonement, because the drama is a cosmic drama, and the victory over the hostile powers brings to pass a new relation, a relation of reconciliation between God and the world.[25]

Aulén also points out that in the early fathers the language of Christ's victory over the enemies of the race alternates with statements indicating these same enemies "are also, from another point of view, the executants of God's judgment on sinful man,"[26] making it "next to impossible to construct a rationally consistent theory of the atonement."[27] We read frequent appeals to Hebrews 2:14 for a dualistic picture of Christ's triumph over death and the Devil,[28] but there can be no "absolute dualism" since the deliverance of human beings from these enemies "is at the same time . . . deliverance from God's judgment."[29] As in the New Testament, there is in the fathers no "developed theological doctrine of the Atonement, but rather an idea or *motif* expressed with many variations of outward form."[30] Cyril of Alexandria can, for example, without altering the basic configuration of the salvation drama or changing the number of principal players, still turn it very decisively in another direction, anticipating the fully articulated penal theories of a later age:

> The penalty for transgression of God's law and contempt of the Lord's will is death. But the Creator had pity on human nature thus doomed to destruction; and the Only-begotten became man, and wore a body by nature liable to death, and bore the name of flesh, so that, by submitting to the death which hung over us as a result of our sin, he might annihilate sin, and put an end to Satan's accusations: for in the person of Christ himself we paid the penalty of the sins of which we stood accused.[31]

The Price of Impunity

Human guilt, the need for forgiveness, and the idea that God actively punishes instead of simply allowing the natural consequences of human sinfulness to take their course are, like the notion that Christ pays the penalty for human sin demanded by God's justice, less prominent in the early Christian literature. Where the problem is cast as a legal predicament with a saving adjudication, we find appeals to Galatians 3:13 and 2 Corinthians 5:21. Galatians reads: "Christ redeemed (ἐξηγόρασεν, *exēgorasen*) us from the curse of the Law, having become a curse for us—for it is written, 'Cursed is everyone who hangs on a tree'—in order that in Christ Jesus the blessing of Abraham might come to the Gentiles, so that we might receive the promise of the Spirit through faith" (Gal. 3:13). Second Corinthians reads: "He made Him who knew no sin to be sin on our behalf, that we might become the righteousness of God in Him" (2 Cor. 5:21). Here Christ's identification with sin and the making righteous of believers stand in a corresponding relation, though it is not clear whether Paul intends a fully reciprocal *exchange* of sin for righteousness. The nature of the transaction remains enigmatic. Notwithstanding this, both passages appear together repeatedly in readings that insist on this saving quid pro quo precisely and sometimes on the fully substitutive death of the redeemer.

The juridical view also draws strength from some of Paul's language in Romans, like this passage from the third chapter: "Now we know that whatever the Law says, it speaks to those who are under the Law, that every mouth may be closed, and all the world may become accountable [ὑπόδικος, *hupodikos*—from *hupo*, "under" and *dikē*, "judgment"] to God" (Rom. 3:19). Later he adds that "being now justified (δικαιωθέντες, dikaiōthentes) by His blood, we shall be saved from wrath through Him" (5:9). This language contrasts sharply with the rescue from satanic enslavement envisioned in Hebrews 2. What is the wrath from which Christ saves? The Devil plays no part in the epistle's long argument, though Paul mentions him briefly in the salutations of chapter 16 ("And the God of peace will soon crush Satan under your feet" [16:20]).

In chapter 8 we read that God sent "His own Son in the likeness of sinful flesh" and "condemned sin in the flesh, in order that the requirement of the Law might be fulfilled in us" (8:3b–4a), with the result that "there is therefore now no condemnation for those who are in Christ Jesus" (8:1a). The question here is whether Jesus suffers and dies in our place as though culpable for our sins. Is God's wrath against human sin spent on Christ without remainder? Is that how we are reprieved? If the language of the New Testament witness does not answer these questions in so many words, later Christian reflection on the atonement turns time and again for help to Isaiah 53.[32] As a prophetic anticipation of Christ, the vicarious sin-bearing of the Servant of Yahweh appears plainly ("Surely our griefs He Himself bore, And our sorrows He carried" [53:4a], "As He will bear their iniquities" [53:11b], "Yet He Himself bore the sin of many" [53:12b]). He suffers in the place of sinners ("But He was pierced through for our transgressions, He was crushed for our iniquities" [53:5a];

"Who considered that he was cut off out of the land of the living, for the transgression of my people to whom the stroke was due" [53:8b]). His suffering is restorative ("The chastening for our well-being fell upon Him, And by His scourging we are healed" [53:5b]). Isaiah goes further still with something the New Testament never says: "the Lord was pleased [חפץ *chāphēts*] to crush Him, putting Him to grief" (53:10a).[33] Notwithstanding these rather more vivid statements to which later tradition appeals to explain Christ's death as an act of substitution, the scriptures as a whole remain difficult to reconcile, let alone systematize on the question of how Christ saves.

For early signs of the idea that it is God's justice and not the Devil who demands payment, we look to Tertullian (second to third centuries), who appears to have introduced the term "satisfaction" to Christian discourse, though not in reference to the death of Jesus.[34] He writes instead that he who repents "make[s] satisfaction to the Lord," whereas he who repents of his repentance "make[s] satisfaction to the devil, and will be the more hateful to God in proportion as he will be the more acceptable to His rival."[35] Tertullian insists that "to expect pardon of sins" when penance has not been done "is to hold out your hand for merchandise, but not produce the price,"[36] for, he says, "the Lord has set [a price] on the purchase of pardon, [namely] he offers impunity (*impunitas*) to be bought in [compensating] exchange for penitence (*paenitentia*)."[37] Because "penitence is so serious a matter, it must be tested in a way which is proportionately laborious,"[38] that exceeds the private act of conscience. Tertullian's word for this fitting demonstration is *exomologesis*, or public confession: "herein we confess our sin to the Lord, not as though He were ignorant of it, but because satisfaction receives its proper determination through confession, confession gives birth to penitence, and by penitence God is appeased."[39] It is therefore a

> discipline which leads a man to prostrate and humble himself. It prescribes a way of life which, even in the matter of food and clothing, appeals to pity. It bids him to lie in sackcloth and ashes, to cover his body with filthy rags, to plunge his soul into sorrow, to exchange sin for suffering. Moreover, it demands that you know only such food and drink as is plain; this means it is taken for the sake of your soul, not your belly. It requires that you habitually nourish prayer by fasting, that you sigh and weep and groan day and night to the Lord your God, that you prostrate yourself at the feet of the priests and kneel before the beloved of God, making all the brethren commissioned ambassadors of your prayer for pardon. *Exomologesis* does

all this in order to render penitence acceptable and in order to honor God through fear of punishment, so that in passing sentence upon the sinner it may itself be a substitute for the wrath of God and, by temporal punishment, I will not say prevent eternal torments but rather cancel them. Therefore, in humbling a man it exalts him. When it defiles him, he is cleansed. In accusing, it excuses. In condemning, it absolves. In proportion as you have had no mercy on yourself, believe me, in just this same measure God will have mercy upon you.[40]

We mark here the idea of making "satisfaction" as an obeisance of fear, the *substitution* of transitory self-inflicted "suffering" for "eternal torments," the submission to priests and their mediation, and an emphasis on strict proportionality between penitential works and God's mercy. With this idea of "satisfaction" comes that of "merit," which may accumulate in acts exceeding obligation, making it possible to earn a surplus. "A good deed has God as its debtor, and a bad deed also, because every judge settles a case on its merits," he says.[41] "Now since God presides as judge in order to exact and safeguard justice, something so precious in his sight, and since it is for this that He establishes every single precept of His moral law, can it be doubted that, just as in all of our actions, so, too, in the case of repentance justice must be rendered to God?"[42] This heavy emphasis on God's justice (like his honor, with which it is inextricably tied) returns in the soteriologies of Anselm of Canterbury and Thomas Aquinas, which push the implications of what it means to give satisfaction for sins in a number of ways that we will discuss below. It is precisely God's justice that obliges him not only to punish sin but to reward meritorious conduct. With this, a crucial distinction enters in: acts that exceed requirement, like martyrdom, realize a cumulative merit unlike those that merely discharge an obligation. Tertullian's *On Exhortation to Chastity* argues that sexual abstinence too is a work of supererogation: there are things such as marriage that God allows in a spirit of *indulgence* and "*unwilling* volition"—so that "if you sin not, still you deserve no reward."[43] Other things proceed from his "pure" and "superior" volition, like chastity, which accrues a positive balance.[44]

Tertullian does not himself teach the transferability of merit from person to person, but Cyprian clearly does,[45] completing the template of penitential theology. His language sows the seeds of the later dogma of supererogation on which the Church would one day predicate the selling of indulgences.[46] Although the reformers excoriated the teaching and practice of indulgences, the idea of satisfaction will live on in their theology, long after "the penitential system and the idea of penance, on which it had originally been built up, had completely disappeared."[47] If the language of making satisfaction to God for one's sins and the sins of others does not even begin to take root until the second and third centuries, it takes even longer to find its way into Christian thinking on how Christ saves. Though traces of the idea appear throughout the patristic record, it is not until Anselm's pivotal *Cur Deus homo* (1099) that it receives its first extended theoretical formulation, one that continues to structure Protestant thinking on the atonement to the present day.

The Scapegoat in Early Eschatology

None of the New Testament scriptures noted makes explicit reference to the Day of Atonement goats, although some have been construed to supply the substitutive suffering and death absent from the Leviticus scapegoat prescriptions. Given the undeniably vicarious character of the scapegoat's sin-bearing errand and statements like that in 1 Peter that "He Himself bore our sins in His body on the cross, so that we might die to sin and live to righteousness" (2:24), it seems only a matter of time before Christ and the scapegoat become one in a moment of rhetorical inspiration, if not dogmatic statement. Indeed, what medium could better ensure this eventuality than the fast and loose typological readings of the fathers, which seize so avidly on Old Testament figures and events as shadows of coming Christian fulfillment? Kelly notes that typological exegesis

> was a technique for bringing out the correspondence between the two Testaments, and took as its guiding principle the idea that events and personages of the Old were 'types' of, i.e. prefigured and anticipated, the events and personages of the New. The typologist took history seriously; it was the scene of the progressive unfolding of God's consistent redemptive purpose. Hence he assumed that, from the creation to the judgment, the same unwavering plan could be discerned in the sacred story, the earlier stages being shadows or, to vary the metaphor, rough preliminary sketches of the later. Christ and His Church were the climax; and since in all His dealings with mankind God was leading up to the Christian revelation,

it was reasonable to discover pointers to it in the great experiences of His chosen people.[48]

The New Testament ends without an explicit reference to the scapegoat, but we do not have long to wait before the first patristic typologies take the field and they plainly identify the animal with the crucified Christ. What might they offer in the way of vicarious soteriology? Rather little, as it turns out. Our three earliest sources—*The Epistle of Barnabas*, Justin Martyr, and Tertullian—all read the scapegoat as a type of Jesus' earthly suffering but there is really nothing to indicate its substitutive character. The still embattled position of the early church meant different needs and interests: that one of numberless victims crushed beneath the wheels of Roman justice was, in defiance of every indication to the contrary, not just a god but the God of the whole world, made the gospel a rather hard sell. A concern for the vindication of the Redeemer trumped many other considerations, and these early typologies seem to reflect this.

The first document that explicitly links Jesus to the scapegoat is the *Epistle of Barnabas* (second century). Some scholars think it uses an earlier source on which Justin Martyr and Tertullian might have drawn. Although there is some question as to when it first appeared, Paget notes the developing consensus for "a Hadrianic date sometime in the 130s."[49] The relevant portion follows:

> *Take a couple of goats, unblemished and well-matched; bring them for an offering, and let the priest take one of them for a burnt-offering.* And what are they to do with the other? *The other,* He declares, *is accursed.* (Now see how plainly the type of Jesus appears.) *Spit on it, all of you; thrust your goads into it, wreath its head with scarlet wool, and so let it be driven into the desert.* This is done, and the goat-ward leads the animal into the desert, where he takes off the wool and leaves it there, on the bush we call a bramble (the plant we usually eat the berries of, if we come across it in the countryside; nothing has such tasty fruit as a bramble). Now what does that signify? Notice that the first goat is for the altar, and the other is accused; and that it is the accused one that wears the wreath. That is because they shall see Him on That Day clad to the ankles in His red woolen robe, and will say, "Is not this he whom we once crucified, and mocked and pierced and spat upon? Yes, this is the man who told us that he was the son of God." But how will He resemble the goat? The point of there being two similar goats,

both of them fair and alike, is that when they see Him coming on the Day, they are going to be struck with terror at the manifest parallel between Him and the goat. In this ordinance, then, you are to see typified the future sufferings of Jesus. But why should they put the wool on the thorns? This too is a type of Jesus, meant for the Church's instruction. For if one wanted to take the scarlet wool for himself, it would cost him much suffering, since the thorns were fearsome and could only be mastered with anguish. Similarly, says He, those who would behold Me and possess My kingdom must go through affliction and suffering before they can reach me.[50]

The author is clearly interpreting a number of extrabiblical details—among them, the twining of the scapegoat's horns, its likeness to the immolated goat, and abuse en route to the wilderness. The scapegoat typifies Christ in his suffering as cursed, spat upon, and pierced, but a concern for his recognition at the Second Coming dominates the passage. As a type of his rejection and death, the scapegoat makes up one half of an equation that the return of the glorified Christ completes. There is a dawning awareness that the one who died has returned, and the scapegoat points to this moment of eschatological fulfillment, but nothing here suggests the vicarious efficacy of Christ's punishment. Indeed, the typology of the wool amid thorns emphasizes sufferings that believers must themselves undergo to lay hold of Christ. An appeal to conflicting recognition motifs confuses the passage, but we should see that both work to underscore the central idea: in one place the twined wool and high priestly robe establish a decisive connection between the suffering of the scapegoat as a type of Christ's Passion and his second coming—scarlet signs connecting his two advents and enabling recognition by those who put him to death; later it will be the scapegoat's likeness to its immolated twin that crystallizes awareness. In either case Christ's self-vindicating apotheosis is what counts.

Justin Martyr's typology, which dates to 160, is less ambiguous than *Barnabas* in representing the two goats as declarative of Christ's two appearances:

Likewise, the two identical goats which had to be offered during the Fast—one of which was the scapegoat and the other the sacrificial goat—were an announcement of the two advents of Christ: of the first advent, in which your priests and elders sent him away as a scapegoat, seizing him and putting him to death; of the second advent, because in that same place of Jerusalem you shall recognize him whom you had subjected to shame, and who was a sacrificial offering for all sinners who are willing to repent.[51]

Here too the emphasis falls on Christ's recognition upon his return. Although Justin's scapegoat is the type of Christ's death, it is the immolated goat he interprets as "a sacrificial offering for all sinners willing to repent."[52] This short remark is all we get in the way of soteriological explanation. Sometime in the early fourth century, Tertullian's *Contra Marcion* says:

> If I may offer, moreover, an interpretation of the two goats which were presented on "the great day of atonement," do they not also figure the two natures of Christ? They were of like size, and very similar in appearance, owing to the Lord's identity of aspect; because He is not to come in any other form, having to be recognized by those by whom He was also wounded and pierced. One of these goats was bound with scarlet, and driven by the people out of the camp into the wilderness [*perditionem*], amid cursing, and spitting, and pulling, and piercing, being thus marked with all the signs of the Lord's own passion; while the other, by being offered up for sins, and given to the priests of the temple for meat, afforded proofs of His second appearance, when (after all sins have been expiated) the priests of the spiritual temple, that is, the church, are to enjoy the flesh, as it were, of the Lord's own grace, whilst the residue go away from salvation without tasting it.[53]

Maclean rightly notes that "the typology of the immolated goat is problematic" in all three citations, as "there is nothing about that goat (other than its physical similarity to the scapegoat) that can be directly likened to Christ's Parousia without recourse to forced exegesis, since a goat, slaughtered and burnt whole, is hardly a fitting image for the triumphant Christ."[54] She thinks the typology so forced that it is probable "the impetus for [the] identification had already been forgotten or even rejected."[55] Punitive details like those found in the Mishnah Yoma probably explain the scapegoat's identification with Christ's suffering and death. Tertullian's extended list of abuses makes the scapegoat a better exemplar than its twin—it is cursed, spat at, bound, torn, pierced, and then killed. This leaves the immolated goat filling a role for which it is rather ill suited. The typologies of later interpreters, who appear to be reading the text of Leviticus alone, make the immolated goat the type of Christ's Passion.[56] One further detail of this typology warrants mention:

Tertullian calls the place to which they drive the scapegoat *perditio* (perdition). Here we need only note that the scapegoat will find itself increasingly entangled with the doctrine of Christ's descent into hell, which does not acquire creedal status before 370 A.D.

Finally, we note the strong resemblance between Christ and the personified Azazel who is driven out amid cursing and killed by Second Temple celebrants. The earliest typologies identify the scapegoat with Jesus, not Azazel, but otherwise the two figures are nearly identical. A kindred curse unites them and drives them to destruction. If there is little to tell them apart as figures of reprobation and punishment, in another sense they are now also perfectly antithetical: one divine, the other diabolical. In the first moment of Christian interpretation, the scapegoat simply doubles as in a mirror, reproducing itself over a vanishing but intraversible distance.

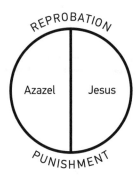

CHAPTER 3

The Sulfurous and Sublime

The Hell-Bound Goat

At a symbolic and structural level, the scapegoat begins its life as a Christian type divided from itself. The personification of Azazel in later Jewish ritual becomes a type of Jesus in the first Christian readings, but the scapegoat's itinerary remains unchanged. It walks a path of abuse and exile that leads to the netherworld, *perditio*. With Origen (third century) the scapegoat reverts unambiguously to its demonic identity. "The goat which in the book of Leviticus is sent away (into the wilderness)," Origen says, "and which in the Hebrew language is named Azazel was none other than this [the Devil]": he is the "wicked one . . . having fallen from heaven . . . the cause of man's expulsion from the divine Paradise."[1] This is why "it was necessary to send it away into the desert and to treat it as an expiatory sacrifice, because on it the lot fell. For all who belong to the 'worse' part, on account of their wickedness, being opposed to those who are God's heritage, are deserted by God."[2]

In one of his homilies on Leviticus, Origen compares the two lots cast on the Day of Atonement to the two thieves crucified on either side of Christ. The one who confesses Christ is taken without delay to paradise, while the other who reviled him "was made the lot of the scapegoat."[3] To this he adds that Christ "fulfilled 'the lot of the scapegoat'" by fastening "the principalities and opposing powers upon his cross" and then leading them to damnation:

> As, I say, no one else could do these things besides him, so no one else could "triumph over" and lead "into the wilderness" of Hell "the principalities and powers and rulers of the world". . . . Therefore, for that reason, it was necessary for my Lord and Savior not only to be born a man among men but also to descend to Hell that as "a prepared man" he could lead away "the lot of the scapegoat into the wilderness" of Hell. And returning from that place, his work completed, he could ascend to the Father, and there be more fully purified at the heavenly altar so that he could give a pledge of our flesh, which he had taken with him, in perpetual purity.[4]

This is an important soteriological moment in the history we are telling—striking not simply for its depiction of *Christus Victor* and the humiliation of the powers but for its tight focus on the cross as the instrument of their defeat and Christ's subsequent triumphal descent into hell. That all this action takes place within the context of a Day of Atonement typology is remarkable given how little the first readings had to offer in this regard. Of course, Christ is here the "prepared man," not the scapegoat. The vicarious character of his mission appears briefly in Origen's reference to "a pledge of our flesh" given at "the heavenly altar," but it is hardly the dominant theme.

In another of his homilies on Leviticus, Origen reworks the Day of Atonement goats to show us Christ's Passion in a different perspective. Here, Jesus is the immolated goat "offered to God as an offering to atone for sins," Pilate is the prepared man, and Barabbas the scapegoat.[5] Among the church fathers, Origen is the first to offer an extended interpretation of Christ's death as a propitiatory sacrifice. He cites both Romans 3:25 and 1 John 2:1–2 when he writes of "the day of atonement [that] remains for us until the sun sets; that is, until the world comes to an end," on which Christ "goes to the Father to make atonement for the human race" and so "propitiates the Father for humans," interceding "not indeed for those who belong to "the lot of that he-goat which is sent 'into the wilderness'" but "only for those who 'are the lot of the Lord.'"[6] The motif appears without any attempt to reconcile the idea of divine propitiation with that of satanic conquest. His *Commentary on Matthew* brings the question of the scapegoat's diabolical character full circle with its claim that "Barabbas the robber . . . is figuratively the devil, or some evil power."[7] Jerome (fourth to fifth centuries) produces something very close to Origen's negative reading in a rigidly dichotomizing Easter Sunday homily:

> On the Sabbath day, the Jews do not make a journey, for they have lost Him who said: "I am the way." . . . They crowned the Lord with thorns; but we, as precious stones, shall become the crown of the Lord. . . . They have rejected Christ, but accept the Antichrist; we have recognized and acknowledged the humble Son of God, that afterwards we may have the triumphal savior. In the end, our he-goat will be immolated before the altar of the Lord; their buck, the Antichrist, spit upon and cursed, will be cast into the wilderness. Our thief enters Paradise with the Lord; their thief, a homicide and blasphemer, dies in his sin. For them Barabbas is released; for us, Christ is slain.[8]

Like Origen, Jerome reads the Day of Atonement goats dualistically, by contrast with the earliest readings that see both goats as Christ. The immolated goat assumes some definition here as Christ in his suffering and death, while the scapegoat extends its significations to include with the Devil a number of his cohorts—principalities, powers, Antichrist, Barabbas, carnal Christians, and, notably, the Jews.

In the fourth century a letter of Ambrose mentions the Day of Atonement goats as types of the saved and the lost: "For as there are *two men in the field, and one of them shall be taken and the other left*, so there [are] two he-goats."[9] The scapegoat "which presents a deceptive offering, not the sincerity of a diligent confession," must "be sent into the wilderness, where our fathers wandered," and "could not attain to the land of resurrection but the memory of them passed from the land."[10] These earliest citations enunciate one pole of that antithetical structure whose emergence over the course of many centuries we mark in this and the following section. Their negative construal of the scapegoat is alive and well deep into the medieval period, where it picks up a few new emphases, though the steady reiteration of the same diabolical significations is what is most striking.

In a commentary attributed to Bede the Venerable (672–735 A.D.), we read that "while many are called, few are chosen," and that "some are sacrificed to God as sacrificial victims," while "the rest are cast out."[11] The lots cast over the goats show "that each one may either be received or cast forth by its own worth" and, whereas the "lot of God . . . is killed, because we are killed on account of him every day," the one "which is sent into the wilderness" bears "the sins of the people into solitude," having prayers "poured forth over [it]" like the blood of the just upon sinners.[12] A few lines on, it is "the desert of the Jews" to which the scapegoat goes, as a type of Barabbas led away when the people cry out for Jesus' crucifixion.[13] In a collection of glosses on the church fathers attributed to the Benedictine abbot Walafrid Strabo (808–849 A.D.) but more likely compiled in the eleventh century, we read that "the goat which is sacrificed to the Lord represents those who are destined to the grace of God, just as Lazarus, who was carried by angels into the lap of Abraham."[14] The scapegoat, for its part, "represents the wicked, or the Jewish people, who are cast away from the face of the Lord on account of their sins, just as the rich man is buried in hell."[15] Another commentary naming Bruno as author—probably Bruno of Cologne, founder of the Carthusian order (1030–1101 A.D.)—teaches that the "first goat is the mystery of Christ," which "by lot goes to the holocaust for the Lord on behalf of our sin" and is "burned outside the camp" as Jesus "suffered outside the gates" in order to "sanctify mankind through his blood"; whereas the scapegoat "is the mystery of the Antichrist," the "Messiah whom [the Jews] await."[16] By his laying on of hands the high priest "condemns all the iniquity of things as well as the goat to the devil with whatever strength he is able, and curses it all."[17] In this typology the figure of the sin-bearer then takes a precipitously sharp descent: "For the Antichrist bears all the sins of the sons of Israel into hell, into the desert, into the land of solitude because on the behalf of those whom he has deceived, he will be transferred to the eternal fires and will suffer a punishment worthy of his sinfulness."[18]

In the carefully reasoned opinion of William of Auvergne (1180–1249), God intended "the places where Demons lived to be places of impurities and sins" and so "that he might place the sons of Israel far from there," it is as though he said to the goat, "Go there, carry there the impurities of sins, to where their main place is."[19] William's didactic reading leaves no stone unturned. God intends this removal to take place "through the agency of the goat, because it is stinking and because clothes are able to be made from its hairs, which are pungent, and which create and nourish bestial impurities"; from these same hairs "indeed ropes become strong, in which it was easy that the stench, impurity, and roughness be understood as the cords and chains of sins."[20] The goat's expulsion has an absolutory value—"the people were freed from sins"—and a punitive one: "just as the Scapegoat is left and exposed to beasts on account of the sins he bears in his figure," so "the people burdened by sins would become derelict of God's protection."[21] William does not typologize the scapegoat, but the idea that the animal meets a bad end in the wilderness as the prey of other animals appears elsewhere in typological readings that exploit this detail to theological ends. A Pseudo-Jerome quoted in the *Catena Aurea* of Thomas Aquinas (1224–1274), perhaps the most famous Latin compilation of glosses, records that the immolated goat "is slain, as a lamb, for the sins of those who are forgiven," for "the Lord's portion is always slain" while the goat "loosed and sent out into the wilderness of hell with the sin of the people" is "the devil's part (for he is the master of those men, which is the meaning of Barabbas)" who, "when freed, is cast headlong into hell."[22] For reasons that we shall come to, the dualist tradition all but completely dies out in the English typologies of the sixteenth and seventeenth centuries, which are numerous but tend overwhelmingly to read the scapegoat as a prefiguration of Christ. The exception to the rule is the Congregationalist preacher Jeremiah Burroughs, who may have been the sole proponent for his century of the reprobate sinner typology. For him the scapegoat "was to go into the Wilderness, into a desolate place among the wild beasts . . . to note the woful condition of a Sinner that hath the guilt of multitudes of Sins upon him" like "a man, all over from the crown of the head to the soal of the foot, full of plague sores."[23]

The Goat on High

According to the rhetor Libanius, it was "during the long winter nights when other people are usually more interested in matters of sex" that the emperor Julian wrote his antichristian opus *Against the Galileans*, expressly to refute those books "in which that fellow from Palestine is claimed to be a god and a son of god."[24] Julian's well-schooled attack on Christianity will significantly affect the history of scapegoat interpretation with its claim that Moses prescribed apotropaeic sacrifices to the *Averrunci*—evil-averting demons—that differed little from those of the pagans.[25] The Levitical prescription of a goat "for Azazel" becomes therefore something of a liability for the Christian apologists. Against this notion of the scapegoat as an offering to demons, Cyril of Alexandria asserts a new kind of holistic Day of Atonement typology. His refutation of the emperor ventures that "Christ was described by the two goats—as dying for us in the flesh, and then, as shown by the scape-goat, overcoming death in His divine nature."[26] As in *Barnabas*, Justin, and Tertullian, both goats are Christ, only without reference to his advents. They signify instead his humble death and exultant resurrection. Cyril develops this interpretation at some length in a letter to Bishop Acacius of Miletene. He disparages the opinion that "the first of the goats or bucks was allotted to God, who is over all things, as a dedication and a sacrifice, while the other one was sent into the desert to some abominable, wretched and unclean demon, and this by the hand of a priest and as a result of a legal decree"—something he deems at once "simple-minded and ridiculous."[27] For how indeed could "he who is the fashioner of all things . . . endure admitting the apostate, Satan, as a consort . . . of his power and glory"[28] or enjoin gifts to that "depraved power" who some "would name *apopompaios*"?[29] Moses "commanded that two he-goats be brought" because "through both of them the one and only Son and Lord Jesus Christ is signified."[30]

As in Origen's typology of the trial before Pilate, the immolated goat is Christ, the sacrificial victim, but Cyril then pushes this identification in a spate of New Testament and Isaiah 53 references to reveal the saving act as an act of substitution.

> Thus Christ became a victim "for our sins according to the Scriptures" [1 Cor. 15:3]. For this reason, we say that he was named sin; wherefore, the all-wise Paul writes, "For our sakes he made him to be sin who knew nothing of sin" [2 Cor. 5:21], that is to say, God the Father. For we do not say that Christ became a sinner, far from it, but being just, or rather in actuality justice, for he did not know sin, the Father made him a victim for the sins of the world. "He was counted among the wicked" [Isa. 53:12] having endured a condemnation most suitable for the wicked. And the divinely inspired prophet Isaiah will also vouch for this, saying, "We had all gone astray like sheep, each following his own way, but the Lord laid upon him the guilt of us all," "yet it was on our behalf he suffers," "and by his stripes we were healed" [Isa. 53:6, 4, 5]. The all-wise Peter writes, "He bore our sins in his body upon the tree" [1 Pet. 2:24].[31]

Here the immolated goat becomes not only a signifier of Christ's vicarious suffering and death, but something more as well. Cyril uses 2 Corinthians 5:21 ("he made him to be sin who knew nothing of sin") to identify Christ with sin; this identification prompts a corresponding insistence on his sinlessness. The move from surrogacy to identification ends in an impasse: to die for the sins of others is one thing, but how indeed could Christ *become* sin? The vicariousness of his work, which depends for its sense on a distinction, however attenuated, between the bearer and his burden, collapses. The problem calls forth an absolute vindication that serves to foreground Christ's simultaneous, unblemishable innocence. This will in time become the sine qua non distinguishing him from every ritual victim gone before, from all the merely apotropaeic devices of archaic religion. We shall discover this simultaneous identification and distinction in other texts where the same scriptures are in play and where more sophisticated strategies are deployed to explain the paradox of the innocent anathema.

For Cyril Christ's death is, moreover, restorative ("by his stripes we were healed")—a reciprocal effect of his suffering. He makes the Father the source of punishment and Christ the victim condemned for the sins of the world. Cyril's use of the Suffering Servant to amplify his typology of the immolated goat is a decisive addition to the history of our term: *what Cyril says about the immolated goat is almost precisely what the scapegoat now signifies.* The victim suffers vicariously. He is innocent. Jesus "was counted among the wicked" although "we do not say that Christ became a sinner," for he was justice itself. What about the second goat, the scapegoat? "Let us see (Christ) in the other living goat sent away," Cyril says, "not being held fast by the gates of the underworld together with the other dead."[32]

> For he rose again, despoiling death and "saying to the prisoners: Come out, to those in darkness: Show yourselves" [Isa. 49:9], and he ascended to his Father above in the heavens to a position inaccessible to men, having taken upon himself our sins and being the propitiation for them. . . . Consider, therefore, how he calls the second goat the living one, although the first goat was sacrificed. For, as I said, the one and only Son and Lord Jesus Christ, was depicted in both [goats] as suffering in his own flesh, and beyond suffering, as in death and above death. For the Word of God lived, even though his holy flesh tasted death, and the Word of God remained impassible, although he made his own the suffering of his own body and took it upon himself.[33]

With this new reading the scapegoat undergoes a final symbolic division to reveal Christ's Resurrection, his liberation of hell, and divinely impassible nature. Escaping immediate death—*unlike* its immolated fellow—the scapegoat opens a new range of signifying possibilities at the far end of the typological spectrum from where the earliest readings begin. Its transformation could hardly be more sweeping: from Satan in the wilderness of hell to Jesus in celestial imperviousness to suffering. What is more, *Christus Victor* appears in the image of Jesus' prison-breaking resurrection from the dead so that in the two goats, the two principal views of the atonement stand side by side.

In another place Cyril writes that Christ "was resurrected and went up to a region inaccessible to us, that is heaven, as if bearing away our sins," for a rather different construal of the scapegoat's sin-bearing errand than the dualist readings advance.[34] Like him, Hesychius of Jerusalem will reject the idea of "a sacrifice offered to the devil."[35] Because "no one is able to cast off sins except God alone," it is God who sends the scapegoat "carrying over itself their names into a solitary or pathless land."[36] Hesychius then adds that the "pathless desert is sacred, and the home of the Holy of Holies, where it is said that at the time of the passion divinity departed into heaven. . . . confining its virtue from humankind, in order to give space to the passion, remaining in a place worthy of itself, which is of course in the lap of the Father."[37] In this influential reading, to which we shall return, Christ's divine nature, being impassible, simply withdraws from the human suffering of the crucifixion.[38] Theodoret gives us what is perhaps the clearest exposition of the dual nature typology in the dialogue *Eranistes*, when Orthodoxos explains to his interlocutor that "the blessed Paul calls Him sin [2 Cor. 5:21] and a curse [Gal. 3:13]," satisfying the types of the serpent in the wilderness and the sacrifice of the two goats respectively. "But the type of the two goats makes us think of two persons," Eranistes replies. "The passibility of the humanity and the impassibility of the divinity could not have been prefigured at the same time by one goat," says Orthodoxos, "for after its death, it would not have revealed the living nature."[39] Thus "two were taken . . . in order to reveal the two natures."[40]

Had the scapegoat been used to typify the vicarious suffering we have just been canvassing, our search would be near its end. But it is the *immolated* goat that plays this part. These Eastern typologies, which exclude punishment or suffering from their interpretations of the scapegoat, bar our way forward. They were, moreover, hugely influential in shaping English readings during the century or more between Tyndale's coinage of the word "scapegoat" and its first metaphorical uses (mid-seventeenth century), an obviously critical period for the semantic destiny of our expression.

We turn next to the earliest English readings (sixteenth to seventeenth centuries), which identify the scapegoat with Christ's divine nature and life from the dead.[41] A translation of the Swiss reformer Heinrich Bullinger's *Fiftie Godlie and Learned Sermons* gives what is perhaps the earliest English formulation of this interpretive tradition. The two goats "do signifie Christ our Lorde, verie God, and verie man in two natures vnseparated," who "is slaine and dyeth in his humanitie: but is not slaine nor dyeth in his diuinitie."[42] A slim majority of sixteenth- and seventeenth-century English commentators follow suit.[43] Their typologies, which emphasize Christ's escape from death, contain predictably buoyant references to his sin-bearing. Henoch Clapham conflates the two motifs handily, writing of the "humaine" and "invisible" natures of Christ as "foretyped by the two Hegoates," one dying to satisfy "Iehouah for Israels synnes," while "thother scaped carying Syn . . . into the place cut of[f] from the habitation of Synners."[44] Many others note Christ's sin-bearing in this absolutory mood. Once conferred upon the animal's head, sin all but disappears.[45] So the goat "which fled into the wildernesse is a type of Christ taking away all our sins," according to John Preston.[46] He is "that true scape-goat" who carries sins "far from the sight of God," says Edward Leigh.[47] In many readings, the wilderness is simply a metaphor of divine amnesia. Thus Nathanael Culverwell writes that when "sins are laid upon the head of the scape-goat, they are then carried into a land of forgetfulnesse," since "God never forgives, but he doth forget too."[48] The same image appears in a number of other sources from the mid-seventeenth century, including Henry Jessey's book-length interview with the young prophetess Sarah Wight, in whose words Christ is the scapegoat who bears sins "away into the Wildernesse of forgetfulnesse, never to be remembred any more."[49] Richard Coppin uses a similar expression, writing that the scapegoat as a "livelie tipe of Jesus Christ" has both "carried [sins] away into the Wildernesse" and "drowned them in the Sea of forgetfulnesse."[50] The thing to notice is that, alone or adjoined to a typological identification with Christ's divine nature, this construal of what it means for the scapegoat to bear sins is devoid of punitive significations. Amnesty for sinners pairs winningly with Christ's resurrection from the dead, but either way, the scapegoat is no sacrifice for sin. If, in the end, the triumphalism of so many commentators comes to naught and the scapegoat's bright prospects are eclipsed by darker meanings, the reasons lie in other, sharply divergent interpretations of what it means to bear the sins of the people.

In the next chapter we will begin marking changes in the soteriological outlook that quickly begin to register in new scapegoat typologies. Before leaving the first millennium of Christian reflection, we should underscore the emergence of the divine-impassible/demonic-damned antithesis that now stands fully revealed. That interpretations of the scapegoat ventured over such a dizzying span of time should break so evenly to one semantic extreme or the other is striking, when indeed there seem to be so few constraints on typological whim and so many exegetes interpreting the Day of

Atonement. The antithesis achieves its fullest, most divergent expression in a period dominated by the narrative of *Christus Victor*, whose action plays in a cosmos delimited by the poles of its opposition.

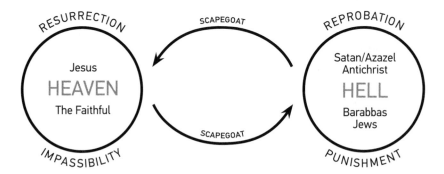

CHAPTER 4

Economies of Blood

Satan Evicted

With the exclusion of the Devil as a player of any consequence—the locus of death and the enemy whom Christ came to defeat—the meaning of the saving operation changes dramatically. The two most important writers associated with this move are Anselm of Canterbury and Thomas Aquinas, both of whom relegate the Devil to a titular role, redeploying the power of death within new soteriological configurations. God did not need "to come down from heaven to conquer the devil," Anselm says, "or to take action against him in order to set mankind free," for God "did not owe the devil anything but punishment, nor did man owe him anything but retribution—to defeat in return him by whom he had been defeated."[1] The standard version of the theory that God ransoms humankind from the Devil is thus abandoned in preference to the idea that Christ offers himself a sacrifice to God in what Pelikan says "could be seen as the one supreme act of penitential satisfaction."[2] Because human sin violates God's justice by depriving him of what he is owed, namely "the honour of his dignity"—and indeed, "there is nothing . . . God preserves more justly"—one of two alternatives obtains.[3] "Consider it, then, an absolute certainty," Anselm tells his interlocutor Boso, "that God cannot remit a sin unpunished, without satisfaction, that is, without the voluntary paying off of a debt."[4] The problem is that no sinner can satisfy this debt since he owes God perfect obedience in the first place. When we consider that he has, moreover, contracted a debt commensurate to the honor of the offended party—namely, an infinite one—his dire predicament appears clearly. The sinner begins in hopeless arrears so that any honor he might contrive to render God is already a matter of obligation. The death of Jesus saves, not by appeasing the wrath of God, who is impassible, but by putting God in obligation to reward a truly *voluntary* offering, for, being sinless, Christ was not obliged to die. This in turn shows us the need for his Incarnation, since "if no one but God can make that satisfaction and no one but man is obliged to make it, then it is necessary that a God-Man make it."[5] To illustrate voluntary action, Anselm recapitulates the same exemplary contrast of marriage to virginity which Tertullian deployed in his contradistinction of that which God allows in a spirit of indulgence and that which he prefers by a superior volition.

> Although a creature possesses nothing of itself, none the less, when God gives it leave to do or not to do something with his permission, he is granting it the gift of having two options, under such terms that, although one option may be better, neither is definitely demanded. . . . Moreover, if it does what is better, it has a reward, because it is giving of its own accord what is its own. For instance, although virginity is better than marriage neither is definitely demanded of a human being . . . [although] if he preserves virginity, he looks forward to a reward for the voluntary gift which he is offering to God.[6]

Anselm uses this example to explain how it is that "when Christ died, he gave what He did not owe."[7] Christ's truly voluntary offering to "the honor of God" earns a compensatory reward that suffices to pay the human debt.[8] In a paraphrase of Jesus' prayer in the Garden of Gethsemane Anselm writes, "Because the Father was unwilling for the restoration of the human race to be brought about by other means than that a man should perform an action of the magnitude of that death . . . it is as if [Christ] were saying: 'Since you do not wish the reconciliation of the world to take place in any other way, I say that you are, in this way, willing my death. Let this will of yours come to pass—that is, let my death come to pass, so that the world may be reconciled to you."[9] Anselm therefore plainly acknowledges the grim alternatives as willed by God. Because "no one else could perform the deed," he says, it was "as if the Father were instructing him to die."[10] This claim stands side by side with Anselm's repudiation of the idea that "God hand[s] over an innocent man to be killed in place of the guilty party," with which it is somewhat difficult to reconcile.[11] "For the Father did not coerce Christ to face death against his will, or give permission for him to be killed," Anselm says, "but Christ himself of his own volition underwent death in order to save mankind."[12] This is critical, in theologian Gary Anderson's view, for understanding how Anselm manages to avoid the implication that God "demands the blood of his Son in order to discharge the debts that are indelibly inscribed in his account books."[13] A clear advantage of *Christus Victor*, which Anselm rejects, is that "it put God in the position of being the unqualified benefactor of humankind. In his passion, God acted on behalf of humanity to abrogate the rights that Satan had previously held. The story of the cross is a story of God's masterful victory over the evil one."[14] If, on the other hand, "God is the holder of the bond, a point of tension can arise. It is possible to imagine God not as the champion of the human race but as an indignant being whose wrath against humanity must be appeased."[15] According to Anderson, Anselm's detractors have missed the "crucial distinction" he draws between punishment suffered as a just consequence of sin and *satisfaction*—"a *voluntary* recompense for wrongdoing."[16] Christ "does not atone for the sins of humankind by becoming a penal substitute. He suffered death solely of his own choosing to redeem the human race."[17]

The distinction is what keeps Anselmian satisfaction from becoming a matter of vicarious punishment, and it proves somewhat difficult to maintain. For one thing, the fate of the world hangs upon Christ's consent to die in such a way that for him to refuse would mean a thwarting of the divine purpose in creation, and that is not much of a choice, as Anselm himself acknowledges. "God does nothing under compulsion of necessity," Anselm says, and yet he nevertheless "put himself under an obligation to bring [man's] good beginning to fulfillment."[18] Once pledged to create he cannot subsequently fail to complete his initiative. What is more, he places himself under this obligation in perfect cognizance of "what man was going to do, when he created him," and knowing, too, the satisfaction he would require to remit man's debt.[19] If this obligation were something God the Father contracted independently of his Son, Christ might then freely elect to save his Father's honor in consenting to die, but the obligation binds Father and Son alike as divinely united in purpose. We are pushing the limits of Anselm's rationalism here in an attempt to see Christ's "voluntary" death in full context. What is properly voluntary in this picture is the divine move to set up a choice that is really no choice at all. Christ's death has less to do with his freely saving God's honor than with the divine initiative to create a world in which it was from the outset a foregone conclusion that he would have to die. In the last analysis there may be no way of keeping Anselm from slipping down the slope to where the more forthrightly penal theologians take their stand. Aulén observes

> that it has been usual to sum up the difference between Anselm's teaching and that of the later scholastics by pointing to the fact that Thomas speaks of Christ's work of satisfaction as also including the endurance of punishment. It is, however, a mistake to lay much stress on this point; at most it is merely a difference of expression, and it involves no change in outlook . . . it is clear that the idea of satisfaction passes over naturally and easily into that of punishment, since the satisfaction which Christ made consisted in the vicarious endurance of a death which, if men had endured it, would have been their punishment.[20]

We recall that what Aulén called the "classic view" scarcely acknowledges, much less reduces, the ambiguity of its simultaneous insistence upon "the deliverance of man from the power of the devil" and "his deliverance from God's judgment," making it "next to impossible to construct a rationally consistent theory of the atonement."[21] Anselm's precise, actuarial description of how Christ saves clarifies things decisively by reducing the role of the devil and extending the pecuniary metaphor. He replays the soteriological action with just three major players, and so makes it more straightforward. God is the creditor, humankind the debtor, Christ the remitter of debt. The ledger of divine justice is one of satisfactions and merits and the saving computation that of a transferable surplus.[22] All the defining features of Tertullian's and Cyprian's teaching on repentance appear together in this rendition of how Christ saves. The emphasis on God's justice to which the problem of death is now fully bound stands clear. A crucial distinction between obligatory and voluntary action sets up the possibility of meritorious supererogation. The vicarious efficacy of that merit completes the transaction, which is so dominated by pecuniary figures that Anselmian satisfaction is sometimes referred to as the "commercial theory" of atonement. Although God graciously pays the price of salvation, it is a price he himself requires. The locus of death has therefore shifted. A diabolical crime against the people of God becomes instead a function of God's retributive justice.

Metaphors of sin as debt are clearly older than Tertullian's use of the term "satisfaction"; but it is equally true that penitential theology influenced the writing of *Cur Deus homo* (1099) profoundly. As a defining religious practice of the Middle Ages, the sacrament of penance ranked second only to the Eucharist.[23] Vicarious satisfaction and transferable merit had become axiomatic features of a system offering a variety of meritorious (pilgrimage, crusade, etc.) and penitential recourses (prayers, fasting, flagellations, etc.) to the faithful. The value of such acts could be realized in a burgeoning economy of absolutions, remissions, commutations, and indulgences, allowing penitents to negotiate terms for themselves and others here and in the world to come. Herwaarden notes that "anyone who visits medieval churches and is filled with awe at the beauty of their architecture should bear in mind that a considerable part of both the buildings and their furnishings was paid for by the revenues from indulgences granted to those who gave money towards the material costs of the church."[24] The meritorious supererogation that saves, according to Anselm's theory, owes far more to the legal framework, terminology, and conceptual resources of the medieval Church's dogmas on repentance than to earlier sources where similar commercial metaphors are in play.[25] Itself a penitential act, Christ's death called forth acts of penance in all who would lay hold of its power to save and sanctioned the church's role in dispensing absolution to sinners. Pelikan notes:

> Satisfaction, then, was another term for "sacrifice," and Christ's sacrificial act of penance made even human acts of satisfaction worthy, since of themselves they were not. It also gave authority to the pronouncement of absolution by a "visible priest," for Christ as the true priest had earned such absolution for all sinners. It was fitting, then, that the act by which "our Christ has redeemed us through the cross" should be appropriated by the individual through penance.[26]

We cannot follow Aquinas through all the labyrinthine paths of his thought on the atonement, but we should mark a few critical thresholds that the angelic doctor crosses. Let us begin by noting the Devil's place in his account. The *Summa Theologiae* says that "Man by sinning became the bondsman both of God and of the devil": he thus contracted (1) guilt and a debt of punishment but also (2) "by God's just permission fell under the devil's servitude."[27] Let us deal with the second of these problems first. Having deceived man, the Devil "held him unjustly in bondage" and God permits this, ordaining it as a penalty.[28] Justice therefore "required man's redemption with regard to God, but not with regard to the devil."[29] It is indeed fitting that "man should be delivered from the devil's bondage by Christ making satisfaction on his behalf in the passion,"[30] although Christ does not satisfy the Devil, who is unceremoniously subsumed under the larger scheme of divine justice. Christ makes satisfaction to God. The drama of capture and rescue depicted in *Christus Victor* is thus bled of its urgency and meaning. The Devil is a player of no consequence. He does only what God permits him to do.

The problem of human guilt and the debt of punishment is more serious. Had God "willed to free man from sin without satisfaction, He would not have acted against justice,"[31] but he did not. "God's 'severity' (cf. Rm. 11: 22) is thereby shown, for He would not remit sin without penalty."[32] The "act of sin makes man deserving of punishment, in so far as he transgresses the order of Divine justice to which he cannot return, except he pay some sort of penal compensation, which restores him to the equality of justice."[33] Christ's death pays this debt of punishment while purging original sin, which as "an infection of human nature itself . . . could not be expiated by the satisfaction of a mere man."[34] There are other benefits accruing, but that his death answers the debt of punishment is arguably "the core meaning of the atonement" for Aquinas.[35]

Where Anselm insisted on the alternatives of satisfaction or punishment, Aquinas simply equates the two: "punishment avails for satisfaction," he says.[36] What is more, "Christ's voluntary suffering was such a good act, that because of its being found in human nature, God was appeased for every offense of the human race."[37] Aquinas even calls it "a sufficient and superabundant atonement," as "when sufficient satisfaction has been paid, then the debt of punishment is abolished."[38] All the major features of Anselm's penitential calculus are therefore operative, with a couple of important differences. Like Anselm, Aquinas writes of Christ satisfying debt, and both thinkers believe only a God-man could make satisfaction for an offense done to "the infinity of the divine majesty."[39] For Anselm, this has everything to do with the uniquely voluntary character of the God-man's death. It obliges God the Father to bestow an infinite and overflowing reward that saves humankind. Aquinas too emphasizes Christ's voluntary suffering, but the coin that satisfies debt is punishment. This means Christ suffers punishment as a substitute. As the God-man, this suffering possesses an "infinite efficiency," which suffices to repay the debt owed.[40] But Aquinas goes further still, and the language of ledger balancing frequently gives way to something stronger: Christ's suffering *appeases* God the Father who in turn "deliver[ed] up Christ to the Passion," having preordained it "for the deliverance of the human race, according to the words of Isaias (53: 6): 'The Lord hath laid on Him the iniquities of us all'; and again (53: 10): 'The Lord was pleased to bruise Him in infirmity.'"[41] Aquinas points to the cry of dereliction as ample proof that God the Father "abandon[ed] Him to His persecutors,"[42] insisting that Christ suffered the Passion "at the command of the Father," its "original author."[43]

Here, we pause to formulate the two things—satisfaction and punishment—as semantic precursors of what we mean today when we say someone is a scapegoat. The idea of being "blamed or punished vicariously" is, like that of being "extolled or credited for the meritorious acts of others," plainly a matter of substitutions. Satisfaction is the Anselmian procedure; punishment avails to save beginning with Aquinas. Either way, we are dealing with vicarious action as a kind of moral operator—a device for meeting the claims of divine justice. The saving operation may be seen as a substitution of Christ's merit for the otherwise fatal human demerit or as Christ's substitution of himself for the condemned, but in each case the shedding of innocent blood deflects the just sentence of death imposed by God.[44] When we recall that punishing the innocent to pardon the guilty all but defines injustice in our world, we catch a glimpse of the cultural turn to come. By modern sensibilities, death by substitution is a moral outrage. In any sphere of life today this kind of exaction would be condemned out of hand, though in Anselm's world it still made binding sense. It matters little here whether we understand the Son's consent to die as a meaningful act of surrender to the Father's will, or whether we see the divine persons as primordially united in setting the price of forgiveness beyond human reach—a price that must be paid in their behalf. Either way, innocent suffering is the coin that buys reprieve in a strict exchange established by immutable decree. As the homicidal work of human beings, the crucifixion leaves nothing to wonder: Jesus dies like countless victims of religious violence before him under conditions abhorrent, but mundane. When the demand for blood is divine, the whole procedure can seem deranged, a plain travesty by present standards of personal accountability and fair play—standards so nearly universal their late advent and historical contingency can be hard to reckon. The medieval world may not have questioned the fitness of such procedures, but we soon cross new thresholds of incredulity and misgiving on our way to the modern age. By what new standard of justice may God's justice be found unjust? Where would it come from? On whose authority would it be founded?

The New Coin of the Realm

As inherently self-reproducing, the act of substitution extends itself through like acts, value quantifications, and rules of exchange in a process of religious efflorescence driven by the problem of death as God's just recompense for sin. Aquinas's teaching on the atonement forms an exemplary instance of this tendency in full flower. Here, the salvific power of Christ's substitutionary death may indeed be superabundant and able to answer the problem of human sin, but it remains immured within a system of incremental and occasionally hopeless appropriations. "Christ by His Passion delivered us from our sins causally," Aquinas says, "that is, by setting up the cause of our deliverance, from which cause all sins whatsoever, past, present, or to come, could be forgiven: just as if a doctor were to prepare a medicine by which all sicknesses can be cured."[45] This cause, however, "needs to be applied to each individual for the cleansing of personal sin" and "this is done by baptism and penance and the other sacraments,"[46] through which the living unite themselves to Christ's Passion, or rather, those among them *only* in whom a requisite "faith living through charity"[47] is active. Baptism remits all debt of punishment but once. For sins committed after baptism penance becomes the means of making satisfaction to God by punishments "equal [to] the pleasure contained in a sin committed."[48] The metaphor may be medicinal but its logic is strictly quid pro quo.

This appears most clearly in Aquinas's teaching on Christ's descent into hell, where "the power of the Passion . . . is applied to the dead," though not to all of them.[49] Infants who died unbaptized did not make the cut.[50] Too young to respond in faith, infants in hell at the hour of Christ's descent also lacked Christian parents whose faith would have been vicariously applied to save them. Failing this transfer, plainly no hope remained. That original sin may be purged in a child by his or her parents' faith is but one provision among many governing vicarious remittances. Aquinas lays down a number of other rules stipulating under what conditions a person may "merit an increase of grace for another" or "fulfill satisfactory punishment" for him.[51] Quinn suggests that "medieval legal codes provided models for vicarious satisfaction" so that Aquinas "would not have felt the force of this problem to the extent we do."[52] In these codes "the debt of punishment for even such serious crimes as killing was literally pecuniary; one paid the debt by paying monetary compensation. What was important for such purposes as avoiding blood feud was that the debt be paid; who paid it was not crucial."[53] McNeil, too, notes that "the belief in the sharing of merit, arising as it did out of early and deeply

rooted ideas of the communion of saints and the solidarity of the whole fellowship, was one of the fundamental religious conceptions of the age."[54] Of
course the line dividing religious from secular life was more intermittent and
uncertain in the thirteenth century than it is now. The "ethic" of vicariousness, which informs the *Summa's* rulings on everything from the meaning
of Christ's death to the damnation of infants was, like democratic notions
of guilt and personal responsibility today, in the air Aquinas breathed. His
teaching on indulgences, which was so influential on the development of
Catholic doctrine, is exemplary in this regard:

> Hence we must say . . . that indulgences hold good both in the Church's
> court and in the judgment of God, for the remission of the punishment
> which remains after contrition, absolution, and confession. . . . The reason
> why they so avail is the oneness of the mystical body in which many have
> performed works of satisfaction exceeding the requirements of their debts;
> in which, too, many have patiently borne unjust tribulations whereby a
> multitude of punishments would have been paid, had they been incurred.
> So great is the quantity of such merits that it exceeds the entire debt of
> punishment due to those who are living at this moment. . . . Now one man
> can satisfy for another, as we have explained. . . . And the saints in whom
> this super-abundance of satisfactions is found, did not perform their good
> works for this or that particular person, who needs the remission of his
> punishment (else he would have received this remission without any indul-
> gence at all), but they performed them for the whole Church in general.
> . . . These merits, then, are the common property of the whole Church.
> Now those things which are the common property of a number are dis-
> tributed to the various individuals according to the judgment of him who
> rules them all. Hence, just as one man would obtain the remission of his
> punishment if another were to satisfy for him, so would he too if another's
> satisfactions be applied to him by one who has the power to do so.[55]

Driving this economy of salvation is the threat of divine retribution. It means
the end of the human race except for a legal maneuver providing for the
substitution of merit or satisfactory punishment between parties. Since God
in Christ enacts the most important transfer, we acknowledge his gracious
initiative, but the fact remains that someone has to die. It is a matter of divine
honor, according to Anselm; an expression of God's severity, says Aquinas.
With the Devil reduced to a mere functionary in the divine court system,
there is no ambiguity left, no merciful paradox. The will to punish is God's

will. As an expression of his justice, death provides the threat and impels each saving exchange—from Christ's vicarious offering of himself to every last remittance of indebting pleasure by satisfactory punishment, personal or vicarious.

Unlike Anselm, Aquinas will speak of God's wrath. The problem of an affronted and angry God is not new. It belongs to an ancient tradition of self-mortification premised upon the possibility of preempting death by passing sentence on oneself here and now, of *substituting* temporal pangs for eternal torments, as Tertullian taught. A contemporary of Anselm's, Peter Damian, put it like this:

> O what a delightful, what a wonderful sight, when the celestial Judge looks forth from heaven, and man punishes (sacrifices) himself below for his sins! There the accused himself, presiding over the tribunal of his inmost being, holds a three-fold office: in his heart he constitutes himself the judge, in his body the accused, and with his hands he rejoices to hold forth as executioner, as if the holy penitent were saying to God: "There is no need, Lord, for you to order your officer to punish me, nor is it necessary for you to strike me with the fear of the vengeance of a just trial. I have laid hands upon myself, I have taken up my own defence, and I have offered myself in place of my sins." ... This is the victim (*hostia*) which is sacrificed while still alive, born away by the angels and offered to God; thus the victim (*victima*) of the human body is invisibly commingled with that unique sacrifice that was offered on the altar of the cross. And thus every sacrifice is stowed away in one treasure, namely both that which each and every member and that which the head of all the elect has offered [to God].[56]

The core sense of an exchange that Tertullian was the first to articulate for Christianity is therefore alive and well in the eleventh century, someway transfigured by Damian's rhetoric, the sublime participation in Christ's sacrifice that he envisions, though it remains at bottom a negotiation with judgment and death. We recall here Tertullian's indignant observation that "to expect pardon of sins" when penitence has not first been made "is to hold out your hand for merchandise, but not produce the price." "Let me pay now, not later," reasons Damian. The persistence of the pecuniary symbolism, here in the language of mystical union, reminds us that a contemporary of Damian's, John of Salisbury, was already decrying corruption in the trade of intangible tender for which an exchange rate to hard coin was established fact. Writing on the venality of religious who "receive confessions" and "presume to bind and loose" even as "they release their scythe upon harvest belonging to others," John goes on to say:

> Moreover, they too readily exonerate the powerful and the more wealthy upon receipt of favours or payment and, placing upon their shoulders the sins of others, they order them to go out in tunics and mourning garments as penance for whatever deeds they lamented they had committed. They extend the mercy of the Lord, who wishes no one to perish, which they proclaim to be open and accessible just as much to penitents as it is closed only to those without hope. They meanwhile make allowance for those who are ardently and tenaciously involved in crimes to sin in hope; yet they are always paid something in advance for the redemption of such men and they boldly promise forgiveness, because just as water extinguishes fire, so alms extinguish sins.[57]

This was written in the twelfth century, long before the reformers began their assault on this kind of corruption in the church. For Anselm and Aquinas the problem facing humankind is one of debt and remittance. Salvation is an economic negotiation. As in Tertullian's thinking on repentance, the threat of eternal death is divine and the metaphors of exchange and substitution preponderate.

The Goat Devoured

The changing soteriology registers in new interpretations of the scapegoat that take us to the heart of our lexical interest. Let us deal with three exemplary cases, the first two but faint adumbrations of the truly pivotal reading in Calvin. We note a fleeting reference to the scapegoat's *vicarious suffering* buried deep within the *Summa Theologiae*. Aquinas does not interpret this detail typologically. Like Cyril, he remarks that the beast "was let loose into the wilderness: not indeed to offer it to the demons, whom the Gentiles worshipped in desert places, because it was unlawful to offer aught to them; but in order to point out the effect of the sacrifice which had been offered up."[58]

> Hence the priest put his hand on its head, while confessing the sins of the children of Israel: as though that goat were to carry them away into the wilderness, where it would be devoured by wild beasts, because it bore the punishment of the people's sins.[59]

The ninth-century Syrian exegete Ishodad of Merv also mentions the scape-goat's being "devoured by wild animals"—a foregone conclusion, according to him.[60] But neither he nor Aquinas reads the animal's death as an anticipation of Jesus' passion. Aquinas gives two typological readings of the scapegoat in the following section of the *Summa*, which is devoted to what he calls "the figurative reason of these things."[61] The first recalls Hesychius, whose scapegoat prefigures the divinity of Christ withdrawing while his humanity suffers the passion. For Hesychius the place to which Christ withdrew is heaven, "the lap of the Father." Aquinas gives a darker rendition of this idea. The immolated goat "offered in expiation for the sins of the multitude" prefigures Christ coming "in the likeness of sinful flesh" since the "he-goat is an evil-smelling animal" and as such signifies "the stench, uncleanness and the sting of sin," whereas "the scape-goat typifies Christ's Godhead which went away into solitude when the Man Christ suffered, not by going to another place, but by restraining His power."[62] As in Cyril's typologies, the scapegoat typifies the impassible divinity of Christ, but with none of the triumphal fanfare. Its sojourn in the wilderness provides an image of Christ's immortal nature waiting out his human torment on the cross in "solitude." This solitude is less a place than a state of suspension. Aquinas's more somber accounting of the two goats, precisely in terms of Christ's few terrible hours on the cross, provides a glimpse of what is coming. The scapegoat may also represent the "the base concupiscence which we ought to cast away from ourselves, while we offer up to Our Lord acts of virtue," he adds,[63] without indicating a preference for either reading.

The theologian and mystic Denis the Carthusian (1402–1471) also mentions the goat "left in the desert to be devoured by wild beasts," concluding that "it is very suiting to divine justice that animals be punished for the sins of men."[64] Here we discover what is perhaps the first boldly substitutionary reading of the scapegoat as a type of Christ:

> Finally, by the scapegoat sent to the solitude, carrying on himself the sins of the people, Christ is signified, upon whom the Father placed all our iniquities: who, *carrying his cross, went out,* and *paid* for what he had not stolen [Ps. 69:5]; also *Christ on Mount Calvary* was exposed, to be devoured by mad dogs and cruel beasts, who opened their mouths against him in insults; and they struck him on the jaw and were satiated with his sufferings.[65]

With this typology we pass an important threshold. Denis emphasizes the Father's agency in the sufferings that Christ must undergo, which are here explicitly vicarious. The reference, however, is brief, an inconspicuous bit of Latin tucked away in a Catholic commentary on Leviticus and as such without currency in Reformation England, where the fate of our English expression will be decided.

Calvin's Pharmakos

Calvin is the last of the major writers on the atonement that we shall consider and the only Protestant Reformer among them. His language pushes the sub-stitutionary character of Christ's work and the problem of God's wrath well beyond the limits reached by Aquinas. The influence he exerted on English Protestantism would be, moreover, difficult to exaggerate. Although a full reckoning of his role in our account must await the English Calvinists, his interpretation of the scapegoat is itself a decisive moment in the semantic evolution of our word.

> And he shall take the two goats. A twofold mode of expiation is here pre-
> sented to us; for one of the two goats was offered in sacrifice according to
> the provisions of the Law, the other was sent away to be an outcast, or off-
> scouring (κάθαρμα *vel* περίψημα, *katharma* or *peripsēma*). The fulfillment
> of both figures, however, was manifested in Christ, since He was both the
> Lamb of God, whose offering blotted out the sins of the world, and, that
> He might be as an offscouring, (κάθαρμα), His comeliness was destroyed,
> and He was rejected of men. A more subtle speculation might indeed be
> advanced, viz., that after the goat was presented, its sending away was a type
> of the resurrection of Christ; as if the slaying of the one goat testified that
> the satisfaction for sins was to be sought in the death of Christ; whilst the
> preservation and dismissal of the other shewed, that after Christ had been
> offered for sin, and had borne the curse of men, He still remained alive. I
> embrace, however, what is more simple and certain, and am satisfied with
> that; i.e., that the goat which departed alive and free, was an atonement
> (*"piaculum"* or "une beste maudite"), that by its departure and flight the
> people might be assured that their sins were put away and vanished. This
> was the only expiatory sacrifice in the Law without blood; nor does this
> contradict the statement of the Apostle, for since two goats were offered
> together, it was enough that the death of one should take place, and that
> its blood should be shed for expiation; for the lot was not cast until both
> goats had been brought to the door of the tabernacle; and thus although

the priest presented one of them alive "to make an atonement with him," as Moses expressly says, yet God was not propitiated without blood, since the efficacy of the expiation depended on the sacrifice of the other goat.[66]

Of the three interpretations that Calvin offers the first is clearly the most striking because of his use of the Greek terms *katharma* and *peripsēma*, from 1 Corinthians 4:13, where the apostle Paul observes ὡς περικαθάρματα τοῦ κόσμου ἐγενήθημεν, πάντων περίψημα, ἕως ἄρτι, or "we have become as the filth (*perikatharmata*) of the world, and are the offscouring (*peripsēma*) of all things unto this day." The expression περικαθάρματα is an intensive form of καθάρμα, whose historical use to designate *pharmakoi* and similar human victims is on record (see the appendix). Is Calvin comparing the scapegoat to the *pharmakos*? His treatment of this same verse in *Commentary on Corinthians* states plainly that the term περικαθάρματα

> denotes a man who, by public execrations, is devoted, with the view to the cleansing of a city, for such persons, on the ground of their cleansing the rest of the people, by receiving in themselves whatever there is in the city of crimes, and heinous offense, are called by the Greeks sometimes καθάρμα, but more frequently καθάρματα.[67]

"Those unhappy men were led round through the streets," he writes, "that they might carry away with them whatever there was of evil in any corner, that the cleansing might be the more complete."[68] The Greek rites were clearly on Calvin's mind. He points out that "Paul, with a view of expressing his extreme degradation, says that he is held in abomination by the whole world, *like* a man set apart for expiation, and that, like offscourings, he is nauseous to all"; in this he "does not mean to say" that he had become "an expiatory victim for sins" but merely "that in respect of disgrace and reproaches he differs nothing from the man on whom the execrations of all are heaped up."[69]

As we began our discussion with scholarly grumbling about the scapegoat and the *pharmakos*, the heaping of blame on Frazer and Girard for recklessly comparing the two, it is worth noting here that Calvin, not Frazer, is the first to juxtapose them. The double meaning of the Greek terms that Calvin uses is, moreover, striking. On one hand, words like καθάρμα / καθάρματα / περικαθάρματα, and περίψημα specified the victims of Greek expiatory rites; on the other, they enjoyed popular currency as terms of abuse. Paul uses them in this second, pejorative sense. A roll call of testimonia confirms the twofold meaning that does not quite correspond to that of our English "scapegoat." Both Greek and English expressions refer to religious rites, but their informal use differs inasmuch as those called καθάρματα and περίψημα are merely contemptible in their lowliness and misfortune—"the scum of the earth," whereas our scapegoat is less an object of contempt than one punished *unjustly*, a victim of irrational hatred.

For Calvin the sacrifice is paramount. God cannot be propitiated in any other way. The confluence in his typology of an implicit reference to the Greek rites with an interpretation of the scapegoat as an expiatory "sacrifice" is, furthermore, unprecedented. By 1659, the gap between the scapegoat ritual and its pagan analogues like the *pharmakos* has closed, at least in the margins and fine print of biblical commentaries, like that of Henry Hammond, whose annotations on this verse (1 Cor. 4:13) inform us that the expression καθάρματα "signifies those things that are used in the lustrating of a city among the Gentiles" like περίψημα itself—"the very same thing in another expression"—namely, "the vilest, refuse creature in a city, such as used to be the expiation in a publick calamity."[70] Hammond includes an impressive list of ancient sources before concluding that all such customs are "but a transcript of the *Azazel* among the Jewes, the *scape-goat*, that was sent into the wildernesse with all the sinnes of the people upon him."[71]

Things are hardly as clear-cut as this when, a century earlier (1563), Calvin is writing his opinion on the scapegoat, and while his Greek references stand out for the reasons we have just given, the typology he offers is conventional; with it he mentions the "more subtle speculation" that the scapegoat was "a type of the resurrection of Christ" before voicing his preference for a third reading as free of punitive meanings as the καθάρμα is loaded with them. What counts is that "the goat which departed alive and free . . . was an atonement, that by its departure and flight the people might be assured that their sins were put away and vanished."[72]

What made Calvin think of the *pharmakos* while interpreting the scapegoat, assuming that any connection between the two figures was less conspicuous in the sixteenth century than it was in the seventeenth and is today? The cited portion of *Commentary on Corinthians*, read alongside the typologies in *Harmony of the Law*, with Calvin's strong insistence that both goats atone and not merely the one who is slain, makes clear that what joins the Greek victim to the scapegoat is *vicarious sacrifice*. The immolated goat plainly dies in place of the people, as a substitute; this, as we shall see, is what being an expiatory sacrifice means to Calvin. How does the goat that escapes become a vicarious sacrifice also? The answer is *vicariously*, in virtue of the death of the other goat.

Fifteen centuries of Christian scapegoat exegesis leading up to this moment prepare us little for the sacrificial duplication in Calvin's typology, the move that turns the scapegoat into a sacrifice for sin and, theologically, into *a propitiatory substitute for the people*. "The statement of the Apostle" with which he appears concerned to square this reading is that in Hebrews 9:22. It stipulates that "without the shedding of blood, there can be no remission of sins." For Calvin this means that God can be appeased in no other way. If the guilty are to be spared, a substitute must be found to die in their place. Because the ritual prescriptions in Leviticus 16 stipulate that the scapegoat, like the immolated goat, "makes atonement," Calvin concludes that it too must be a sacrifice. So much for the straining logic of Calvin's unprecedented interpretation; the problem now becomes how to account for the fact that the scapegoat's life is spared.

The scapegoat is still a sacrifice for sin, but its sacrificial efficacy is borrowed, Calvin reasons. It becomes a sacrifice by taking a share in the atoning power of its twin's immolation. The equivocal character of the ritual goats who are not even formally named until the moment of their "decision" at the door of the tabernacle is preserved in a relationship of sacrificial consanguinity afterward, notwithstanding the diametric outcomes of the lottery—life and death respectively. The blood of one makes both goats sacrificial.

Before moving on let us note that Calvin emphasizes the punitive and substitutionary character of his reading with an allusion to another sacrificial figure—the Suffering Servant of Isaiah 53. "His comeliness was destroyed," Calvin says, applying the words of the prophet to the goat driven into the wilderness; "He was rejected of men."[73] Like the *pharmakos* and the Servant of Yahweh, the scapegoat is one who cleanses the people, being heaped with sin and expelled. Physically disfigured, universally abominated, and punished vicariously, the two victims join, superimposing themselves upon the scapegoat, imbruing it with sacrificial color. The references are brief but their confluence here is momentous. Calvin appears to have touched off a symbolic fusion, with an interpretation he ultimately rejects, deliberately passing it up in preference to that brighter image of the scapegoat's absolvingly sin-laden flight into the wilds. By the time Frazer is writing about so-called scapegoat rites, the sacrificial meanings that begin to mingle in Calvin's "also-ran" typology will have long since hardened in a word.

CHAPTER 5

The Damnation of Christ's Soul

An Incomprehensible Judgment

The creedal item of Christ's "Descent into Hell" (*descensus ad infernos*) is at the heart of one of the "lesser but vigorous controversies of the Reformation era"[1] (late sixteenth to early seventeenth century), where the last, crucial determinants of the scapegoat's semantic formation are evident. A single chapter of that long-running debate over how literally Protestants should interpret the confession that Christ "descended into hell" stands out for the extended disputation of Day of Atonement typologies it contains.

In an acrimonious exchange of treatises between the exiled Puritan leader Henry Jacob and the Anglican bishop of Winchester, Thomas Bilson, a good deal of the patristic record on the scapegoat is rehearsed and contested. The mystery of the expression "Azazel" is noted, the sages consulted, and the fathers weighed in the balance. Major theologies at stake in the "Descensus controversy" keep the rhetoric sober. That sermonizing genius calling the tune nearly everywhere else in English scapegoat interpretation here falls silent.

The dispute begins with a sermon preached at Paul's Cross in 1597 by the reverend Thomas Bilson, who refutes the opinion of "some conceited and too much addicted to nouelties," who spare not "to vrge the suffering of the *verie paines of hell* in the soul of Christ on the crosse, as the chiefest part, and maine ground of our Redemption by Christ."[2] At this early moment in the debate Bilson is merely picking a fight with Calvin and his followers, who interpreted the descent into hell as Christ's bearing in his soul God's wrath against fallen humankind.

What, precisely, does Calvin say? In places he merely repeats the metaphors of "satisfaction" for sin as "debt," so that a number of commentators think he remains more or less within the ambit of Anselm's thinking on the atonement; in others he writes of Christ having been judged and punished in the place of sinners, using forensic language to evoke the desperation of the human predicament before God and the legally substitutive character of Christ's death. "The curse caused by our guilt was awaiting us at God's heavenly judgment seat," Calvin writes. "Accordingly, Scripture first relates Christ's condemnation before Pontius Pilate . . . to teach us that the penalty to which we were subject had been imposed upon this righteous man."[3] Christ's trial is important for its orderly disposition of the facts in the case, the significance of which then appears most plainly:

> To take away our condemnation, it was not enough for him to suffer any kind of death: to make satisfaction for our redemption a form of death had to be chosen in which he might free us both by transferring our condemnation to himself and by taking our guilt upon himself. If he had been murdered by thieves or slain in an insurrection by a raging mob, in such a death there would have been no evidence of satisfaction. But when he was arraigned before the judgment seat as a criminal, accused and pressed by testimony, and condemned by the mouth of the judge to die—we know by these proofs that he took the role of a guilty man and evildoer. Thus we shall behold the person of a sinner and evildoer represented in Christ, yet from his shining innocence it will at the same time be obvious that he was burdened with another's sin rather than his own. He therefore suffered under Pontius Pilate, and by the governor's official sentence was reckoned among criminals. Yet not so—for he was declared righteous by his judge at the same time, when Pilate affirmed that he "found no cause for complaint in him" [John 18:38]. This is our acquittal: the guilt that held us liable for punishment has been transferred to the head of the Son of God [Isa. 53:12]. We must, above all, remember this substitution, lest we tremble and remain anxious throughout life—as if God's righteous vengeance, which the Son of God has taken upon himself, still hung over us.[4]

It is clear that Calvin, like Aquinas, reckons satisfaction in terms of actual punishment, and for this meaning the picture of Christ condemned to die before a court of law is crucial. With a nearly theatrical deliberation Calvin shows us Christ in two aspects—though fully identified with the criminal, he remains immaculately pure. The substitutive character of the death Christ must die could hardly be more explicitly formulated. "What was the purpose of this subjugation of Christ to the law," he asks, "but to acquire righteousness for us, undertaking to pay what we could not pay?"[5] The debt that humankind contracts through its disobedience Christ must satisfy in his obedience unto death—this emphasis is important and unmistakable; but when Calvin writes of "God's curse and wrath" as "the source of death,"[6] we begin to glimpse the terrifying straits that Christ consents to enter in our behalf.

As "no one can descend into himself and seriously consider what he is without feeling God's wrath and hostility toward him," we do "anxiously seek ways and means to appease God and this demands a satisfaction," for "he is a righteous Judge, he does not allow his law to be broken without punishment, but is equipped to avenge it."[7] This threat is something that each one of us senses intuitively, according to Calvin. By becoming the guilty one in our place Christ makes himself liable to "all the signs of a wrathful and avenging God."[8] He thus "bore the weight of divine severity," Calvin says, "since he was stricken and afflicted [Isa. 53:5] by God's hand."[9] Here, as in the passage quoted above, Calvin turns to the Suffering Servant of Isaiah 53, this time for an explicit reference to the divine agency in Christ's punishment. If things were not dire enough, he then introduces a fateful distinction that will extend the sufferings of Christ to a nethermost extremity undreamed by Anselm and Aquinas.

> If Christ had died only a bodily death, it would have been ineffectual. No—it was expedient at the same time for him to undergo the severity of God's vengeance, to appease his wrath and satisfy his just judgment. For this reason, he must also grapple hand to hand with the armies of hell and the dread of everlasting death.[10]

These are momentous lines and not just for their unprecedented double assertion about Christ's descent into hell, which runs the most punitive language yet into an image of Christ's conflict with the enemies of humankind, for an unholy amalgamation of *Christus Victor* and juridical substitution. It betokens a larger movement of symbolic collapse we may now begin to register.

With the "dread of everlasting death" we are properly into what Calvin thinks Christ must suffer in addition to merely physical torments. The difference is critical for making sense of Jesus' agony in the Garden of Gethsemane, which otherwise seems but puling cowardice. "What shameful softness would it have been . . . for Christ to be so tortured by the dread of common death as to sweat blood and. . . . to be revived only at the appearance of angels," when "thieves and other wrongdoers . . . despise [death] with haughty courage."[11] Why then was he "stricken and almost stupefied with the dread of death?"[12] For "the fierceness of his torment, drops of blood flowed from his face," Calvin writes, "and he did not do this as a show for others' eyes, since he groaned to his Father in secret."[13] In the end, "what Christ suffered in the sight of men" little compares with that "invisible and incomprehensible judgment which he underwent in the sight of God."[14] Though "Christ's body was given as the price of our redemption . . . he paid a greater and more excellent price in suffering in his soul the terrible torments of a condemned and forsaken man."[15] The creedal article that Christ descended into hell must be understood as a reference to his torment on the cross, where he drains the cup of divine wrath to its dregs. Calvin finds the most consummate expression of this in Jesus' cry of dereliction:

> And surely no more terrible abyss can be conceived than to feel yourself forsaken and estranged from God; and when you call upon him, not to be heard. It is as if God himself had plotted your ruin. We see that Christ was so cast down as to be compelled to cry out in deep anguish: "My God, my God, why hast thou forsaken me?"[16]

Calvin's language on supererogation, which he calls "an absurd fiction,"[17] provides us with a compelling index of the new soteriology. The "idea of meriting reconciliation with God by satisfactions, and buying off the penalties due to his justice, is execrable blasphemy," writes Calvin, "in as much as it destroys the doctrine which Isaiah delivers concerning Christ—that 'the chastisement of our peace was upon Him.'"[18] The Father is the bearer of death, but the fatal blow he deals is deflected onto Christ alone. There will be no participation in that suffering. Our religious habits and penitential observances surrender all power to appease and any claim they once had on divine favor. This registers in a corresponding explosion of wrath, which Christ then quenches without remainder. The saving operation stands revealed in a single horrific act of divine violence, transcending mere physical torture so utterly there is no human analogy for it and inflicted on a divinely innocent man. "Thus in a marvelous and divine way," writes Calvin, quoting Augustine, "he loved us even when he hated us."[19]

The Descensus Controversy

Jacob's 1598 *Treatise of the Sufferings and Victory of Christ, in the work of our Redemption* will demur at Calvin's interpretation of the creedal article: the hell of the creed is the place of the dead, and the article should be amended to read, "Hee descended among the Dead," even though, strictly speaking, the place of the dead is "for Christ as for the patriarchs . . . in God's presence."[20] Christ must indeed suffer in his mind and soul the pains of hell or their equivalent according to Jacob, but this ordeal has nothing to do with the descent into hell. His argument runs as follows: "Christ tooke on him the nature of man . . . that he might suffer in that nature which he assumed, & by suffering in it he might save it."[21] Since "he assumed (all men know) our humane *soule* as well as our flesh, and he saued our *soule* as well as our flesh, *ergo* he suffered both in *soule* and in flesh."[22] Jacob then adapts the Day of Atonement goats as types of Christ for an unprecedented reading.

> The Iewes sacrifices, that is certaine of them, did signifie more then the *bodily* sufferings only, they set forth the sufferings of the soule of Christ also. In the 16. Chapt. Of *Levit. verse, 5.* we have a *sinne offering* consisting of Two Goates, the one *slayne*, the other the *scape goate:* yet both of them *a sacrifice for sinne,* as the text speaketh. What doeth the *slayne Goate* figure but the *body* of Christ slayne, the *scape-goate* the *soule* which *also bare our sinnes,* and was a *sinne* offeringe, but yet suruiued and dyed not as the body of Christ did. The *scape-goate* heere surelie muste of necessitie signifie the *Soule* or the *Deitie* of Christ. The *Deitie* it can not signifie, because that can not bee a *sinne offering.* Therefore it signifieth that the immortall *Soule* of Christ was a *sinne offeringe:* and being a sinne offering, or a sacrifice for sinne, it did properlie beare our sinnes, and suffer for our sinnes.[23]

Here the scapegoat as a type of Christ's deity is noted but passed over in favor of a fully sacrificial identification of the animal with "the suffering of Christ's soul." The phrase means not "that Christ suffred *Hell* properlie, that is hell torments in the verie place & condition of the damned," Jacob avers.[24] "God forbid. This grosse cogitation neuer came into our mindes, but only he suffred for our sinnnes Gods *seuere Wrath and iust vengeance* . . . which we affirme is equal to Hell it selfe and all the torments thereof in sharpnes and vehemencie of payne. And thus we say *Christ suffered Hell or Hellish sorrowes* for vs."[25] As in Calvin, the vicariousness of Christ's suffering

and its salvific efficacy translate readily into debt metaphors ("He gaue himselfe a price of redemption for vs, which wee els should have payed")[26] and
forensic ones:

> then was Christ *by the iust sentence of the Law* hanged on the tree, & so
> he bare in deed the true *Curse of the Lawe.* Not in respect that he was an
> innocent man, nor as the Iewes Magistrates had to doe with him, for so
> they did him most foule wronge that Crucified him: but as he took on him
> our *person,* as he was *made sinne* for vs, and as he stood forth in our name
> to aunswere Gods iustice, So was the *iust* sentence of our condemnation
> according to the iustice of the Lawe inflicted on him.[27]

Here Jacob grounds Christ's substitutionary status and the punitive character of his sin-bearing on the same two Pauline formulas Theodoret used in
his typology of the immolated goat. For the strong identification of Christ
with sin and the Father's agency in punishment, Jacob compares 2 Corinthians 5:21 ("*He hath made him sinne fore vs whiche knewe no sinne, that we
might bee made the righteousnes of God in him*") with Isaiah 53:10, which he
renders: "*The Lord will breake him and make him subject to infirmities, when
he shall make his soule sinne,* that is to say, a sacrifice for sinne."[28] The other
ontological formula is that in Galatians: "Christ redeemed us frō the curse
of the Lawe, when he was made a Curse for us"—a curse that can be nothing
other than "Gods wrath for our trãssgressions imputed to him."[29]

As strong as this identification with sin and "the curse of the law" may
be, Christ must remain throughout untainted, for though he "suffered for
sinne" he was "sinles indeed."[30] Jacob then deploys a legal distinction. Christ's
sufferings, he says, "were for our sinnes now made his by Gods accoumpt"
and unlike the sins of "the Reprobats and damned," which are "inherent,"
Christ suffers for "sinnes only *imputed*."[31]

The rigidity of the economy of redemption appears in Jacob's repeated
insistence that "Gods strict *iustice* requireth it so, therefore it was so, and
it must be so."[32] This demand for justice is finally so implacable that the
Father appears "the proper and principall Ordayner, Author and Executor
of [Christ's] punishment."[33] The other actors in the Passion are accordingly
reduced to mere puppets in the drama that unfolds: "The Divells and wicked
men his Persecutours did their parts also indeed for other ends, but yet they
were all as Instruments only, & vsed by God vnto his owne end,"[34] so that
Christ "having most horrible sinnes imputed to him as the damned haue also
. . . suffered for them from Gods hand euen as the damned do."[35] This is the

reason for Christ's "dismay" in the Garden of Gethsemane, "wherfore also he saith, *Father, saue me from this hower*" and "*if it be possible lett this cuppe passe from me.*"[36]

Jacob reproduces all of Calvin's attitudes, scoffing at the suggestion "that only his bodilie death and outward paines should so terrifie and dismay him," something he deems "no lesse then impious."[37] It is rather "his howor of suffering for sinne, *This cuppe* of affliction and sorrowe which nowe he felt and was to feele yet further" [that] "caused him so to mourne and feare," for "he both *feared* and *felt* Gods anger for the sinne of the worlde."[38] It was "Gods owne hand did it to Christ," Jacob concludes, "no lesse then to the damned"[39] with, here again, an appeal to Isaiah 53, for the emphasis on divine agency in punishment: "As it is written, *The Lord laid upon him the punishment of vs all.*"[40]

The Anglican bishop answers the following year (1599) with a treatise in which the human soul of Christ descends to hell quite literally and in a triumphal fashion—to destroy the power of the devil.[41] The "bloud of Christ Iesus" is "the sufficient price of our Redemption, and true meane of our reconciliation to God," Bilson writes.[42] The "*sacrifices* of the Lawe" prefigure Christ's bodily death;[43] it is this the church has "receaued and beleeued . . . fourteene hundred yeares, before anie man euer made mention of hell paines to bee suffered in the soule of Christ."[44] In a second treatise of 1604, Bilson holds up the typology of "the wicked and reprobate" as preferable by reason of its venerability and sundry patristic attestation alone (Origen, Ambrose, Bede), like that of Barabbas (Origen, Bede) and even "the impassible godhead of Christ, as Theodoret, and Isychius affirme since power to take away sin and to cleanse it, without any suffering for it, is proper to God."[45] Jacob's rejection of the fathers is so much the worse in that the type of Christ's soul in hellish sorrows is proffered "vpon the bare surmise of your own braine."[46] Calvin himself, whom Bilson credits as "a man of sharpe iudgement" though "in some sense a mainteiner of the sufferings of Christes soule," can be no ally since he "doth not applie the Scape-goat as you doe."[47] He, therefore, "whom you would seeme most to follow" exposes "that your assertion . . . is but your meere imagination" since Calvin maintained "*the force of cleansing sinne depended on the sacrifice of the other (slaine) goat.*"[48] For Calvin, the scapegoat stood "either to witnesse the *resurrection of Christ*, as the slaine goat did declare his death; or to shew that Christ was a *man deuoted* to beare *the shame* and punishment of sinne for others."[49] Nowhere is Christ's soul even mentioned. He rather embraces "*that which is more simple and certaine*": the scapegoat departed "*alive and*

free," so *"that by his departure and leading away, the people might be assured
their sinnes did vanish,* and were *carried farre out of sight."*[50] Invoked here
at the eye of the Descensus controversy, Calvin's formulation is perhaps as
deft a summation of escape and absolution motifs as the scapegoat literature
contains. The emphasis falls on the scapegoat's life and liberation; for, after
all, only a living goat may bear sins, but there is nothing sacrificial in its
sin-bearing. Sins vanish, that is all.

Bilson acknowledges that "if the vsage of the people towards the Scape-
goate were such as Tertullian describeth; which was to spit at him, punch
him, and curse him, as he was caried out of the Citie," the scapegoat might
then prefigure "the detestation and hatred the Iewes had of Christ when they
cryed, *away with him, away with him"*[51]—although it can hardly be deemed
on that basis a "sacrifice for sinne,"[52] nor credibly said to suffer a punishment
so plainly meted out upon the other goat. It is *this* note of incredulity that
marks the real parting of the ways: "if you can not shew, as you neither doe
nor can, that the Scape-goat by the Scriptures suffered any thing; how will
you bring it about, that the Scape-goat figured the sufferings of Christes
soule? shall no suffering be a figure of suffering? such may your figures be;
but the wisdome of God maketh figures for similitude and resemblance to
the trueth; and not for contrarietie to it, as you do."[53]

Of course, Bilson's reading of the scapegoat fares no better than his tri-
umphalist and literal understanding of the creedal descent. Both simply drop
out of currency along with Calvin's explanation of the creedal article, which
"waned, even among Puritan writers who continued to accept his view that
the soul of Christ suffered the torments of hell."[54] Typological interpretation—that ancient hermeneutic tradition bequeathed to Christendom by
the fathers—is itself on the wane. Though punitive significations have shadowed the scapegoat at least from the time of the Second Temple ceremony,
the polarization of types during sixteen centuries of exegetical reflection
conceals until the last historical moment just how the term would slip into
common usage, if at all, and with what meanings. Jacob's typology stands
out, if not for its rootless innovation, then for its eleventh-hour entry to a
millennial debate and the controversy surrounding its publication. All but
flouting tradition, the Puritan divine extemporizes a new scapegoat typology
in which the vicarious suffering of the innocent for the guilty takes prece-
dence over all other meanings. The popularization of this new meaning owes
more to later Puritan sermonizing than to Calvin's bookish allusion to the
pharmakos, which predates Bilson's debate with Jacob by a few decades, but
then it is the distinction Calvin introduces between Christ's corporeal and

incorporeal sufferings that sets up the new terms to which Jacob predictably, maybe inevitably, attaches the goats as types.

How does the scapegoat, which escapes, become a signifier of sinless and vicarious suffering? The answer is: *theologically*, through its identification with that "greater and more excellent price" he paid.[55] Jacob is the first to drive this identification home. Others echo his witness, using the same references in Paul and Isaiah to insist on substitution averting the just punishment of guilt, and to maintain that although Christ is punished like the damned, he remains blameless. The condemnation achieves cosmic scale with the subsuming under divine wrath of every malefactor, human and demonic. In this vision, God transforms the entire world into the gallows on which Christ dies at once universally condemned and surpassingly innocent.

The Sacrifice of the Scapegoat

A superstition enriches the English discussion in this period. "Adamant is so hard a stone, that it can be softened with nothing but the bloud of a goate," writes George Abbot about a decade before his preferment to archbishop of Canterbury. "Mans heart was grown so hard, mans case was growne so hard, that it could be lenified by nothing, but by the bloud of him, whome the skape-goate in Leuiticus, so liuely did represent."[56] This reference to adamant as a metaphor for impenitent hearts and to goat's blood as an unrivaled solvent or shatterer is found in a fair number of references to the scapegoat across the period literature. "God be thanked that even an Adamant, as hard as it is, may bee mollified by the blood of a goat," writes John Jackson, appealing to an ancient and still popular fallacy.[57] "Christ Iesus is this goat, hee is *hircus emissarius* the scape goat, carrying our sinnes into the wildernesse."[58] Edmund Calamy condenses this still further: "Have we not trampled the bloud of Christ under our feete, and shall not the *bloud of this Scapegoate* melt our adamantine hearts?"[59] This conjuration of the scapegoat's blood finds an echo in Sir Richard Baker's *Meditations and Disquisitions*, which reminds Christians that "though God love a whole heart in affection; yet hee loves a broken heart in sacrifice. And no marvell, indeed; seeing it is even hee himselfe that breakes it: for, as nothing but the blood can breake the Adamant; so nothing, but the blood of our scape-goate Christ Iesus, is able to breake our Adamantine hearts."[60] In 1646 Sir Thomas Browne publishes his *Pseudodoxia Eepidemica, or, Enquiries into Very Many Received Tenets and Commonly Presumed Truths*, which deflates, among other superstitions, the belief that "a Diamond, which is the hardest of stones . . . is yet made soft, or broke by the bloud of a Goat."[61] He finds this view espoused in "many Christian Writers, alluding herein unto the heart of man, and the precious bloud of our Saviour, who was typified indeed by the Goat that was slaine and the scape Goat in the wildernesse . . . at the effusion of whose bloud, not onely the hard hearts of his enemies relented, but the stony rocks and vaile of the Temple was shattered."[62] Browne notes the storied power of the substance "is easier affirmed then proved,"[63] like that of goat's blood electuaries said to dissolve kidney stones: "Wherein notwithstanding, we should rather relie upon the urine in a Castlings bladder," he writes, "a resolution of Crabs eyes," or a "digestive preparation drawne from species or individualls, whose stomacks peculiarly dissolve lapideous bodies."[64] What is most striking here, given the ultimate fate of the English expression, are the invocations of the scapegoat's blood. Why was the legend figuratively linked to the scapegoat, rather than to the immolated goat whose blood *is* shed?

In some commentators the bearing of sin means little more than its purging or cancellation. Among others, darker implications prevail. Jacob is perhaps the most striking instance of this. His move to reinvent the scapegoat as a type of Christ's vicarious suffering is something he will share with a number of other period writers, many of them Puritans like himself, whose typologies of the scapegoat echo Calvin's language on the atonement. The vice chancellor of Oxford University, George Abbot, is a case in point. He publishes *An Exposition upon the Prophet Ionah*—from which the above reference to the lenifying effect of goat's blood was taken—in 1600. In it he goes on to say that "to procure our peace" he "whome the skape-goate in Leviticus so lively did represent"

> plucked warres on himselfe; and what we should haue borne, his humanity did sustain with a louely chaunge of our parts. For the vnrighteous sinneth, and the righteous man is punished: *the guiltie man did offend, and the innocent one is beaten, the vngodly had transgressed, and the godly was condemned: what the wicked man had deserued, that did the good one suffer, what the seruant had endomaged, that did the maister pay: and what man had committed, that he a God tooke upon him.*[65]

Like Jacob, Abbot casts what it means to bear sins in crimson. He reads Christ's innocent and vicarious suffering back onto the scapegoat, who is plainly a sin-bearer too, unlike its immolated fellow, who receives no mention. The scapegoat's substitutionary punishment is amplified through a second typology to which the animal is frequently tied by like features, in this case, the act of expulsion: "This is the assured comfort, which the wounded conscience hath," says Abbot, "although the tempest of Gods wrath be ready to swallow him, yet notwithstanding the casting in of this Ionas, procureth a calme vnto him . . . to cease the rage of the sea, to stoppe the wrath of the Father."[66] Like those storm-tossed mariners who jettisoned the prophet and "found their best ease, by putting him to paine,"[67] sinners are spared when God vents his wrath upon a surrogate. That weightiest of Puritan theologians, John Owen, renders the scapegoat with something like this in mind.

> In [Christ] hath he made his *Iustice* glorious, in making all our *iniquities to meet upon him,* causing him to beare them all, as the *Scape Goat* in the Wildernesse, not *sparing* him but giving him up to death for us all. So exalting his *Iustice* and *Indignation* against sinne, in a way of freeing us from the condemnation of it: Rom. 3. v. 25. Rom. 8: 33, 34. In him hath he made his *Truth* glorious, and his *Faithfullnesse* in the exact accomplishment of all his absolute *threatnings* and promises; that fountaine threat and commination, whence all others flow, Gen 2:17. *in the day thou eatest thereof thou shalt dye the death*, seconded with a Curse; Deut. 27.26 *Cursed is every one that continueth not &c.* is in him accomplished, fullfilled, & the truth of God in them layd in a way to our good. *He* by the Grace of God *tasted death for us,* Heb. 2. 9. *and so delivered us who were subject to death,* v.14 and *he hath fullfilled the curse, by being made a curse for us,* Gal. 3: 13.[68]

We note the same radical identification of sin-bearer and burden by way of the Pauline formula in Galatians, the same insistence on God's agency in punishment, although Owen features the benefit of acquittal to the guilty as a provision of divine grace rather more prominently. The rector of Saint Matthews, Henry Burton, also a zealous Puritan, whose fulminations against the bishops from his London pulpit and anti-Episcopal pamphleteering led to numerous imprisonments and the severing of both ears, gives a standard version of the dual-nature typology ("figuring the humanity the slaine Goate, and the diuinity of Christ, the scape Goate: or the slaine Goate the death of Christ; and the scape Goate his resurrection"),[69] which then drops precipitously into a darker meditation on the meaning of imputed sin by way of the high priest's laying on of hands.[70] Here Christ "offering himself vpon the Crosse, was clothed in filthy garments, euen with the menstruous cloth of our sinnes imputed vnto him, or imposed vpon him," although the reciprocal effect of the savior's humiliation is just as important: "because he was attired in filthy rayment, we rising againe in him, may alwayes haue white garments vpon us."[71]

Another Puritan divine, Anthony Burgess, writes of "some kinde of sinne and pollution" laid on Christ "that he should become sin, and a curse for us, that he should be under the displeasure of God for us" who "of himself had no uncleanness, being then *holy, undefiled, and separate from sinners.*"[72] He deploys both Pauline formulas alongside the claim of Christ's pristine sinlessness and a familiar pecuniary image—"he was our Surety, and undertook our debt bearing our sinnes upon him. . . . Even as "the *scape-goat* had the sinnes of the people laid upon it."[73] Burgess then connects the scapegoat as sin-bearer with Christ's ordeal in the Garden of Gethsemane, recalling vividly the opening pages of Jacob's *Treatise* and the sixteenth chapter of Calvin's *Institutes.* "Because our sins were laid on him," he writes, "therefore did he so much strive in prayer, with those excessive agonies in his soul, because of the sense of Gods anger for our sins."[74] John Jackson—another "good old Puritan and member of the Assembly of divines at Westminster"[75]—who we read urging goat's blood for the breaking of stony hearts, treats the paradox rather more colorfully. Jesus is our *hircus emissarius* with the following qualification: he remains "*agnus immaculatus*, an innocent sweet-breathed lambe in regard of the purity of his owne nature; but as our sinnes are imputed to him, hee is *hircus foetidus*, a stinking goat."[76]

In this symbolism the scapegoat decisively parts company with the herd of its sacrificial fellows—the scarlet bound and pestilential Hittite animal, the Greek *pharmakos* and even with itself, that reviled and jettisoned creature of the Second Temple—to become something new. It doubtless remains indistinguishable from them insofar as the strong imputation of sin makes Christ the curse with which he is cursed, but the scapegoat must become something more than a maledicted apotropaeic device and byword, something other than a victim whose life and meaning ends in the pollution with which it is identified. Though every mouth revile him, he must continue blameless, an innocent, sweet-breathed lamb.

This is why "Christ crucified must bee the subject of all our preaching," Jackson says, wrapping up his sanguinary meditation on the "warme blood" we apply "when soever therefore we meet with any that have a stone in their heart."[77] For "if thou wouldest come to God for grace, for comfort, for salvation, for any blessing," he says, "come first to Christ, hanging, bleeding, dying on the crosse, without whom there is no hearing God, no helping God, no saving God, no God to thee at all."[78]

Other commentators will link the scapegoat even more explicitly to Christ crucified. Richard Steward's advice to sacramental reflection is a good example of this. "Here bee fat things full of marrow," he writes, and "wine upon the lees . . . that goes down sweetly":

> Here wee see Christ crucified before our eyes; now wee see him hanging, and bleeding upon the Crosse, we now see him pressed and crushed under the heavy burthen of his Fathers wrath. Now wee see him in the Garden in his bloody sweat. Now wee may behold him under the bitter conflict with his Fathers wrath upon the Crosse. *Behold the man,* saith *Pilate.* This is our duty by meditation, to present unto our selves the bitterness of Christs passion, *Exod.* 24. 8. *And* Moses *took the bloud, and sprinkled it on the people, and said, Behold the bloud of the Covenant.* So here, *Behold the Lamb of God which taketh away the sins of the world:* And behold the bloud of that innocent, and spotless Lamb; yea behold him now shedding his precious blood to take away the sins of the world, and look upon him as the Scapegoat, bearing and carrying our sins upon him.[79]

The passage is exemplary for its recapitulation of Calvin's emphases on Christ's trial, his ordeal in the garden, and his crucifixion as a fulfillment of Old Testament prophecy, as for its conflation of the scapegoat with the crucified Christ. Bishop George Downame writes in a similar vein: Christ "taketh away our sinnes by taking them upon him, or bearing them as it is said of the scape Goat," and is thus "offered upon the crosse . . . who himselfe doth beare our sinnes in his own body upon the tree."[80] Note, too, how Samuel Purchas elides the immolated goat in favor of the scapegoat in this revision of the imagery of Hebrews 9:11–14:

> IESUS CHRIST, the eternall high Priest, who hath alone wrought our atonement, entered into the Holy place of heauen, and laide our sinnes on the scape-Goate, bearing them, and satisfying for them in his owne person on the Crosse, and by the sprinkling of his bloud sanctified vs for euer to GOD his Father.[81]

We end our review of English scapegoat typology with a citation from the divine George Stradling, written in 1692, with its even more glaring omission of the immolated goat in this comparison with the Akedah:

> For when we were prisoners to Death by sin, God made an exchange, delivered his Son over to it for us, became our Scape-goat, like the Ram substituted in the place of *Isaac* and, as the Apostle speaks *tasted death for every man*, that we might not be devoured and swallowed up by it.[82]

We recall that the Akedah ram was slain in the place of Isaac, yet Stradling compares it to the scapegoat rather than its immolated twin. In a move that—given the citation's late date—seems to indicate that the English word's bifurcation into a literal sense, on the one hand, and a new metaphor on the other, is more or less complete, Stradling uses the scapegoat in the sense of "one punished in place of another," overwriting the textual fact of its escape from death. On the Levitical evidence the scapegoat compares far better with the amnestied victim Isaac, whose life, like its own, is spared, but the scapegoat's primary meaning now competes with a second. Even here, in a comparison of Old Testament figures, the sense of the metaphorical expression comes more readily to hand.

CHAPTER 6

Anthropologies of the Scapegoat

Frazer and Girard on Archaic Religion and Atonement

We have come to the end of our typological history of the scapegoat. What remains is to adduce the word's earliest nonexegetical, metaphorical uses. Before we do this, let us pause to situate our corrected history within a broader theoretical framework or two. Patterns in the data under review in this first portion of our study need to be reckoned, especially in view of the citations we shall come to in the final chapters of this book with their curious distribution into "types." We are, moreover, finally in a position to check the two most important theorists of the scapegoat—Sir James Frazer and René Girard—against the actual record. How well do they anticipate the textual evidence? What help might they give us interpreting the data? Frazer is regarded as the first to insist on persistent features, repeating sequences, and a unity of meaning for the scapegoat. He is of course reading ethnographic data, rather than theological typologies. As we shall see, the radically foundational place of the scapegoat in Girard's thought furnishes an account of the pattern common to both.

Having submerged the crucifixion of Jesus along with the Greek *pharmakos* and the Levitical scapegoat in a sea of expulsion ceremonies from every age and abode under heaven, the British ethnologist J. G. Frazer famously reserves the word *scapegoat* as a title for one large volume of *The Golden Bough*. It was apparently a last-minute decision. Until "the very eve of the publication of the relevant section of the Third Edition, he thought of this portion of the argument as 'The Man of Sorrows'"—a reference to Isaiah's Suffering Servant.[1] He writes,

> The aspect of the subject with which we are here chiefly concerned is the use of the Dying God as a scapegoat to free his worshippers from the troubles of all sorts with which life on earth is beset. I have sought to trace this curious usage to its origin, to decompose the idea of the Divine Scapegoat into the elements out of which it appears to be compounded. If I am right, the idea resolves itself into a simple confusion between the material and the immaterial, between the real possibility of transferring a physical load to other shoulders and the supposed possibility of transferring our bodily and mental ailments to another who will bear them for us. When we survey the history of this pathetic fallacy from its crude inception in savagery to its full development in the speculative theology of civilized nations, we cannot but wonder at the singular power which the human mind possesses of transmuting the leaden dross of superstition into a glittering semblance of gold. Certainly in nothing is this alchemy of thought more conspicuous than in the process which has refined the base and foolish custom of the scapegoat into the sublime conception of a God who dies to take away the sins of the world.[2]

We note that the scapegoat, the *pharmakoi*, and the Suffering Servant assemble under Frazer's category heading, as they did centuries earlier in Calvin's Day of Atonement typology. They are joined to a myriad of other rites and customs by what Frazer understood as a common error, the confusion of material and immaterial burdens, combined with a rather shabby attempt to foist the latter onto some unfortunate who then bore the brunt for everyone else. Although the "scapegoat" frequently undergoes expulsion and is sometimes put to death, Frazer emphasizes the category mistake underpinning the ritual transfer. It is what unites the scores of rites and customs collected in his volume.

In festivals like the Saturnalia celebrated across the ancient world and marked everywhere by "the inversion of social ranks" and the sacrifice of a man in the role of a god, Frazer saw phenomena that dated "to an early age in the history of agriculture," when small communities were "presided over by a sacred or divine king, whose primary duty was to secure the orderly succession of the seasons" along with the fecundity of both cattle and women.[3] Though he appears to have held at least one other, fully incompatible view on the subject, Frazer surmises in *The Scapegoat* that the king's original term of office corresponded to one cycle of the seasons, at the end of which his subjects put him to death. Each year "a man, whom the fond imagination of his worshippers invested with the attributes of a god, gave his life for the world," thus "infusing from his own body a fresh current of vital energy into the stagnant veins of nature."[4] He was succeeded by another "who played, like all his predecessors, the ever-recurring drama of the divine resurrection and death."[5] If the king in time "contrived by force or craft to extend his reign and procure a substitute, who after a short and more or less nominal tenure of the crown was slain in his stead," the first of these surrogates was probably his own son, although "the growth of humane feeling" soon demanded that "the victim should always be a condemned criminal" and still later, a mere effigy when even a criminal seemed "too good to personate a god on the gallows or in the fire."[6]

The ancient significance of these festivals was purely *magical* insofar as they sought "to direct the course of nature."[7] In this sense they typified the primitive stages of phenomena that Frazer saw as superseded by more advanced and properly *religious* forms, marked as they invariably were by ethical sensitivities, however inchoate and confused. Beyond a certain threshold, one glimpsed the first signs of a concern for the clearance of evil and the expiation of guilt. Inasmuch as the rite aimed at the riddance of sin or impurity, it could be deemed a properly religious phenomenon. Those used ritually in this connection Frazer termed "Scapegoats."[8]

The "hard facts of cruel ritual" will of course be "diluted into the nebulous abstractions of a mystical theology" by the most advanced forms of ethical religion, but even these must give way to science, which surmounts them all in Frazer's evolutionary program.[9] His contempt for the earliest, nonethical phenomena, which he saw as situated at the bottom of a progression extending from benighted savage to modern man, is today infamous.

During his research on the Saturnalia, Frazer came across a Babylonian custom in which "a condemned criminal" was enthroned, "dressed in state regalia," allowed "to swill and guzzle to his heart's content" and even "to make use of the royal concubines"[10] before being stripped, whipped, and strung up—which could mean either "hanged or crucified."[11] If Frazer's attempt to dispose of the scourging and crucifixion of Jesus as a late case of the same thing ends in failure,[12] the relevant portion of his argument that he ultimately consigned to an appendix at the end of the third edition was "very much the *coup de théâtre* up to which the whole foregoing discussion leads."[13] In the end, the unprecedented burial of Jesus under a mountain of slain and reanimate gods that *The Golden Bough* so formidably endeavors remains susceptible to a counterinterpretation, as Frazer wryly acknowledges in the closing paragraph of his appendix. His tone is hardly acquiescent: the choice between them is hereafter more stark and infernal than ever.

> In the great army of martyrs who in many ages and in many lands . . . have died a cruel death in the character of gods, the devout Christian will doubtless discern types and forerunners of the coming Saviour—stars that heralded in the morning sky the advent of the Sun of Righteousness—earthen vessels wherein it pleased the divine wisdom to set before hungering souls the bread of heaven. The skeptic on the other hand, with equal confidence, will reduce Jesus of Nazareth to the level of a multitude of other victims of a barbarous superstition, and will see in him no more than a moral teacher, whom the fortunate accident of his execution invested with the crown, not merely of a martyr, but of a god. The divergence between these views is wide and deep.[14]

Once primitive religion crosses the ethical threshold, and notwithstanding its late, rarefied theological formulations, the idea remains more or less the same: a transfer of sin or impurity takes place followed often by the mistreatment or death of its designated bearer. What unites so many divergent customs and rites under the *scapegoat* is this thematic common denominator. Although Frazer might just as easily have chosen the name of any other victim, the word *scapegoat* must have struck him as a highly serviceable option. The generalized sense of the expression made it a fitting category name and allowed him to avoid the scandal of a more explicit reference to Christ (Isaiah's "Man of Sorrows").

For Girard, the trouble with Frazer is that he is onto something but only half sees what it is. Struck by the close resemblance between certain rites, Frazer invents a thematic category "which is otherwise non-existent, like all categories," one he calls "scapegoat rituals" because a transfer of curse or impurity takes place. If Frazer's intuition of a kinship among rites was not mistaken, he ultimately misses what truly unites them.[15] Though "we [must] reject the Frazerian rationale for 'ritual transference' (i.e., the confusion between a physical and spiritual burden) can we deny that some victims, in rituals the world over, are expelled, persecuted, and killed for the sake of the entire community?" Girard asks.[16] The essential thing is that the scapegoat's persecution and death redounds to the common good. The kinship Frazer sensed, if he also failed to understand it, is based in something more fundamental than he expects, and as such inescapable, for "to expel religion is, as always, a religious gesture—as much so today when the sacred is loathed and abhorred as in the past when it was worshipped and adored."[17] Girard writes,

Modern thinkers continue to see religion as an isolated, wholly fictitious phenomenon cherished only by a few backward peoples or milieus. And these same thinkers can now project upon religion alone the responsibility for a violent projection of violence that truly pertains to all societies including our own. This attitude is seen at its most flagrant in the writing of that gentleman-ethnologist Sir James Frazer. Frazer, along with his rationalist colleagues and disciples, was perpetually engaged in a ritualistic expulsion and consummation of religion itself, which he used as a sort of scapegoat for all human thought. Frazer, like many another modern thinker, washed his hands of all the sordid acts perpetrated by religion and pronounced himself free of all taint of superstition. He was evidently unaware that this act of hand-washing has long been recognized as a purely intellectual, nonpolluting equivalent of some of the most ancient customs of mankind. His writing amounts to a fanatical and superstitious dismissal of all the fanaticism and superstition he had spent the better part of his lifetime studying.[18]

This excoriation risks misrepresenting Girard's gratitude to Frazer, whom he sees as having come close to the truth in his contrivance of a false category. Though Girard will demur at the theory of ritual transference, he thinks Frazer rightly saw that the victim "[gives] his life for the world," that he dies *for the sake of the people.*[19] In Girard's work, this truth is no mere theme, but a principle of structure that as such belongs at the threshold of human thought and social existence.

Given the foundational role of violence in his thought, Girard's critique of Frazer issues less from beyond the circle of expulsions in which the ethnologist remains unwittingly trapped than from a point of illumination within it. The circle may even be inescapable since what drives it is a fundamental, human predisposition for imitation, something so banal it remains nearly invisible though it simultaneously engenders severe perceptual distortions. Its role in social conflict is rarely glimpsed, almost never fully appreciated, and least from within the conflagrations to which it endlessly gives rise. The putative causes of social conflict—contested objects—the exclusive possession of which is superficially at issue, only eclipse the real source of fascination and rivalry—the *mediator* or *model* who exemplifies what it means to possess and enjoy them; from whom, as it were, "a mysterious ray" descends, causing the objects to "shine with a false brilliance."[20] When a person is drawn to something his mediator enjoys, he threatens that enjoyment and the mediator turns rivalrous. The mediator seems to invite emulation, but should that emulation succeed too well, the injunction to imitate changes swiftly into a threat of retaliation and the model becomes an obstacle. Girard thinks this the basic existential contradiction. We mark its power to falsify and delude in that the more insuperable antagonists feel their differences to be, the more indistinguishable these same antagonists become. As conflict worsens, the contested objects diminish in importance and may even cease to matter, replaced by fascination with the model-turned-obstacle as such. Girard calls this mix of infatuation and loathing that fuses rivals to one another *scandal.* At least initially, rivals may behave very differently, distinguishing themselves from one another by acting in completely opposite ways, though with each new privilege claimed and denunciation issued they grow more and more alike. The disposition of each toward the other converges on perfect identity, since to distinguish oneself from one's rival at all costs is paradoxically to become indistinguishable from him, insofar as he, too, is animated by the same intention.

If the conflict continues to worsen, soon every word and gesture seems doubled as in a mirror. Unless it is deflected, this angry pantomime of accusation for accusation and curse for curse tips over at last into real violence as rivals join in a tangle of kicks and blows. And this violence is nothing if not contagious. What begins with two antagonists spreads quickly to involve others as more and more are drawn into the conflict, which mounts in reciprocating attacks. Girard writes,

> Why does the spirit of revenge, wherever it breaks out, constitute such an intolerable menace? Perhaps because the only satisfactory revenge for spilt blood is spilling the blood of the killer; and in the blood feud there is no clear distinction between the act for which the killer is being punished and the punishment itself. Vengeance professes to be an act of reprisal, and every reprisal calls for another reprisal. The crime to which the act of vengeance addresses itself is almost never an unprecedented offense; in almost every case it has been committed in revenge for some prior crime.

Vengeance, then, is an interminable, infinitely repetitive process. Every time it turns up in some part of the community, it threatens to involve the whole social body. There is the risk that the act of vengeance will initiate a chain reaction whose consequences will quickly prove fatal to any society of modest size. The multiplication of reprisals instantaneously puts the very existence of a society in jeopardy.[21]

This tendency of human violence to escalate unchecked leads Girard to a properly anthropological question—that of cultural origins and the growth of religion. How do people come together to form stable groups, build cities and states, given their mimetic propensity to spiraling violence? What keeps the manifold from descending into the amorphous and obliterating "mob"? The answer he gives explains the universality of sacrifice as an institution in primitive cultures and the dual character of pagan deity—the gods of the primitive sacred who are both good and evil, protectors and destroyers by vicissitude. Girard theorizes that at the height of conflict to which human groups invariably tend, in a veritable "paroxysm" of mob violence, a sudden polarization occurs. The group turns against and kills a single, arbitrarily chosen victim. A common enemy or scapegoat unites it in an act of murder that coincides with a sudden and profound cessation of all the foregoing hostility. "In a single decisive movement," the discharge of what Girard calls the scapegoat mechanism "curtails reciprocal violence and imposes structure on the community."[22]

The death of the victim corresponds to a moment of violent disintegration and mimetic symmetry that is then "stabilized by the mechanism of scapegoating—time T_0 of culture, degree D_0 of structure."[23] All the most basic strata of meaning will be delaminated here. Human thinking itself, "beginning with [the] ability to discriminate anything from anything else," is therefore sacrificial in origin, according to Girard, and "discrimination as a purely intellectual exercise is inseparable from discrimination as exclusion, expulsion, ostracization."[24] He writes that "because of the victim, in so far as it seems to emerge from the community and the community seems to emerge from it, for the first time there can be something like an inside and an outside, a before and after, a community and the sacred."[25] The victim's death coincides with a moment of total unanimity and pure mystification. The sudden transition from all-out war to common peace is something so unforeseen that supernatural intervention seems the only explanation. Though the community deems the scapegoat a villain at his death, it must ultimately take him for "divine," believing he both willed and survived his own demise. The victim could be said to incarnate the violence threatening the community, which it expels. He will then transcend the community as its god—a figure signifying all things from the diabolical to the divine—a god hereafter invoked and propitiated as both the exalted representation of disorder and the mysterious foundation of peace. Thus the world of the primitive sacred unfurls in the victim as "at once good and evil, peaceable and violent, a life that brings death and a death that guarantees life."[26] "Every possible significant element seems to have its outline in the sacred," Girard writes, "and at the same time to be transcended by it."[27] At the dawn of the social order the victim becomes a prelinguistic "universal signifier. "[28]

A scrupulously naturalistic explanation is being ventured here, one that reduces the metaphysical character of the primitive sacred in the multiplicity of its expressions to the universality of a psychosocial event. The channeling of violence against a single victim produces a reciprocal cohesion within the group, allowing it to survive "the intensification of mimetic violence . . . already very much in evidence at the level of primates."[29] By situating the scapegoat mechanism and the birth of the primitive sacred at a point where dominance patterns that check the escalation of violence in primate societies have begun to break down, Girard's thesis becomes sensu stricto ethological.[30] Of course, the peace obtained by the death of the victim is only temporary. The mimetic tendency in humans is so insistent that these early societies are soon embroiled in other conflicts and face the same threat of disintegration all over again. Beset by the problem of mimetic escalation without limit and impelled by fear, the community seeks to reproduce the peace of the founding murder through a scrupulous reenactment of its conditions. This will mean the substitution of other victims for the first, each signifying and so far as possible reproducing the moment of primordial epiphany. What becomes in time a fully religious operation begins with the deliberate reproduction of something that took place at first spontaneously, in a paroxysm of mob violence. This first *conscious* act of the human community qua human community will predate the development of rite and language, which themselves emerge from the collaborative effort, and yet this "first" act is already a repetition. The pattern is not unfamiliar: the surrogate victim "participates in" or "reproduces" the sacrificial power of the original victim to reconcile the people, to atone in the sense of binding them together as one. The founding murder is repeated and this repetition stands at the paradoxical origin of the group as its first collective act, but one that is "radically generative" as such.[31] It ends "the vicious and destructive cycle of violence" while initiating "a constructive cycle, that of the sacrificial rite—which protects the community from that same violence and allows culture to flourish."[32]

The very first surrogate victims probably die in what amount to little more than crude mimetic reproductions of the founding event. "Ritual, in its earliest stages," Girard writes, "is more like a reflexive mimetic repetition . . . much like a child's earliest reactions as it begins to learn." Only much later does "the scapegoat phenomenon and its ritual repetition create the possibility of representation, which requires some degree of reflection," a process that "may have taken hundreds of thousands of years."[33] In time and with the development of a fully human representational capacity the community will come to see the ritual act as a *propitiation* of the victim whose apotheosis identifies the fount of divine blessing with a persistent threat of violence. "It is the god who supposedly demands the victims," Girard writes, "he alone, in principle, who savors the smoke from the altars and requisitions the slaughtered flesh. It is to appease his anger that the killing goes on, that the victims multiply."[34]

The superimposition of two incommensurate notions of *substitution* mark the properly religious logic of this interpretation, so let us pause to disentangle them.[35] If the original victim perishes in the oblivion of mob violence, at a moment of purely reflexive polarization that "saves" the group, the killing of surrogates is deliberately staged and will come in time to be understood as an "exchange" of the one for the many. "Whatever god has caused this plague, for you behold these rams," says Ashella. "Be herewith appeased!" The definitively religious gesture of propitiation is then joined to the appeal to take these rams "fat in liver, heart, and member" and so "let the flesh of humans be hateful to him."[36] *The rams will die in our place*, Ashella reasons.

Let us approach the second mode of substitution by way of Girard's revision of Frazer on kingship and its origins. For Girard the institution of kingship emerges directly from sacrificial ritual, where the community "replay[s] the scenario of an indubitably guilty victim capable of first disrupting the entire community and then of reunifying it through the victim's death."[37] He will therefore read the requirement that ritual victims violate taboos and take unwonted liberties as preparing these same victims for slaughter as criminals by forcing them to imitate "all the crimes that the first victim was supposed to have committed"—a clear sign of the community's "unshakeable conviction that the victim is guilty."[38] The "original victim is endowed with superhuman, terrifying prestige because it is seen as the source of all order and disorder," and some of this prestige rubs off on the surrogate. What may begin as a brief period of "enthronement" and the temporary accordance of unrestricted powers will develop with time into the political institution of monarchy, as other surrogates fill in to extend the king's reign: "The king is at first nothing more than a victim with a sort of suspended sentence."[39]

An unsurprising consequence of the foundational role Girard assigns the victim in his theory of cultural genesis is the emergence of not just kingship but of *all* cultural institutions from sacrifice. The inherently substitutive character of ritual itself, which gradually replaces human victims with animal ones, and these in turn with variously invested objects and forms of ritualized action, eventually screens the victim's presence at the threshold of culture, which tends naturally to outgrow its sanguinary origins. The victim is gradually lost in time and institutional oblivion.

We could situate the rite of Ashella at a still early point in this immemorial process, which began with the killing of human surrogates in blind imitation of the founding murder, the group's constitutive act. By the time of the Hittite ritual, a few rams suffice as surrogates for the plague-stricken army. In the larger scheme of Girard's theory, "surrogacy" expresses a relationship between the victim of the founding murder and all who "die" in like manner, whether in fact or symbolically, as substitutes, by participating in and reproducing the cohesive power of his death. We shall treat the question of structural coincidences at some length in the following chapter; let it suffice here that the same pattern of propitiation (God was not appeased without blood) with a double mode of substitution marks Calvin's Day of Atonement typology, where the immolated goat dies in place of the people (substitution 1) and the scapegoat too becomes a vicarious sacrifice, but one whose power to atone "depends on the sacrifice of the other goat" (substitution 2).

The bewildered response of the human mind to an experience of being "surpassed and transcended by a force that appears to be exterior to it"[40] is of course mistaken, but hardly irrational. "Victims are transfigured into all-powerful manipulators of disorder and order, founding ancestors, or divinities," Girard writes. "Later on, the descendents of the scapegoaters will draw spiritual sustenance from their distorted recollections of the community's ordeal."[41] These recollections are what myths disclose. They conceal only what the community perforce fails to see, namely, "that the choice of the victim is arbitrary, that the causal link between the victim and whatever disaster is ascribed to him is not real."[42] Girard therefore discovers in myth a connection to the generative violence that founds culture, since myth preserves the victim, who is later completely effaced, in its misrepresentation of who he is.

In this view mythology is a garbled history that as such retains an impression of the violence out of which human groups are born. This is why in myth symbols of crisis and disorder abound. "The modern mind has difficulty conceiving of violence in terms of a loss of distinctions," Girard writes, "or a loss of distinctions in terms of violence,"[43] whereas primitive peoples see this connection clearly. The prevalence across primitive cultures of taboos and interdictions against twins, mirrors, reflections, and other "doubling" phenomena suggesting the collapse of stable boundaries reflects this sensitivity; so too the plagues and monstrous births that permeate mythology—vivid expressions, in Girard's view, of a common experience, descriptors of violent liquidation. These same themes curiously recur in the history of our first scapegoat metaphors. It is thus that the question of mythology, its origin and fate, becomes critical to the historical analysis endeavored in the balance of this monograph.

Let us underscore here that if myths relate the death of the divinized victim in different ways, they tend to misrepresent what really happened—not deliberately, of course, because the community is itself blind to the truth. The "texts of mythology are the reflection, at once faithful and deceptive, of the collective violence that founds the community," Girard writes.[44] As such they "bear witness of a real violence" and "do not lie even if in them the victimage mechanism is falsified and transfigured by its very efficacy."[45] In the different accounts given "we must recognize a mask of the collective violence that terminates the crisis."[46]

> Generative violence constitutes at least the indirect origin of all those things that men hold most dear and that they strive most ardently to preserve. This notion is affirmed, though in a veiled and transfigured manner, by the many etiological myths that deal with the murder of one mythological character by other mythological characters. That event is conceived as the origin of the cultural order; the dead divinity becomes the source not only of sacred rites but also of matrimonial regulations and proscriptions of every kind; in short, of all those cultural forms that give man his unique humanity. . . . Sometimes the central character breaks away from the group and flees, taking with him [an] object in dispute. Generally he is overtaken and put to death; occasionally he is merely wounded or beaten. Sometimes it is he who demands to be beaten, and at each blow extraordinary benefits accrue, giving rise to a fertility and an abundance that assures the harmonious functioning of the cultural order. The mythical narrative sometimes takes the form of a contest or game, a quasi-sportive or pugilistic event.[47]

As a linguistic phenomenon, myth can only be a late reflection upon origins. Its narrative elaborations may in time submerge the ritual logic of propitiatory substitution, so explicit in ceremonies like Ashella, where the community remains a violent actor in the urgency of a saving exchange. The displacement onto primordial deities of murderous impulses and deeds reduces the local violence to a shadow thrown by eternal realities. Immemorial, even timeless mythic events, foreordained by the inexorability of divine purposes, serve to found the communal sacrifice, assimilating it to the cosmic order of existence. So often in myth a prized possession changes hands and a murder ensues that in turn gives birth to the polis. This narrative may overwrite the naked exchange of a victim for the life of the people, but rarely effaces it completely. Myth retains an imprint of the transaction. As a retelling of events from the dawn of time, the mythologization of violence represents a final stage in the efflorescence of religion, a process marked initially by ritualized acts whose aim is placatory and whose modus operandi is substitution. If the surrogate is a "stand-in" for the people (in the sense of dying in their place), he is also a substitute for the original victim (as participating vicariously in the power of his death). Myth encodes this violence in the narrative of a time before time, dramatizing the predestination of the sacrificial act at the expense of the group's culpability.

Girard is therefore more radical than Frazer in his insistence on the priority of ritual over myth: because myth presupposes representation and language as a medium of transmission, it takes shape last in a process driven by the evolutionary pressure of the rite.[48] We recall here that what Girard terms "the theological superstructure of the [sacrificial] act"[49] is itself built upon a misrecognition (*méconnaissance*)—the arbitrarily chosen victim *theologized* into an object of ritual placation. Myth then embroiders this error into a replete vision of the universe wherein the actual role of sacrifice is even more hopelessly lost. The truth is that the immolation of the victim propitiates no one, nor is it written in the stars. That the sacrifice "serves to protect the entire community from *its own* violence"[50] never appears to view.

Two Versions of Jesus

Today we can see through the sacred transfigurations of violence in myth, which have gradually broken down, and with them religion itself—from its more pagan and overtly sacrificial forms, which have largely disappeared, all the way through to its most exalted theological formulations in Christianity itself. The latter has been submitted to the most damaging scrutiny and revision at least since the Enlightenment. "For centuries religion has been declining in the West," Girard writes, "and its disappearance is now a global phenomenon. As religion recedes and allows us to consider it in perspective, what was once an insoluble mystery, guarded by formidable taboos, begins to look more and more like a problem to be solved."[51] The pivotal figure in this long process of historical collapse in which we stand looking back is Jesus. Both Girard and Frazer mark his strong resemblance to the *pharmakoi* and other ritual "scapegoats," although this point of agreement between the two thinkers is also a parting of the ways. Girard will read the accounts of Jesus' death in the Gospels as "reproduc[ing] the mythological process with extreme exactitude in order to reveal and completely subvert that process."[52] What they reveal, finally, is something myths never do—that the victim is blameless, that the mob that put him to death acted murderously.[53] Oriented as they are toward the Passion—"the same drama found in all world mythologies"[54]—the Gospels nevertheless culminate in a full disclosure of the scapegoat mechanism. Jesus will bear a striking resemblance to the heroes of myth, and the drama of his death will conform itself to the established pattern in order "to discredit point by point all the characteristic illusions" of myth.[55]

Blackened by the usual false accusations, he dies without a word in his own defense. When from the cross he asks forgiveness for his accusers, he says something that is today so familiar and overdetermined by sentimental piety it barely registers. Girard insists that "the almost technical role" of this prayer, which stands at the heart of the Passion narrative, is "scarcely ever recognized" although its meaning is crucial to understanding what is taking place: "It says something precise about the men gathered together by their scapegoat. *They do not know what they are doing.*"[56] The mob that crucifies Jesus acts in a state of hermetic incomprehension, in the belief that it is doing a service to God. What makes the Passion original is not the "falsely Christian" idea of an incomparable evil perpetrated against Jesus, but what Girard calls "its dimension of revelation."[57] Something unprecedented emerges at the heart of a drama that is otherwise indistinguishable from its countless depictions in myth. For Girard, the death Jesus willingly dies is something neither he nor his Father brings to pass, *as though the violence of the community were somehow an expression of the divine will.* This is precisely the myth of the persecutors. Instead, he yields himself to an inexorably violent process in such a way as to expose its myth for a lie. When the Passion "is regarded not as revelation but as only a violent event brought about by God," Girard writes, "it is misunderstood and turned into an idol."[58]

The Gospels spell the beginning of the end for religion whose constitutive act—the deflection of violence onto a scapegoat—functions less and less well to quench mimetic violence at the heart of communal life. The more arbitrarily blamed and innocent the victim appears, the less susceptible he is to sacred transfiguration. Without this his expulsion stands ever more nakedly exposed to incredulity and suspicion. Its power to bind the group begins to slip. What may have once sufficed to save the city from itself suffices no longer. This opens history into an apocalyptic dimension as violence mounts unchecked by the rites that kept peace from time immemorial. By modern times, which is to say *late* in the historical aftermath of the revelation, the scapegoat mechanism is so weakened that the states it founds are foundering in what is, historically, no time at all. The sacrificial unanimity that built Rome has become unsustainable. The demonization of victims now leads to sacrifice on an unprecedented scale, but its constitutive force is not what it once was. As "the eternal return of religion" nears an end, its seemingly "inexhaustible power of renewal" runs out.[59] The "Thousand Year Reich" that lasted scarcely a hundredth part of its vaunted millennium and the Soviet Union under Stalin furnish Girard with exemplary moments of the mechanism's enervation in a prevailingly demystified world, a world in which the violence needed to build even these short-lived states will be reckoned in the millions and tens of millions of lives. The operative principle that returns on the symbolic level in the following chapter is this: the more exposed the mechanism of scapegoating stands, the greater the expenditure of violence required to achieve the same effect.

CHAPTER 7

The Goat and the Idol

Pagan Religion and Christian Theology

The revelation of the scapegoat progressively disables the religious forms and cultural institutions that depend for their efficacy on its occlusion. One of the first casualties is pagan religion, with its mythology and overtly sacrificial rites. We recall the Roman world of the apostolic age, its temples, shrines, and sacred groves, its games and festivals in honor of the gods from every corner of the empire. Under the roomy pavilion of religious life in the imperial period, the storied denizens of Greek, Roman, and Egyptian myth lounged comfortably alongside local and familial divinities, some of them in more than one regional or civic embodiment, many with priesthoods devoted to their veneration. "There was also no pagan concept of heresy," notes Roman historian Robin Lane Fox.[1] "Pagans performed rites but professed no creed or doctrine. They did pay detailed acts of cult, especially by offering animal victims to their gods, but they were not committed to revealed beliefs in the strong Christian sense of the term."[2]

> Honours for the gods were like dealings on an ever more complex heavenly exchange. Everybody invested, hoping to profit and sometimes to enjoy the gods' close protection. . . . In this pagan religiousness, there is, I believe, a common core despite the many variations in local practice. . . . From Britain to Syria, pagan cults aimed to honour the gods and avert the

misfortunes which might result from the gods' own anger at their neglect.
. . . Any account of pagan worship which minimizes the gods' uncertain
anger and mortals' fear of it is an empty account. This fear did not preclude
thanksgiving, but thanks in Greek prayer . . . were interwoven with ideas
of propitiation. These ideas centered on the offering of gifts. . . . The gods
were concerned with honour and the due offering of gifts. . . . They were
not just superior patrons, but powers of immense superiority: they were
particularly touchy, then, about honour.[3]

Many gods presided over Rome as bestowers of blessing and bringers of curse.
The empire's replete paganism could therefore be seen as a late, fully blown
religious expression of something that transpires at the dawn of history, on
the margin of human self-awareness, in a constitutive act of murder—an act
transfigured by its very power to save. Thus victims presided, each in his or
her own way mercurial and Janus-faced, benignant and bloodthirsty, over
a fear-ridden but reconciled people from time immemorial. Within a few
hundred years of Jesus' coming all this is gone, at least in the West, though
not quite without vestige. Because the death of Jesus so closely resembles that
of innumerable mythic victims, it lends itself to what Girard calls "secondary
and superficial mythological crystallizations."[4]

We could push the implications of Girard's insight here, turning back
to where we began with the early Church Fathers and Justin, whose *Christus
Victor* overwrites the stories of the gods and their exploits in what seems at
first glance an indistinguishably mythic idiom. Its main features are familiar
from the many etiological myths staging the rivalry of two mythological
characters over some contested object. One deceives the other, takes possession of the object, and flees. A pursuit follows that ends in murder. This
death "is conceived as the origin of the cultural order" and the "source not
only of sacred rites" but of all the rules that constitute the basis of communal
life.[5] Girard notes that "the mythical narrative sometimes takes the form of
a contest or game, a quasi-sportive or pugilistic event," behind which we
glimpse "the outline of reciprocal violence, gradually transformed into a
unanimous act." If we apply this insight to the evolving story of how Christ
saves, it quickly becomes evident that with *Christus Victor* we are still at the
stage of discrete, reciprocating attacks. Satan deceives humanity, absconding
with God's people. God deceives Satan and retakes possession of them. The
fathers provide a host of details that render the contestants, their motivations,
and ploys in all too familiar colors. All the strategies of scandalized desire are
on full display, from the Devil's envy of Eden's blessedness and inveiglement

of human credulity, to the feigned inadvertence of Christ's exposure to death and his rival's homicidal covetousness, which he outfoxes. All belong to a repertoire of narrative devices at once purely mythic and cannily descriptive of human conflict. The divine hero even founds a new community, a race remade in his own image.

To see what is unprecedented here, let us recall that myth amalgamates the power of life and death and divinizes it. Any violence is therefore caught up and enclosed in the round of divine agency. The victim's death is depicted as inevitable in view of spectacular crimes laid to his account but above all as *divinely* self-willed because it founds the social order. This representation occludes the violent role of the human community in the exchange of a merely human victim to save its own skin. That human beings play a passive role in *Christus Victor*, first as dupes, then captives set free, means that little is revealed of their culpability, which pales in comparison with the malevolence of Satan, the undisputed agent of destruction. The Father is for his part not merely gracious and favorably disposed toward his people, but completely averse to violence. With this strict division between rivals of the power to kill and give life we come to something unprecedented in the text of myth. We might even say the early versions of *Christus Victor* cleave pagan deity, which is at once good and evil, into two opposing faces, fissuring the integrity of the sacred. Satan now incarnates the power of death *simpliciter*, while his rival becomes the God of life whose justice demands that he remain pristinely nonviolent. For at least ten centuries the scapegoat marks out the distance between them, as first the signifier of one, then the other, back and forth, in readings that progressively extend the range of significations on each side. As divine, the goat stands for Christ's indestructible life beyond suffering, exalted among the faithful on high. As diabolical, it signifies the Devil in hellish torment amid a fair crowd of adjutants, followers, and fools.

With the gradual mythic elaboration of *Christus Victor* to include the idea of a deception perpetrated by God in Jesus, whose incarnation then appears to be little more than a cunningly devised hoax, divine justice will seem to have been compromised. If Jesus avoids gross acts of seizure, the premeditated fraudulence of his ploy cannot but tarnish his innocence. He is nobly intentioned but tainted by the basest political instincts like a thousand heroes of myth. It is precisely against these portrayals that the first juridical theories move—to rescue divine honor from the shadow of moral turpitude under which it has fallen. The innocence of the Savior appears to have outgrown the myth. Soon flourishing in its place is a penitential economy established by his innocence precisely and the consequently voluntary, surplus-generating sacrifice that he alone can make.

This emphasis cleaves the sacred once again. We recall that if human guilt and God's just condemnation of sin are but minor and intermittent motifs in *Christus Victor* to begin with, the myth's increasingly psychodynamic plot tends to overwhelm them completely. The withdrawal of the Devil in the juridical accounts clearly foregrounds these motifs as soteriological problems of the first order. A partial demythologization has therefore taken place. The victim is now completely innocent and the people stand fully condemned. But then the God of *Christus Victor* has also undergone a fearsome transmogrification. The Devil may no longer be a player of any consequence but the polarization of divinity into opposed faces has scarcely been reduced. The axis of opposition has merely shifted. As divine victim Christ alone repudiates violence by consenting to die without reprisal, becoming the source of life for all; but the Father consequently turns deathward and dark. His justice, that guarantor of divine pacifism in *Christus Victor*, now demands bloody retribution. Death, as an expression of God's justice, undoubtedly serves to drag human guilt from the shadows, but the violence evicted in the person of the Adversary is henceforth unleashed inside the Godhead itself. Corresponding now to the divine victim (God the Son) is a divine killer (God the Father). A process of symbolic implosion is now well under way that gradually reveals all that ritual and myth serve to occlude, a process that proceeds in stages so that what breaks with the sacred pattern appears a little at a time.

Here let us end by noting that, while the meritoriousness of Christ's death is more than sufficient to save, a number of rules and procedures govern its applicability to sinners in the penitential economy of the scholastic period. Unless these are observed, one cannot but remain pitifully exposed to the wrath of God. We recall that in myth, too, the sacred is at once the promise of salvation and a continuing threat of death for which religion furnishes, as it always has, the ways and means of divine appeasement. If culture itself begins in acts of sacrificial substitution, which come to full religious flower in Roman paganism, Christianity must be seen as largely quenching the outward, bloody manifestations of sacred cult, but not without internalizing its constitutive rationale, *not without enshrining it in new forms of sacrificial endeavor.* The threat of death gives urgency alike to the pagan rites as to the sublimated offerings of Christian penitents. Inscribed in all their different rhetorical gestures—from Aquinas's pleasure-equivalent punishments to Peter Damian's direct, physical participation in the passion of Christ—is an act of substitutive exchange, a transitory mortification that preempts eternal death. "Deliver me wholly and entirely from your justice," says Damian, "so that having been configured to the Crucified in punishment, I shall deserve to be the companion of the Arisen in glory."[6]

The Innocent Anathema

Something seen only from beyond the closure of theology is working itself free in the "symbolic collapse" of reflection on the meaning of Christ's death. If what begins at the threshold of culture as a crude mimetic duplication of the founding murder is gradually ritualized and later theologized, becoming an act of divine propitiation, the fully theologized ritual is at last fenced round by the narrative interpretations of myth. This process gives us "religion" fully fledged, without regard to any particular historical instantiation. A process of demystification then subverts this development, toppling paganism and, eventually, Christian theology itself. The first thing to go is also the last to develop in what Girard posits as the growth of religion from communal violence, namely, religion's mythological integument, already reduced to a single narrative layer in the first Christian centuries: the consolidated "pagan" myth of *Christus Victor*. The dissolution of this paradigmatic narrative gradually exposes the violent exchange at its core. Ritual's propitiatory gesture—its bloody quid pro quo bid for peace—must then itself begin breaking down. The more revealed it stands, the less well it functions. As it fails, the saving transaction grows correspondingly more violent, but also more senseless and confused. What the historical trajectory of the scapegoat shows us is a process of religious degeneration that proceeds in stages symmetrical with those of religion's inception and growth, a process that ends in the coalescence of our secular metaphor.

Let us recall that as a *mythic* account of origins the integrity of *Christus Victor* is already meaningfully broken. Though it remains indistinguishable from its pagan archetypes as a tale of death and resurrection, and the birth of a people by divine fiat, it nevertheless polarizes the values of the primitive sacred into two unmingled rivals—exemplars of life and death, peace and destruction, respectively—something myth never does. Against the exalted conception of divinity this division produces, the pagan gods cannot but seem adulterate and corrupt, and this obviously hastens their demise.

But where justice establishes God's nonviolence in contradistinction to the violence of his adversary in *Christus Victor*, the juridical theories oppose this same virtue to the increasingly sordid machinations of *Christus Victor* itself. Jesus must therefore be radically vindicated. He must be hereafter unsullied by acts of bribery and low deception. Gone, too, is the wily but pacific deity of *Christus Victor*, replaced by the divine avenger. The two polarized faces of *Christus Victor* reunite in the Godhead, which comes more nearly to resemble one of the old pagan deities—a bestower of life but jealous of his honor and armed to defend it. The religious response so intent on propitiation and preemptive substitution grows correspondingly less distinguishable from pagan cult. The high convertibility of such gestures, pagan and Christian alike, to pecuniary metaphor—their extreme susceptibility to the dynamics of exchange—must give us pause. As all economic activity resolves itself into a series of discrete substitutions, so the value of penitential acts must themselves begin to *circulate* like ghostly coin made palpable by fear. From Britain to Syria and the imperial age to the present, substitution is the animating principle of trade—the religion in business no less than the business of religion.

There is, however, at the center of the penitential system a value found nowhere in the old pagan economy. As in Roman times, anyone hoping to win favor and avert divine anger was obliged to invest, but the sine qua non of this economy—the thing driving it—is the *innocence* of Christ, formulated in the first case by Anselm as his *unindebtedness*, a doctrine in which the robust metaphysical economy of the period stands reflected. It is not yet everything it will become theologically, but it is already the standard of currency on the new "heavenly exchange."

In the language of Calvin and the Puritans things begin to change once again. The Father's vengeance becomes something colossal and all-consuming. The Son here plays the role of divine victim whose death protects and reforms the people under new auspices. The most extreme formulations of this reduce all creation and every being in it to a homicidal manifestation of the divine will so as to once again lose the thread of *human* violence in the dazzling brocade of the sacred. This will is the divinized energy of the mob, violence writ large. A more unanimous act of murder could hardly be imagined. Christian soteriology now undergoes a last, unprecedented, and ultimately fatal transformation. With Calvin's anathema of the Catholic penitential system, the entire compensatory economy of merits and satisfactions collapses into a single exchange. The killing stroke deflects onto a lone substitute, invalidating all the smaller self-inflicted privations by which the faithful had long endeavored to preempt punishment. There is but one act of substitution, the act of Christ. Faith alone avails to give us a part in it, says Calvin. No self-arraignment here and now means anything, no chipping away at God's punishment in penances and mortifications, personal or vicarious. A single paroxysm of divine wrath annuls the usual religious expedients. Calvin's chilling descriptions of its fury plainly exceed previous formulations, which seem weak and tentative by comparison.

The mere triumphalism of *Christus Victor*, like the penitential rationalism of the Schoolmen, has given way to something more turbulent and congested, a nightmare of violence abolishing every distinction and limit. In Jacob's language, even the lately illuminated guilt of the people recedes into the darkness of a will to punishment so cosmic and pervasive that distinct human agency is confounded. Christ's persecutors "were all as Instruments only, & used by God unto his owne end," Jacob says. "God's owne hand did it to Christ." The mythic architecture of a quasi-pugilistic game, with its discrete reciprocal attacks between contradistinguished enemies, is swallowed by an act of violence that not only converts each persecutor (human and, even, demonic) into an instrument of the divine will, but threatens even the discriminability of victim and victimizer. As something that the Father inflicts on Christ, Death now expresses a relation of the divine to itself.

This penal conception of the atonement is sometimes defended by appeal to Trinitarian formulas. There can be no question of the Father torturing his son to death, it is said, for *opera Trinitatis ad extra sunt indivisa* (the works of the triune Godhead toward the world are indivisible). If so, a single agency unites inflictor and inflicted in an act that obliterates them both. Trinitarian indivisibility makes the violence only that much more sweeping and abyssal. The move to redeem punishment as an act of love by surrendering the final distinction between Father and Son—the last conceivable difference in a *process* of violent undifferentiation we grasp only from an anthropological perspective—is an expression of the mysticism of violence at the point of no return. As a manifestation of God's wrath the act belongs wholly to myth, which has always seen violence as an expression of divinity and as such inscribed in the very order of creation. Here again is the god who both wills and survives his own death—a mythic formula and convention. Only this time, the two faces of pagan divinity, on which the sacred economy of favors and propitiations has always depended, run together in a flash of obliterating heat. Rather than opening the flow of trade, this annuls it. The act of violence still discharges itself within the closure of the sacred as answering a divine necessity, and its deflection belongs undeniably to an *economy* of salvation. This economy is, however, petrified at inception, reduced to a theological symbol.

The reduction of paganism's mythic plethora to a single "myth," and the historical paring back of this one to expose a single act of soul-destroying violence, is something that finally exceeds theological formulation or dogmatic pronouncement. If there is little that does not belong to the vocabulary of myth in *Christus Victor*, the earliest formulations of this idea nevertheless begin to polarize the sacred, in such a way as to allow us a glimpse of the God beyond death, the one whose infinite resources of wisdom and counsel mean he never need resort to violence. Here is indeed "the Father of lights in whom there is no variableness, neither shadow of turning"—something unprecedented and demythologized, inasmuch as the pagan deities stood undecidably for life *and* death, good *and* evil confounded.

However, this cosmos and its soteriology, too, caves in upon itself. As it does, the mechanism of substitution is gradually exposed. A worsening threat of punishment, remythologized in the dogma of God's justice and its demand for satisfaction, marks the transition from Aquinas to Calvin, during which a whole system of discrete transactions is consolidated into a single, glaring exchange. The efflorescence of a religious system that takes seriously this demand, providing a host of institutionally mediated remediations, is finally overwhelmed by an apotheosis of divine wrath, whose universal scale and intensity beggars human response. The malefactors are so helplessly culpable that literally everything depends on the innocence of the victim who consents to die in their place.

Calvin tells us we are saved when divine wrath exhausts itself on this victim. He thus begins to build the city of myth once more, only this time on the sacrifice of *one* man who pays with his life and a torment past imagining for crimes he did not commit. His suffering is wholly unsubsidized and solitary. The punishment inflicted could not be more intentional or thoroughgoing, nor the victim more "shiningly innocent." As the officiant and scribe of his own symbolic Golgotha, Calvin, like his counterparts fifteen hundred years earlier, proclaims the expediency of Jesus' death as substitute: "that one man should die for the people, and that the whole nation should not perish." Like them, he fails to glimpse the world-historical fault line where he stands, or that the order he reforms is itself passing away. A new day is breaking well beyond the precincts of Catholic orthodoxy and its would-be Protestant successors, not unlike that which illuminated the world of pagan cult in the first Christian centuries. With the coming of the Age of Enlightenment the hegemony of Christianity's medieval past has reached its end. The blow that

Calvin deals to Catholic teaching is one of the first among many that will reduce the domination of religion as such to a rubble of sectarianism in the West, all of it historically surmounted by science and the advent of the secular age. Calvin's divinization of violence enshrines at the heart of his bequest to the Protestant sects that continue to promulgate one adaptation or another of his language on the atonement, an act from which every modern notion of justice and fair play could take its leave as from a negative standard—as from *injustice* itself: the destruction of the weak and innocent party in the service of the multitude. The gesture that elevates the victim's death into a sacred mystery no longer conceals this.

It is thus that a Girardian anthropology allows us to situate Christian soteriology on a single trajectory extending from that liminal burst of violence at the dawn of the primitive sacred, through the turbid symbolism of myth and radiantly fissured cosmos of *Christus Victor*, to where the latter begins to contract, imploding till the poles of exalted divinity and satanic torment fuse in Calvin's vision of a God who is damned. Can this display of bottomless suffering be the revelation of divine love? Is it not rather the last gasp of the old primitive sacred, the collapse of its metaphysical vectors and symbolic field? In the "marvelous way he loved us even while he hated us," a last, ruined mask of pagan deity flares out of the darkness, transfixed and scandalized. Like so much in the soteriological panorama from Justin to Calvin, this face too now seems only a reflection, staring back from the glass in which we peer so darkly.

When we consider the final stages of our word's evolution, two moments stand out above all. The first, which is purely semantic, occurs in Calvin's "offscourings" typology, connecting the type of the scapegoat with the idea of vicarious sacrifice. The second is properly lexical. Jacob, who is reprising Calvin theologically, uses the English word specifically to designate the vicarious damnation of Christ's soul. If we understand Jacob to be making explicit what Calvin only implies for the scapegoat, a final observation on patterns in the scapegoat data is warranted.

At what is arguably the semantic origin of our English metaphor, in Calvin's typology of the scapegoat—the earliest reference we have linking the animal to the idea of vicarious sacrifice—a sacrificial duplication takes place. Any account of the scapegoat that neglects this typology and its prodigious interpretive fiat remains fragmentary and partial. There are two sacrifices, says Calvin, not one. The demand for blood as the price of atonement overwhelms all the merely textual considerations in Calvin's reading of Leviticus 16. If the scriptures say the scapegoat "makes atonement" for the people, he reasons, it is a *sacrifice* in virtue of this fact alone (substitution 1: *the one for the many*). To overcome the detail of the scapegoat's escape from death he then conjures up a paradox, something new and scripturally unexampled by his own admission. Of course, Calvin's *bloodless sacrifice* is not really bloodless at all, inasmuch as the scapegoat is hereafter steeped in the blood of its immolated twin. Only thus may it duplicate (substitution 2: *the surrogate for the original victim*) the sacrificial power to atone—*to make one*.

This same pattern appears in the act of communal self-constitution, wherein the death of one saves the rest from a violence threatening to destroy them all, a death deliberately reproduced in the group's first collective act: the sacrifice of the surrogate victim. The surrogate victim, like Calvin's scapegoat, recapitulates an original act of vicarious bloodshed; he is at once a sacrifice for the people (substitution 1) as taking their place, and a surrogate or stand in for the original victim, as reproducing the unifying force of that victim's death (substitution 2). What could possibly account for the correspondence between Calvin's reading and Girard's originary scene? The structural anthropologists who observed and theorized about the meaningfulness of patterns across widely divergent phenomena might speak here of "homologous structures," although we are simultaneously confronted by two cases of repetition at origin, the deconstructor's paradox par excellence. At the threshold of communal existence the power of the original victim's death to reconcile and bind is "doubled," in striking parallel to what occurs in Calvin's typology, the semantic threshold of our English metaphor. The coincidence lets us know we are on the borderlands. Could it be the twilit perimeter of thought itself?

By situating the scapegoat—as psychosocial phenomenon—at the inception of human self-awareness, at the genesis of *time* and *structure*, Girard opens a perspective in which the recurrence becomes susceptible to explanation in a chronological narrative of stages, a narrative that begins with the submerged pattern of a proto-*event* that surfaces in the course of a historical revelation. This occurs at a moment of linguistic formation whose result—the metaphor of the scapegoat—discloses something the event served to conceal. Let us recall that long before the appearance of language, the victim opens up the dimension of human signification as at once "good and evil, peaceable and violent, a life that brings death and a death that guarantees life."[7] He is thus divinized so that "every possible significant element seems to have its outline in the sacred and at the same time to be transcended by it."[8] Concealed behind this phantasmatic production is the truth that he was arbitrarily chosen and therefore innocent. If the first victim is transfigured by the sacred array of meanings that his death unfurls—the "last victim" (*Christi ad Infernos*) collapses that array precisely and in so doing bequeaths something new to language. In what we are calling the final, imploded myth of Christ in hell, Calvin shows us this victim reducing the sacred and all its constellated antitheses in extremis. Every possible significant element has its outline in the sacred save one, and it is this one that surmounts the obliteration of them all—the victim as *innocent.* Jacob then calls this victim: the scapegoat.

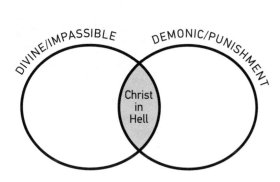

CHAPTER 8

A Figure in Flux

The Translated Goat

"Ultimately, everything we say here is an attempt to understand the semantic evolution of the word and evaluate its impact," Girard writes. "Our whole hypothesis has existed silently in common language since the emergence of what is called rationalism."[1] The huge importance he assigns the scapegoat proceeds from a theoretical intuition—ventured in the late 1970s without benefit of the facts uncovered in this monograph—that the word becomes a signifier of emergent historical truth when it splits to reveal a second meaning. What the new evidence allows us to see is that this truth quickly explodes the theological matrix in which the word takes shape. Though it impresses the scapegoat with the form of a relation between parties in an act of deflected violence, the theology of penal substitution will itself soon face the music of an annihilating new critique that it very nearly defines—nearly, but for an implicit judgment that soon attends every use of our secular metaphor.

We now know that less than a century after Calvin's typology of 1563, the "scapegoat" escapes theological commentary to become an expression in common speech, a descriptor of purely terrestrial violence. In the final stage of its linguistic evolution we witness the eclipse of divine wrath by a sign undeniably fired in its heat, but hereafter signifying *human* inhumanity alone. The dimension of the sacred fades quickly, and as metaphysical determinations even "guilt" and "innocence" dim to no more than implied meanings. As one blamed or punished for the sins of others, the scapegoat hereafter expresses no more than a preferential relation of the accused to his accusers.

That the semantic value of our expression is still very much in flux until sometime in the early eighteenth century, when it begins to lock tightly with the sense it has today, can be judged from a handful of early uses that fall outside the margin of biblical commentary. Two things stand out from the citations adduced in this chapter and the next. First, the scapegoat's linguistic fate is very much up for grabs during the first century of its life as a metaphor: there is no question of improbably fateful patristic typologies determining its current meaning and usage.[2] Though readings like those of Calvin and the Puritans will ultimately prove decisive, the sense of the expression varies widely for some time after leaving the orbit of theological commentary. Second, the earliest informal uses of the expression in a sense approximating its current meaning will be inflected by judgments like those that inform usage today.

We could plot the earliest metaphorical use of the term on the index of typological motifs we have just staked out, at the far end of all the darker significations, as a metaphor of escape, though it remains for all that most prescient and mysterious. The English topographer John Norden, who is said to have penned devotional works from penury and a lack of steady patronage, publishes *A Christian Familiar Comfort and Incouragement vnto All English Subiects, Not to Dismaie at the Spanish Threats* in 1596, about midway through the Anglo-Spanish war. In it he urges his readers to look "euerie man into himselfe, and the magistrates into the whole state" for the cause "whereby it cannot bee denyed but God may . . . suffer vs to tast of the sword of this ambitious and blasphemous nation":

> And therefore surely it will hardly appeare that we haue deserued to be punished, if wee looke no further than into other men, & so let our selues passe like the scape goats: for if euery one couet to find the cause in others, and prie not into himselfe, there wil be neuer a free man, yet all free, for euerie man will condemne all but himselfe, and yet though none will condemne himselfe, hee shall bee condemned of all. And therefore let euerie man acknowledge himselfe worthie to bee punished, so all men shall be condemned by theyr owne mouthes, and seeke no further witnesse. And this (no doubt) is the waie to finde the cause why God hath called this nation agaynst vs, as *Ionah* was founde guiltie by casting of lots.

For doubtlesse if wee seeme to seeke the cause of this daunger without our selues, we doo wrong to the iustice of God, who is not as enuious man, that will strike one for an other, but *the soule that sinneth shall die.* Lo then it is sinne that draweth on this *hoobub* to pursue vs, euen to our subuersion, if wee repent not of our sundrie euills. Wee are called Christians, and our aduersaries Antichristians, but if wee looke into the fruites of both, a man may bee in doubt who is lykest Christ.[3]

The reference is striking for its fully-fledged statement of what it means to scapegoat others in the modern sense of that verb, including even the blind-ness of accusers to their own faults. It reminds us that for Girard the word "scapegoat" is but a sign, the crystallization in a word of a new critical spirit afoot in the world, although it can hardly be said to crystallize lexically here: Norden's scapegoats are those who let themselves off the hook. They are pre-cisely the accusers and not the accused. Even so, the darkness of persecution, the war of all against all, and the cold light of repentance are vividly evoked. To be sure, God is still the agent of punishment. But he is rather an impar-tial enforcer of justice than the wrathful avenger and—this is telling—*God punishes no one by proxy.* Norden formularizes the modern ethic of personal accountability with a line divining its advent in the prophet Ezekiel. No one is struck down for the sins of another: it is "the soule that sinneth shall die." Let each look to himself and his own sin for it "draweth on this hoobub to pursue us."

Nathaniel Pownall makes a similar use of the expression in *The Young Divines Apologie for his Continuance in the Vniuersitie,* which he publishes in 1612 after recovering "in a manner, at Cambridge, that life, which he lost at his departure from Oxford."[4] In it Pownall bids his reader "Behold the boun-tie, and seueritie of God: seueritie towards mine enemies, that haue fallen; bowntie towards mee, that when I, and they stood before thine Altar, as the two Goats, one of vs to be sacrificed, to appease thy wrath, and as *Ionas* with the Marriners, in the tempest of thine anger, one of vs to be cast out, hast pleased to let the lot of the scape-goate, fall on mee, and to make them the sin-offring."[5] Like Norden's scapegoat, Pownall's figures escape, the reprieve of punishment. Here Pownall evokes the story of Jonah with the same emphasis on expulsion we discovered in George Abbot's reference, without neglect-ing to exploit that other feature of the narrative whose sacrificial character Girard notes—the casting of lots.[6]

In 1678 Jean Barrin's *The Monk Unvail'd: Or, A Facetious Dialogue, Dis-covering the Severall Intrigues, and Subtil Practises, together with the Lewd and*

Scandalous Lives of Monks, Fryers, and Other Pretended Religious Votaries of the Church of Rome plays the expression in a slightly different register. The book takes the form of a dialogue between the country curate Florimond and the "secularized monk" Patrick, who regales his interlocutor with tales of monkish venery behind cloister walls, which are met with exclamations of scandalized disbelief and a moist enthusiasm for the details. In response to the ludicrous tale of an aged Jacobin who advises two maids that "to keep those innocent Brests imprisoned" not "suffering them to breath in the open air" is to "renew the Martyrdom and Persecutions of the Primitive-Church," Florimond mentions others like him but worse, with the wish "that those Goats might not dare any more to appear, but be forc'd to flee to some solitary place, like unto these Scape-goats, laden with the sins of the people, whereof mention is made in Leviticus."[7] Here the scapegoat is plainly the sin-bearer as reprobate, one who departs under the burden of his own transgressions. That the lechery connoted by goats and satyrs might have claimed the expression as a slur is evident in at least one other citation from the period. Bewailing vexations that attend the fixing of dowries and the marrying of daughters, *The Pleasures of Matrimony* by satirist Edward Ward cautions:

> Neither is it safe always to divulge what a Man intends to give with his Daughter; for if that be once spread abroad, 'tis Ten Thousand Pounds to a Nut-Shell, but there comes one smooth Chinn'd *Slipstring* or other, and makes a *Pye-Corner* Ensurance of his Affection upon her Belly. She is betray'd by this Midwife, and t'other Nurse, or another Old Beldam Conveyor of *Billet deux's*, and all her Father's Carping and Caring, squandered away upon a Scape-Goat of an Attorney's Clerk; or Coach'd away in a Moon-Shiny Night, from a Boarding School, by a young Squire of Seven Hundred a Year in *No-Land*. We have heard of some too, that have been Courted upon the Report of being Heiresses, to that Condescention, as to suffer themselves to be let down from their Guardian's Garret-Window in a Dust-Basket, as if they were making their Escapes for Felony; then away to Bed and a Clean Pair of Sheets, and so home again by Five a Clock in the Morning, before any body is up, but the dear Conspiratress that sits up to let her in.[8]

Here the scapegoat is a synonym for the scoundrel in amorous exploits and its biblical meanings a far-distant echo; if the word still connotes escape, it is in the unprecedented sense of absconsion. One would think Ward had in mind "scapegrace' or even "scamp,' only those words appear to have an even later date of origination than our metaphor.[9] In another droll piece of 1705 entitled *City and Country Recreation*, the expression is used twice in very different ways. Recounting the fair promises of a seducer whose talk of marriage persuades an overfond girl to spend "a few Night's Recreation at Lovers In-and-in," the author, J. S., tells how she is then sent "a great Way on a sleeveless Errand, with her worst Cloaths on" while "he removes his Quarters to some secret Place," so that "returning, and finding herself stript, and deceived of a Husband, her Eyes are opened too late."[10] The jilted girl "cries, wrings her Hands, makes search after her Scape-goat, though all in vain," while "the growing Burthen of her Womb brings her Folly perpetually into her remembrance."[11] This usage differs little from the previous one, so it is all the more striking to find the expression deployed again in the same text, only this time to name a dupe, the prey of sharpers who "haunt blind Ale-houses and such Ninny-broth Houses as were not too publick" in search of young fools down on their luck to deceive.[12] "Our scapegoat" will be persuaded with empty promises "of both Money and a Mistress" to throw an alehouse party where his better-heeled friends may "spend their Money most liberally, as coming easily by it" and there be—unbeknownst to him—sized up for the easy marks among them.[13]

One other transitional usage detains us for its better approximation of the figure in current use. In the *Preface* to a poem in six cantos called *The Dispensary Transvers'd*, the poet apologizes for "the many Faults this poem has for want of those judicious Correcting Hands," which *The Dispensary* of Samuel Garth—to which it replies—"underwent before it was publish'd."[14] There are besides the "gross Errata of the Printer" that are apt to make it appear "sent into the World, like the Scape Goat into the Wilderness, bearing the Errours and blunders of the Author."[15] Here we find the motif of the sin-bearer adapted for a secular use, although the transfer of blame that the poet hopes to preempt is noteworthy. "The fault is not all mine," he seems to say, "though I am blamed." The scapegoat is of course less one blamed than an occasion of blaming.

In another citation taken from a 1712 issue of *The Examiner*, the author advises the Whig party, to which he does not belong, upon the occasion of "the annual Choice of all their great Officers of State" that "if a Viceroy happens to be proposed to them" whose "Tyranny and Avarice are alike Boundless, his Power without any superior but Providence, a Being he has not yet acknowledg'd; and who, like the Scape-Goat of Old, can only serve to Transport the Sins of a whole Nation into a strange Country; I think the Commonwealth ought not to be over-hasty in Declaring for him, *lest he should be the first to expose their Judgment*, and, like one of the Popes, immediately after his Accession, make his Footman Prime Minister."[16] Once again the motif of the sin-bearer appears in a nonreligious context where the question of consequent blame is paramount: choose carefully whom you send as you will have to answer for his sins.

The Plague Goat

We turn next to citations identifying the scapegoat with plague. The earliest of these is found in *The Prophecies, and Predictions, for London's Dliverance*, an astrological tractate printed in 1665 at the height of the Plague of London, when as many as seven thousand deaths were reported in the city each week. It includes variously calculated prognostications of the plague's progress and dénouement, enjoining "Patience the best Plaister against Sores" and "Repentance the best Restorative," like "Prayer the best antidote."[17] Because the plague "is God's doing, repine not at his Providence,"[18] neither think to flee the city, the astrologer John Gadbury advises, since "the Rod of his Anger is of such a *Longitude*, that it can reach us every where."[19] He adds that "*London* hath at present been the Patient, and hath felt the force of the Almighties scourge to purpose; while most other places of *England* have escaped the *lash*. I wish with all my soul, that *London* might be the Scape-Goat for them all."[20] Gadbury here deploys the expression to designate one who suffers vicariously and so as to spare the guilty. London is doubtless being punished for its own sins, but his wish that it might draw the sting for other cities is striking not merely for the logic of substitution invoked, but for its context—the plague he would thus forestall. The reference recalls another of 1721, penned during the Plague of Marseilles. In it the author recounts that at the height of the crisis the bishop

> went out of his Palace in Procession, accompanied with the Canons . . . and the Curate, and Parish Priest of St. *Feriol,* and appear'd as the Scape Goat, sent out loaded with the Sins of the People; and as if he had been a Victim destin'd for the Expiation of their Sins, he march'd with a Halter about his Neck, and a Cross between his Arms, and bare footed . . . [At the Gate of *Aix*] he celebrated Mass in Publick, on a Alter which he had order'd there to be erected . . . [exhorting the people] in order to perswade them to Repentance, that thereby it might asswage the Wrath and Anger of God, and obtain Deliverance from this cruel Pestilence. . . . The Tears

which trickled down from his Eyes during this holy Ceremony, together with his soft and healing Words, excited a Remorse in the Hearts of the most obdurate, and every one was penetrated with so lively a Sorrow, that they cried out aloud for the Mercy of God.[21]

In the outbreak that by some estimates will claim half the city's population, Marseilles's very survival hangs in the balance. The priest here plays the part of the scapegoat as sacrificial substitute, recalling the myths and public rituals of the ancient world in which the *pharmakos* and like human victims figure so prominently. Whether these invocations of the scapegoat allude deliberately to the *pharmakos* it would be difficult to say. But the wish they express—that the penalty owed the many might be deflected onto one—is feckless, at least according to Gadbury, who says as much: "but ah, I fear, before the Planet *Saturn* be gotten quite out of *Capricorn* that those other parts of this Nation will drink deep of the same *Cup. God* and *Nature* punish none by *proxy*. It will not be this Cities suffering, that can excuse other Towns and Cities, from the violent stroak of so insatiate an Enemy."[22] The violence is that of God himself, a severe but impartial punisher who, moreover, like Nature, accepts no surrogate but exacts by strict recompense alone. Between the conception of a God who demands the blood of his own Son to assuage his wrath against humankind and that of a judge who balks at punishing substitutes, we may chart the descent of our expression that is here, as it were, midway between metaphysical and profane violence. A scapegoat will not work, says Gadbury. The Avenger never stoops to this expedient. We saw this same idea in John Norden's contention that when "wee seeme to seeke the cause of this daunger without our selues, we doo wrong to the iustice of God, who is not as enuious man, that will strike one for an other."[23] There, of course, Norden was using the expression "scape-goat" in a very different sense than Gadbury, whose deployment of it here approximates the current meaning quite closely. Gadbury's scapegoat is a wishful substitute, one who would suffer for the sins of others were it not an affront to divine probity. If, as we have been contending, the scapegoat acquires its meaning from the language of penal substitution, which establishes God's demand from the innocent of a price owed by the guilty, here those terms are being overwritten and with them a fundamental conception of who God is: not the enraged deity propitiated by blood (a fundamentally pagan notion) but the judge beneath whose dignity it stands to punish any but the culpable, an indifferent enforcer of the law, like nature herself. The implications have yet to be fully spelled out, but God's just disdain of all such deflections onto the innocent means the scapegoat is cast to earth, where it hereafter remains a descriptor of something human beings do in their injustice and enmity toward one another. Who today would say that "God *scapegoats* Jesus" to explain what many theological traditions more or less contend? The dissonance of that statement is an index of the word's semantic descent, a long echoing trace of just how far it has fallen under blood and shadow in the centuries since it first named Christ's satisfaction of divine vengeance. The negative connotations are already in evidence here, the henceforth ineradicable marks of violence desacralized.

Around the time of the Plague of Marseilles, Englishmen John Trenchard and Thomas Gordon begin publishing a series of vividly conceived attacks on tyranny, championing the rights and liberties of the individual against the despotism of government and majority rule alike. Among their essays (published under the nom de plume "Cato"), which so influenced American colonists in the coming generation, is one of March 1721 that warns against recourse to a scapegoat at the height of yet another plague:

> But what shall be done! Where is the Remedy for all these Evils? We hope for it, we expect it, we see it: and we call for it, from the healing Hands of our most gracious King, and his dutiful Parliament. There is a Crisis in the Health of Governments, as well as of private Persons. When Distempers are at the Worst, they must mend, or the Patient die. . . . What then is this Remedy?—We *must begin with letting out some of our adulterate and corrupt Blood,* one Drop of which is enough to contaminate the Ocean. We must first take full Vengeance of all those we can discover to be guilty. . . . Let us not, Oh, let us not suffer the Sins of all *Israel* to be at this Time of Day laid upon the Head of the SCAPE-GOAT. When we have taken this first and necessary Step to prevent an Apoplexy or malignant Eruptions, let us prescribe strong Emeticks, proper Sudorificks, and effectual Purgatives, to bring up or throw off the noxious Juices and morbifick Matter than oppresses us. . . . *But above all, and for the sake of all,* let us avoid the Beginning with Lenitives and palliating Medicines, which will only cover and foment our Evils, make them break out more violently, and at last, perhaps, turn into dangerous Swellings and epidemical Plague-Sores, and by such Means spread a general Infection: Let us not suffer any of our great or little Rogues to escape publick Vengeance.[24]

Here of course the plague is only an extended metaphor for the corruption afflicting the body politic. Is this coincidence of plague references in the earliest informal uses of the expression an indirect sign of the degree to which the scapegoat and more forthrightly substitutionary victims of religious violence like the *pharmakos* have become entangled in the popular *imaginaire*? We recall that only the Greek victim was ever used to halt plague. Or does it express something more unthinking and reflexive? Cato's letter urges against recourse to this all too convenient "cure" in a prevailingly vengeful mood. The problem with scapegoats is that the guilty get away scot free. Implicit here is Cato's insistence that *personal* accountability is the only true standard of right. A scapegoat only serves to divert attention from other malefactors who may then all too easily lose themselves in the crowd. Justice demands that each and every great and little rogue be brought to account. No mere substitute will do.

CHAPTER 9

Early Modern Texts
of Persecution

The whole development of the world tends toward the absolute significance
of the category of the single individual, which is the very principle of
Christianity.

—Søren Kierkegaard, *Journals and Papers*

The Half-Decomposed Myth

The intersection of two lives provides a point of altitude from which to take
the lay of the land in seventeenth-century New England, where a series of
related public scandals discloses the scapegoat's transformation from type
into metaphor. When we speak of the scapegoat as a revelation of human
violence, it is to these persecutions that we turn, not simply for references
to victims but because the episodes have long been recognized as iconic
moments in the cultural shift under way in early modernity. They furthermore open an arresting perspective on how "scapegoating" became a rough
synonym for the "witch hunt."

We recall here an exemplary moment in the history of successive
demystifications that Girard adduces to illustrate the presence of the
scapegoat as a structuring principle in culture. A work of the Middle Ages
by Guillaume de Machaut (fourteenth century), which blames the Jews
for an outbreak of the plague, appears today to be a transparent case of

scapegoating. Like the Gospels themselves, Machaut's text contains no reference to scapegoats. The Evangelists have, notwithstanding this, much to say about scapegoating. They plainly take the side of the victim against his accusers, representing Jesus as the innocent party, the charges as merely concocted. Machaut also tells us something about scapegoating inasmuch as he believes the accusations and sees the Jews as guilty:

> After that came a false, treacherous and contemptible swine: this was shameful Israel, the wicked and disloyal who hated good and loved everything evil, who gave so much gold and silver and promises to Christians, who then poisoned several rivers and fountains that had been clear and pure so that many lost their lives; for whoever used them died suddenly. Certainly ten times one hundred thousand died from it, in country and in city. Then finally this mortal calamity was noticed. He who sits on high and sees far, who governs and provides for everything, did not want this treachery to remain hidden; he revealed it and made it so generally known that they lost their lives and possessions. Then every Jew was destroyed, some hanged, other burned; some were drowned, other beheaded with an ax or sword. And many Christians died together with them in shame.[1]

A principle to which Machaut remains blind, which we today intuit spontaneously, structures his allegations. "We reject without question the meaning the author gives his text," Girard writes. "We declare that he does not know what he is saying. From our several centuries distance we know better than he and can correct what he has written. We even believe that we have discovered a truth not seen by the author and, with still greater audacity, do not hesitate to state that he provides us with this truth even though he does not perceive it himself."[2] Our certainty on this score is an indication of the degree to which the act of scapegoating stands revealed in our world, though it was hidden from Machaut. On the trajectory of a historical revelation that extends from the death of Jesus to the present, Machaut stands at a midpoint. His text of persecution is a "half-decomposed myth" that, while it still victimizes, has lost the power to divinize its victims.[3] The dimension of the sacred is missing: "medieval and modern persecutors do not worship their victims, they only hate them," Girard writes.[4] Machaut's world was therefore "more deeply immersed in its unawareness of persecution than we are," but "less so than the world of mythology."[5]

The textual history reflects the advance of knowledge which in time exposes the pogroms and witch burnings of the Middle Ages, along with texts like Machaut's. As we enter the early modern period we move decisively beyond Machaut, though we still encounter persecution and texts of persecution. Some texts are so credulous and uncritical they differ little from Machaut's. Alongside them we discover other, fully demystified reports of the same events so dismissive of the incredible accusations that they are indistinguishable from modern, fully scientific interpretations.

Implicit in this history is the rise of natural science, which Girard sees as initiated by the revelation of the victim as arbitrarily chosen, and innocent—of the victim as *scapegoat*. Because "science presupposes the renunciation of a former preference for the magical causality of persecution"—a renunciation which "leads men to the patient exploration of natural causes"—the "invention of science is not the reason that there are no longer witch-hunts," he writes. "The fact that there are no longer witch-hunts is the reason that science has been invented."[6] The latter is therefore, "a by-product of the profound action of the gospel text."[7] This move brings into sharp focus the divide separating Frazer's evolutionary program and popular assumption of science's historical genesis and growth from Girard's theory of history, which prioritizes a critical shift in favor of the victim, making it the precondition of fully scientific thought.

Antinomian Scapegoats and Puritan Mythology

The Quaker chronicler George Bishop records that in 1659 Mary Dyer "came to *Boston* . . . to visit *Christopher Holder*, then in Prison" and being "espied standing at the Window" was taken into custody and "carried to the house of Correction by the Constable."[8] Dyer is eventually hanged for defying an order of banishment. She becomes one of four Quakers who die for their faith in Massachusetts, and the only woman among them.[9] Holder will, for his part, be deported to England, ending a bloody chapter in his own young life, during which he is severally tortured and maimed for evangelizing in the Quaker way. Of the two, Dyer's history in New England is the longer and more prominent. It begins with her emigration from England with husband William Dyer, a prosperous London milliner, in 1635. Governor of Massachusetts John Winthrop will describe her as "a very proper and fair woman" but "of a very proud spirit . . . much given to revelations," and "notoriously infected" with the errors of one Anne Hutchinson.[10] A Boston midwife like Dyer, Hutchinson comes to the attention of Puritan authorities for the fortnightly lectures in her home, at which as many as eighty people might be in attendance. Puritan writer Thomas Weld will see these meetings as diffusing the "venome" of antinomian opinions "into the very veines and vitals of the People."[11] Hutchinson's insistence on the direct revelation of the Holy Spirit and open defiance of the Massachusetts clergy, whom she condemned with few exceptions for teaching religious proprieties in preference to the inner transformation by grace, results in a trial before the General Court in 1637 and banishment to Rhode Island the following year, but not before cleaving the community along an important meridian of political power and group identity. Among her supporters are some of the most prominent members of the colony, including the governor, Henry Vane, and minister John Cotton, whose volte-face late in the proceedings against her seals Hutchinson's fate. Critical to the outcome of the case is the insinuation that any claim of unmediated access to the Holy Spirit is a step down the slippery slope of moral laxity to libertinism. Anne's husband, who will be disparaged by Winthrop as having "a very mild temper and weak parts . . . [a man] wholly guided by his wife,"[12] can little be expected to restrain a woman whom he regards as a saint and to whom he feels in any case "more nearly tied . . . than to the church."[13]

In the transcripts of her examination before the courts Hutchinson appears a formidable opponent, "a Master-piece of Women's wit,"[14] whose nimble deployment of the scriptures and biting sarcasm repeatedly nonplused her examiners. She is above all disinclined to receive admonition in a manner that befits her sex. During the trial the minister Hugh Peter reproves Hutchinson for having "stept out of place" and "rather bine a Husband than a Wife and a Preacher than a Hearer; and a Magistrate than a Subject"[15]—a comment echoed by Winthrop, who, writing of what came to be known as the Antinomian Controversy, wailed that "all things are turned upside down amongst us."[16] He records that "this American Jesabel"[17] and her followers subsequently turned Anabaptist, "[denying] all magistracy among Christians" and maintaining "there were no churches since those founded by the Apostles and Evangelists, nor could be."[18] News of Hutchinson's death at the hands of Indians in 1643 is greeted by the Massachusetts divines as fitting retribution for her recalcitrance. "Let her damned heresies, and the just vengeance of God, by which shee perished, terrifie all her seduced followers from having any more to doe with her leaven," says synod leader Peter Bulkeley.[19]

As was often the case in New England at the time, the charges of heresy were shadowed by innuendos of diabolism. These attach to Hutchinson through Mary Dyer—who makes public her unwavering support for Anne by accompanying her from the meetinghouse when "she was cast out of the church"[20]—and the midwife Jane Hawkins, who according to Winthrop was "notorious for familiarity with the Devill."[21] The latter was said "to give young women oil of mandrakes and other stuff to cause conception"[22] and "utter many speeches in the Latine toungue, as it were in a trance."[23] She consequently "grew into great suspicion to be a witch."[24] Rumors circulated that expectant mothers who consumed her potions sometimes gave birth to monsters. In March 1638, Hawkins was brought before the court to answer questions about the delivery and secret burial of a stillborn infant born to Dyer a month earlier. Though Hawkins was the acting midwife, it appears that Anne Hutchinson was present, too. Winthrop tells us that Hawkins confirmed the child was a female born "about two moneths before her time":

> At *Boston* in *New England*, upon the 17. day of *October* 1637, the wife of one *William Dyer*, sometimes a Citizen & Millener of *London*, a very proper and comely young Woman, was delivered of a large woman childe . . . so monstrous and mis-shapen, as the like hath scarce been heard of: it had no head, but a face, which stood so low upon the breast, as the eares (which were like an Apes) grew upon the shoulders.
>
> The eyes stood farre out, so did the mouth, the nose was hooking upward, the breast and back was full of sharp prickles, like a Thornback, the navell and all the belly with the distinction of the sex, were, where the lower part of the back and hips should have been, and those back parts were on the side the face stood.
>
> The armes and hands, with the thighs and legges, were as other childrens, but instead of toes, it had upon each foot three claws, with talons like a young fowle.
>
> Upon the back, above the belly, it had two great holes, like mouthes, and in each of them stuck out a piece of flesh.
>
> It had no forehead, but in the place thereof, above the eyes, foure hornes, whereof two were above an inch long, hard, and sharpe, the other two were somewhat shorter.
>
> *Many things were observable in the birth and discovery of this Monster.*[25]

Winthrop, who called for the body to be disinterred, reports that "though it were much corrupted, yet the horns, and claws, and holes in the back, and some scales, &c. were found and seen of above a hundred persons."[26] He adds that "at such time as the childe died" in the mother's body "the bed wherein the mother lay shooke so violently, as all which were in the roome perceived it"[27] and "withal there was such a noisome savor, as most of the women were taken with extreme vomiting and purging, so as they were forced to depart;

and others of them their children were taken with convulsions, (which they never had before nor after)."[28] Winthrop gives no indication of how he discovered these details, which suggest the diabolical complicity of all three women. Historian Carol Karlsen notes the shaking bed implied the fetus was itself "a devil, since it was believed that Satan could impregnate a witch and that demon offspring struggled violently against their own demise."[29]

News that Hutchinson, too, suffered an aborted pregnancy some months later was advertized by Weld as a second monstrous nativity. If "Mistris Dier brought forth her birth of a woman childe, a fish, a beast, and a fowle, all woven together in one, and without an head," Hutchinson, for her part, "being big with childe, and growing towards the time of her labour, as other women do . . . brought forth not one . . . but (which was more strange to amazement) thirty monstrous births or thereabouts, at once; some of them bigger, some lesser, some of one shape, some of another; few of any perfect shape, none of them (as farre as I could ever learn) of humane shape."[30] Though "loath to bee the reporter" of "things so strange," Weld insists he knows better than "to delude the world with untruths."[31] He scoffs that God adapted punishments to fit the crimes "in causing two fomenting women . . . to produce out of their wombs, as before they had out of their braines, such monstrous births as no Chronicle (I think) hardly ever recorded the like."[32] The multitude of deformed, inhuman offspring born to Hutchinson is fitting retribution for her role as the fount of antinomian heresy: "as shee had vented mishapen opinions . . . about thirty opinions in number, so many monsters.[33] Mary Dyer soon thereafter leaves Boston for Rhode Island and in 1652 accompanies her husband on an embassy to the English Parliament. None of the women mentioned were ever formally charged with witchcraft, although Winthrop's *Short Story*, with its infamous preface by Weld, was circulated widely on both sides of the Atlantic.

Its monster stories incurred one incredulous rejoinder in print—the *Mercurius Americanus* of Reverend John Wheelwright, who, unsympathetic though he was to the Antinomians, treats the *Short Story* with open contempt. To Winthrop's account of Hutchinson's miscarriage Wheelwright replies: "I question not his learning, &c. but I admire his certainty, or rather impudence: did the man obstetricate?"[34] If the *Short Story*'s author was not himself present, on whose authority does his report depend?

> But what if he had it from any then present? will that suffice to make him
> so confident, as thereupon to take occasion to ingage, and magnifie Divine
> direction, and derive this not known by him to be a truth, from the God

of truth? . . . As for his *Analogy*, which he observes betwixt her productions and opinions. . . . It is a monstrous conception of his brain, a spurious sinne of his intellect, acted upon by a sweatish and Feaverish zeal, which indeed beats almost in every line; and resolves his in themselves imperfect & sometimes, if not feigned facts into phanatique meditations. . . . yet [his] Notion is impertinent, for he brings in defects of Nature, amongst defects of Manners. . . . But he will say perhaps, that this birth was an extraordinary defect: It avails nothing, unlesse he will either raise it to a miracle, or at the least prove a supernaturall remission of the *formative virtue* in her. That will require a most accurate physicall inspection which I think his learning will not reach, although (for ought I can see) his modesty might: for he tels us of women *purging and vomiting*, what if the distemper we usually call *Cholera* did for the present oppresse those women? must it needs be proclaimed? must it needs be in print?[35]

Hunting Quakers in Massachusetts

Karlsen writes that "from almost the beginning of their movement in the 1640s, English Quaker women openly assumed what New England's Quaker women had claimed only indirectly."[36] At stake once again are the role of women as spiritual teachers and belief in the direct revelation of the Holy Spirit. That women "publishers of truth" traveling New England during the first prophetic waves of Quaker missionizing could be outspoken critics of the Congregationalist establishment is something no one disputes. Their public remonstrances and tendency to engage in other, more symbolic forms of protest[37] made them, furthermore, conspicuous targets of Puritan vituperation and ridicule. Myles notes wryly that "although Puritan authorities remained publicly silent about the memories of Hutchinson these radical women must have evoked, her image was surely present for them in this nightmarish return of the repressed."[38] Puritan anxieties during this period echo the charges of masculinization and intimations of sexual license produced against the Antinomians. Salem minister Cotton Mather mentions two women Friends who, arriving "stark naked as ever they were born into our publick assemblies," are swiftly "adjudged unto the whipping post."[39] Assuring his readers that reports of Quaker persecution are not to be credited, Mather tellingly derides the stunt as a "piece of devilism."[40] The comment recalls that if Quaker women assumed more brazenly than the antinomians before them a right to spiritual leadership, both preaching in the streets and proselytizing openly, their paroxystic prayer lives and bold insistence on a continuous revelation of the *light within* made charges of witchcraft nearly inevitable. As early as 1660, John Norton would denounce "that gesture wherewith they are affected, at or about the reception of their revelations," it "being the ancient and known manner of Satan . . . to afflict the bodies of his Instruments with pains" and "agitate them with *Antick and uncouth motions.*"[41] He compares Quaker women to the Greek Sybil, "Satan's Prophetess, at the act of receiving her *Oracles*, from the revelation of the Devil, *pale faced, with eyes wrung, in an unwonted and fearful manner, as also quaking and trembling.*"[42] Their fits disposed "ignorant spectators" to "the expectation of some strange discovery . . . in pretence *divine*, but indeed *diabolical*[43]—a judgment to which Mather would later add that Quakers were a species of "*lunaticks, daemoniacks* and *energumens,*"[44] the first of whom must be sought "at the Delphian Oracle upon Parnassus . . . where the usage was, for a certain woman sitting upon a tripos over a cave, to be possessed with a dæmon" who caused her to be "immediately taken with an extraordinary trembling of her whole body," so that "foaming horribly, there issued from her the prophecies which enchanted all the world."[45]

As it happens, the first Quaker missionaries arriving in Boston from Barbados in 1656—Ann Austin and Mary Fisher—are arrested before their ship even makes landfall, stripped naked, and searched for witches' marks. Their books confiscated and burned, the pair are banished after a five-week detainment at Boston's fetid public jail in what proves to be an unavailing attempt to stop the spread of the sect to New England. The same year, another group of Quakers, including Christopher Holder and John Copeland, two well-educated young men "of good Estates and of good life amongst men,"[46] arrive in Boston, where they, too, are incarcerated, then banished. In early 1657, a third ship of Quaker missionaries anchors at Boston. On board is Mary Dyer, now a convert to Quakerism, returning to Rhode Island after a seven-year stay in England. Like the others, she is arrested and imprisoned at Boston, although her husband manages to secure her release some months later. The Quaker Humphrey Norton, who would accompany Holder and Copeland on their return trip from England aboard the *Woodhouse*[47] later that year—and who was himself severally fined, scourged, and banished, once imprisoned midwinter without candle or fire, and lastly branded with an *H* for "Heretic"[48]—records the "sufferings" that befell his two companions. Being moved by God "to go to *Salem*, a town in *Boston* Colonie,"[49] Holder and Copeland are soon arrested for evangelizing and imprisoned. After a brutal scourging—"the Executioner measuring his Ground, and fetching his

Strokes with all his Strength, which so cruelly cut their Flesh" that "a Woman at the Sight of it fell down as dead"[50]—the men are deprived of food and water three days, then detained nine weeks in "cruel bonds, without fire all the cold season."[51] Things worsen the following year, when Holder and Copeland fall victim to a grisly new law passed by the Boston General Court in October 1657 stipulating that a banished Quaker returning to Massachusetts Bay must "for the first offense have one of his ears cut off."[52]

In August 1658, the Boston hangman severs the right ears of the two implacable missionaries (then "slunck away as a dog when he hath sucked the blood of a Lamb, and is discovered," in Norton's telling).[53] Present at the deed is Anne Hutchinson's sister Catherine Scott, a "grave, sober, ancient Woman," and a Quaker besides "of good Breeding,"[54] whose daughter Mary will eventually become Holder's wife. Catherine is herself taken into custody and given "Ten cruel stripes" with a corded whip for denouncing the amputations as "Works of Darkness,"[55] then threatened with hanging should she ever return to Massachusetts. "If God call us, wo be to us if we come not," she says.[56] "We shall be as ready. . . . to take away your Lives as ye shall be to lay them down," is Governor John Endicott's reply.[57] So virulent does the persecution become that even those supposed to have assisted Quakers are rounded up, fined, and incarcerated. Humphrey records the plight of a sympathizer, Cassandra Southick, who pays for the hospitality shown to Copeland and Holder on their Salem expedition. It is here that the scapegoat metaphor appears for the first time in something like its current sense, inaugurating a new era in the meaning of the term.

> Also one *Cassandra Southick*, with her Husband, a grave couple, were apprehended by their Officer, and brought unto Boston, for the entertaining [of] the two forementioned strangers, her husband being a Member of their corrupt body, which they call their Church, they returned back again that he might receive the defilement thereof, she being as a *scape-goat* from the scattered Tribes, they continued her seven weeks in Prison, fining her fortie shillings for owning a Paper, which was given forth by the Spirit of truth in these its Messengers, for which the Governor said, they deserved death (such was his cruelty) although the thing held forth nothing but what shewed how their Priests and Rulers differed from the holy men of God of old.[58]

This reference to the scapegoat, which predates the earliest *OED* citation for the second sense of the word by 165 years, is striking for its designation of a woman on her way to jail. Except perhaps for the reference to "the scattered tribes," there is no indication of the word's primary signification or ritual context. The use is clearly figurative but somewhat enigmatic, owing probably to the different registers in which blame is assigned. In modern usage one is a scapegoat to the extent one suffers for the sins of others, and in this instance both defendants are at fault, although the law they have broken is itself unlawful; the justice to which Norton implicitly appeals rules furthermore against Mr. Southick's amnesty by affiliation with a corrupt Church. If Cassandra Southick must suffer, Mr. Southick really ought not to be excused, and yet the sentence falls singly on her shoulders. Because she alone is truly innocent, there is no question of the word "scapegoat" figuring "reprobation" here, and her seven-week term of incarceration means the trope cannot designate "one who escapes punishment," leaving substitution—the innocent for the guilty—as the most likely sense of the expression. It is noteworthy that Southick pays for possessing a religious tract in a city that would one day epitomize the democratic ideal for the rest of the world, enshrining speech and press freedoms along with religious toleration as the foremost rights of the governed. Norton's account of Southick's punishment gives us a vignette of the sympathetic recalibration under way in favor of the individual, whose status as a scapegoat of the powers serves to amplify the demand for universal human freedoms.

Accounts of Dyer's execution included in *New England's Ensign*, from which the above reference was taken, and George Bishop's compendious *New England Judged* will call attention to the plight of Quakers when they are published in 1659 and 1661, respectively, like those other more visible witnesses to Puritan cruelty, among them Christopher Holder, who, with fellow amputees John Copeland and John Rous, returns to England—a living testimony of religious persecution abroad. Bishop's book will be conveyed to the newly restored King Charles II, who reads it with favor and swiftly dispatches a missive to Governor John Endicott, effectively suspending further executions.[59] If the royal letter is a clear sign that things have begun to change, there is little relief for Quakers in the short term. The Puritan rulers replace the law of banishment on pain of death with the Cart and Whip Act (1661), which provides that a Quaker "be stripped naked from the middle upwards" and "tied to a cart's tail and whipped through the town, and from thence immediately conveyed to the constable of the next town, towards the borders of our jurisdictions, and so from constable to constable."[60] Anyone returning faced further scourging, branding, and lastly execution "under the old law of 1658"—that is, "if anything is left of him."[61] The persecution continues, and yet the days of unrivaled Puritan domination are numbered. Back in England, King William III's accession to the throne in 1688 will be followed by the passage of the Act of Toleration a year later ("An Act for Exempting their Majestyes Protestant Subjects dissenting from the Church of England from the Penalties of certaine Lawes"), establishing freedom of worship for Protestant Nonconformists and ending government persecution on English soil of Quakers and Puritans alike.[62]

The recognition of "the nonconformists' right to a distinct legal existence" did not, however, mean the end of official church opposition to the sects.[63] It is to the Church of England's ecclesiastical assemblies of the late seventeenth and early eighteenth centuries that we turn next, with their rancorous disputes between the Upper House of Convocation, comprising the archbishop of Canterbury and its diocesan bishops, and the Lower House, made up of lesser clergy who then "enjoyed the liberty of meeting, or arguing controversial points" and of "burning a few impious books—that is, books written against them"; this wry appraisal is Voltaire's, who adds that the latter were in time "reduced [to] the obscurity of their parishes."[64]

If the bishops as a whole took a more lenient and accommodating view toward dissenters in the aftermath of England's Glorious Revolution (1688–1689), the Lower House of Convocation, securing from King William a reluctant concession to sit and act in 1701, lost no time in establishing "a committee on heretical and scandalous books."[65] Leaders of the Lower House like Francis Atterbury saw themselves as defending Anglican orthodoxy against "Heresie" and "Crimes Ecclesiastical" alike;[66] they were as bitterly opposed to the nonconformist sects as to the latitudinarianism of the bishops, which they regarded as itself a form of heterodoxy. In 1711, Atterbury drafts a report to Queen Anne whose censorious and inflammatory rhetoric stirs controversy. A first version of the report, entitled *A Representation Of the Present State of Religion, With regard to the late excessive Growth of Infidelity, Heresy, & Profaneness: Unanimously Agreed upon by a Joint Committee of Both Houses of Convocation of the Province of Canterbury and Afterwards rejected by the Upper House, but Passed in the Lower House*, is ultimately deemed too virulent for presentation to the queen, though it will be printed and circulated. Decrying the "deluge of impiety and licentiousness, which hath broke in upon us, and overspread the Face of this Church and Kingdom,"[67] the *Representation* takes wide aim at a host of ideological threats—atheism, deism, popery, Socinianism, and Arianism—without neglecting to deplore the "licentiousness of the Stage" (yet "another fountain from whence the present corruptions of Religion and Morality have flowed") and "the liberty of the press," which, finding opportunity "by reason of confusions and disorders that usually attend great changes of state," allowed "those who 'sat in the seat of the scornful' to promote the interests of Skepticism and Infidelity"[68] so that today "Mock catechisms," "loose and licentious poems," "profane writings,"[69] and "spurious treatises"[70] flood the land. "Nor ought we, among the several instances of infidelity," writes Atterbury, "omit the mention of those damnable errors which have been embraced and propagated by the sect of Quakers; who, in several of their treatises, in their Catechisms and Primers, have taught the rudiments of the Christian Faith in such a manner, as to make it seem to be little more than a complicated system of Deism and Enthusiasm."[71]

Later that same year (1711) an anonymous tract entitled *Brief Remarks on the Late Representation of the Lower House of Convocation; as Respects the Quakers Only*, appears by way of rejoinder, with this epigraph below the title: "*But considerest not the Beam that is in thine own Eye: Thou Hypocrite*, Matt. 4. 5." The opening paragraphs give what is perhaps the earliest statement of all our metaphor has come to mean.

It may be observ'd, that in most of the Nations of the World, where pub-lick Divisions either in Church or State have prevail'd, they always had one Party or Profession of People among them to make the Object of general Calumny; upon whom the most of publick Reproach is as it were by com-mon Consent promiscuously cast, whether from this side or that, whether with Cause or without. As if these were born only for Contempt, or were suffer'd to live upon Condition of carrying other Men's Burthens; that were always to bear Scandal without Guilt, and be Condemn'd without Crime, or something like the *Scape Goat* under the Law, were to be sent into the Wilderness with other Men's Faults upon their Backs, without any regard to their own.

This has been more especially practiced when the People of these Countries have found it difficult to defend their own Ways, and yet have been under some necessity of keeping the Scandal off from themselves, whoever they injure or oppress.

It would not be difficult to give Instances of this in most of the Nations in the World. Thus the *Pharisees* serv'd the *Publicans* in old Time, whom they treated as People neither fit for God's Mercy, or Man's Society, and reproach'd our Saviour for eating or sitting down with them. Thus afterwards, and deservedly too, the *Jews* themselves were serv'd in most Nations of the World; who in any publick Calamity were always made the Sacrifice on both sides. Thus the Christians were serv'd in time of the Roman Empire: The *Waldenses* and *Albigenses* in their Day: Thus the *Hugonots* in *France:* Thus the *Puritans* in *England* in old Days; and thus the *Quakers* are serv'd now.[72]

The statement is exceptional for its description of the tendency to deflect blame onto a stigmatized group as universal, noting as it does the arbitrary character of this deflection, the unanimity of reproach, and above all the innocence of those blamed. The list of historical scapegoats, dating all the way back to the time of Christ—who is importantly blamed for consorting with the scapegoats of his own day—suggests that if it is not one group, it is another: *some* few will be hated and censured by all, through no fault of their own and as though born to the role. Of course, the argument so patiently advanced in these, the opening paragraphs of the tractate, is all but collapsed by a single clause in which the Jews are "deservedly" scapegoated by the world and by the author himself in a moment of incognizant vindictiveness. The remark hangs like a thread that threatens to unravel the sense of his statement—*that the scapegoat is a merely expedient, therefore guiltless victim.* But then its inclusion—a blind spot at the center of an otherwise radiant elucidation—is also what makes the statement exemplary. At once prescient and regressive, the author converges on something exceedingly hard to see except in peripheral glimpses. The difficulty of isolating a human response so fundamental, reflexive, and unthinking succumbs to gradual exposure: though it quite slips the notice of its author in 1711, we read his anti-Semitic qualification today as embarrassingly discordant and offensive.

Salem and the Crisis of Differences

A good deal has been written about the relationship between Quaker persecution in New England and the Salem witch trials. We could mention that it was only *after* the Massachusetts charter of 1691, imposing complete liberty of conscience and freedom of worship on Massachusetts Bay, "that the wayward Puritans mounted the fiercest campaign against satanic witchcraft in their midst."[73] It is also widely noted that bonds of blood, marriage, and "geographic propinquity to the Quaker community characterized many of the accused witches of Salem Village."[74] Heyrman and others have pointed to Mather's *Memorable Providences, Relating to Witchcrafts and Possessions*, published in 1689, with its contention that "Diabolical *Possession* was the Thing which did *dispose* and *encline* men unto *Quakerism*" as a fair preview of coming attractions.[75] The book contains a lengthy account of the bewitchment of four children, one of whom, an adolescent girl, lived at Cotton Mather's home for a time.[76] The latter, who was beset by "*ludicrous fits*" and variously tormented by devils whenever she was asked to read from the Bible or Puritan tomes—like Cotton's father Increase Mather's *Remarkable Providences*, which "cast her into inexpressible *Agonies*"—was able to "quietly read *whole* pages" of a "*Quaker's Book*."[77] Her brother, for his part, was "cast into such *Tortures* and *Postures*" whenever his father spoke of going to the congregational meeting houses so "that he would sooner *Dy* than go out of *doors*; but if his Father spoke of going to *others* of the Assemblies in the Town, particularly the *Quakers*, the boy in a moment would be as well as could be."[78] In the end the Goodwin children are reclaimed by Mather's prayers and those of his fellow clergyman from "the strange liberty which the *Devils* gave unto [them] to enjoy the *Writings* and *Meetings* of the Quakers."[79]

Theories about what happened at Salem run the gamut from class warfare to ergot poisoning and I do not mean to argue yet another position here. What links the Quaker persecution with the antinomians before them and the subsequent witch trials, for our purposes, are the basic features of the accusations, which remain strikingly consistent, if the accusations themselves also grow increasingly shrill and fantastic. Writing in the aftermath of the trials in 1695, Salem Quaker Thomas Maule would note the work of what he termed "the Devils general Court" in hunting down and punishing suspected witches was "as like in imitation to the work of the former Priests and Rulers against the People called *Quakers*, as the moving shadow of a wicked man, is like to the moving of his corrupted *Body*; for all that would not conform to the Faith of the Priests and Rulers, to do as they did in that day, were by them and their followers esteemed no better than Dogs."[80] Of course the Puritans had other enemies—the French and the Indians—who were seen along with the Quakers as making a common assault.[81] The tendency of these rivals to change places or even merge became strikingly more pronounced as the division of visible from invisible worlds grew more porous and unstable. In 1699, Mather will write that "while the *Indians* have been thus molesting us, we have suffered Molestation of another sort, from another sort of Enemies, which may with very good Reason, be cast into the same *History* with them. If the *Indians* have chosen to prey upon the *Frontiers*, and *Out-Skirts*, of the Province, the *Quakers* have chosen the very same *Frontiers*, and *Out-Skirts*, for their more *Spiritual Assaults* . . . to Enchant and Poison the *Souls* of poor people, in the very places, where the *Bodies* and *Estates*, of the people have presently after been devoured by the Salvages."[82] John Norton will draw the more obvious connection between the "quaking" of Quakers and "the custome of the Pow[wow]'s, or *Indian Wizards*, in this Wilderness; whose whole bodies at the time of their *Diabolical* practices, are at this day vexed and agitated in a strange, unwonted and dreadful manner."[83] Historian Richard Godbeer notes that "accusers at the Salem witch trials in 1692 not only detailed the connections between suspects and native Americans as indicative of their guilt" but "even claimed that the Devil looked like a native American."[84] Guilt by association was so damning that any connection to Native Americans, "however tenuous and whether or not connected with native religion, could be used to incriminate a witch suspect."[85] The very real threat of French aggression during the period of King William's War (1689–1697)—coinciding as it does with the trials and Mather's subsequent account thereof, *A Discourse on the Wonders of the Invisible World*—is, for its part, doubly etherealized: likened to a famed poltergeist haunting and so enacted "by a singular Fury of the Old Dragon inspiring of his Emissaries,"[86] it reappears in Mather's conjecture "that there is a sort of Arbitrary, even Military *Government* among the Devils. . . . Think on, Vast Regiments, of cruel and bloody French *Dragoons*, with an *Intendant* over them, overrunning a pillaged Neighbourhood."[87]

During the trials the shifting of semblances and collapse of stable limits become something truly abyssal with the introduction of an epistemological wild card. The question is that of so-called "Spectral Evidences" and the weight they should be accorded, "especially at a Time, when 'tis possible, some Over-powerful Conjurer may have got the skill of thus Exhibiting the Shapes of all sorts of persons"[88] and innocent ones, especially, thus causing "the Righteous to Perish with the Wicked."[89] While it is likely that "among the persons represented by the *Spectres* which now afflict our Neighbours, there will be found *some* that never explicitly contracted with any of the *Evil Angels*"—known witches having admitted to "plot[ting] the Representations of *Innocent Persons*, to cover and shelter themselves in their Witchcrafts"—this hardly suffices to acquit the accused, for "even so, a Spectre, exactly Resembling such or such a person, when the Neighbourhood are Tormented by such Spectres, may reasonably make Magistrates inquisitive."[90] The scapegoat as a principle of text structure stands here, in Mather's text, as it were, half revealed. Unlike Machaut's, this text of persecution plainly grapples with the possible untruth of the accusations. What strikes us most forcibly here is the hopelessness of the judicial project, given the Cartesian principle of doubt admitted to deliberation: if the Devil and his minions may impersonate the righteous—representing them to others as engaged in acts of witchcraft and other forms of diabolism—and moreover conceal the wicked, then the ground of all things is torn away and every appearance is a lie. Mather seems to acknowledge this. "But such is the Descent of the Devil at this day upon ourselves," he writes, "that I may truly tell you, *The Walls of the whole World are broken down!*" and "the very *Devils* are broke in upon us, to Seduce the *Souls*, Torment the *Bodies*, Sully the Credits, and consume the *Estates* of our Neighbours, with Impressions both as *Real* and as *Furious*, as if the *Invisible* World were becoming *Incarnate*."[91] This coincides precisely with a scene of moblike violence, for Satan himself "improves the *Darkness* of this Affair to push us into a *Blind Mans Buffet*" in which all are found "*Sinfully*, yea, Hotly, and Madly, Mauling one another, in the *Dark*."[92]

Circumstances are ripe for victims and victims there will be. During nine months between the still disputed participation of a few Salem girls in a form of divination based on "common magical folklore"[93] and the end of the crisis in May 1693, over 150 will be accused. Six men and fourteen women are executed. One man, Giles Corey, perishes while undergoing *peine fort et dure*, an ancient procedure reserved for those refusing to enter a plea that involved piling heavy stones upon his chest in a field beside the jail. Five others die in prison while awaiting trial.[94] Two dogs are hanged. But then it all comes to a crashing halt. Governor Phips suspends the Court of Oyer and Terminer and "within just one year after the affliction had begun forty-nine of the accused still in prison were acquitted."[95] The General Court in Boston subsequently proclaims a general pardon. Fuess records that "most of those active in the prosecution ultimately were swayed by remorse and repentance."[96]

> Even the jurors who had condemned so many prepared a statement admitting that not being "capable to understand nor able to withstand the mysterious delusion of the power of darkness and prince of the air," they feared they had been instrumental with others, "though ignorantly and unwillingly," in shedding innocent blood. Frankly, if belatedly, they expressed to the survivors their deep sense of sorrow" and begged forgiveness for their errors.[97]

Mather is but one of a small minority who continue to fan the flame of witch fear in the aftermath of the trials and this "despite meetings with eight confessors who told him they had falsely confessed."[98] Even so, as an early modern text of persecution, his *Discourse* is exemplary for its anguished contradictions. He remains concerned to establish adequate standards of judicial proof for the conviction of witches. For all his credulity he cautions against the sole reliance on spectral evidence: a concern for the fate of the innocent in a conflict so dark and embroiled militates against the urgency to expose the malefactors. Jensen notes that during the trials a "pseudo-scientific demonology" was employed, which relied on "empirical indicators of possession and witchcraft using existing reference books and prior court cases as guides," eliminating medical explanations before moving to supernatural causes.[99] It seems that opposition to the witch trials "grew in strength during the trials" and that "key religious leaders, including Mather's own father, would have put the brakes on the episode earlier were they not preoccupied with pressing issues such as the creation of a new charter."[100]

When former Salem minister Deodat Lawson comes to preach in his old pulpit at the height of the crisis he urges the faithful to "Give no place to the Devil by *Rash Censuring of others without sufficient grounds, or false accusing any willingly*," which "is indeed to be like the Devil, who hath the Title (*Diabolos*) in the Greek, because he is a *Calumniator*, or *False Accuser*."[101] It is precisely through "*unruly Passions, such as Envy, Malice, or Hatred of our Neighbours and Brethren*" that the Devil gains entrance to cause mayhem.[102] "There is an inclination in the best," Lawson says, "to Charge the *Sins of others*, as the procuring cause of GODS Judgments and to reflect severely on the *Pride, Lukewarmness, Coveteousness, Contention, Intemperance,* and *Uneven Conversation* of others; but we can hardly be brought to smite upon our own *Breast*, and say, *What have I done?*"[103] The "inclination" is so insistent that "Unless we be, in particular: *Charged*, and *Convicted*" we remain in ignorance of our part in abetting the discord.[104] Here Lawson invokes David and the prophet Nathan, who rebukes the king's haste to judgment with the revelation that "*Thou art the man.* Thou art he that art concerned in this Provocation by thy Transgression."[105] This is as lucid an indictment of what it means to scapegoat in the fully-fledged sense of the verb as one could ask, including as it does the blindness of the accuser to his role in abetting conflict and even the revelation of knowledge without which he remains trapped in scandalized darkness.

Lawson's call to repentance contrasts sharply with a sermon delivered just three days later from the same pulpit by acting minister Samuel Parris—a chief instigator of the conflict—who chooses as a text from which to preach the words of Christ in John 6:70: "Have not I chosen you twelve, and one of you is a devil?" Parris warns his congregation that "Our Lord Jesus Christ knows how many devils there are in his church and who they are . . . whether one or ten, or 20."[106] The division of these from the other members of the congregation is stark and admits no exception: "we are either saints or devils;

true believers, or hypocrites & dissembling Judases that would sell Christ & his kingdom to gratify a lust,"[107] for "the scripture gives us no medium."[108] Ripped from its context and turned on the Salem community at the height of the interrogations, jailings, tortures, and executions, Christ's words are changed into a threat and commination, congealing in a phrase the rationality of scapegoating in all its paranoid conviction and menace.

"In short," Jenson writes, "Lawson's sermon reflects the modern interpretation of the Salem episode as a product of contention among families and factions,"[109] something other commentators, noting merely a contrast in tone with Parris's monitory words, have missed. This summary remark is striking for all it leaves unsaid. What is it precisely about modern interpretations that distinguishes them from the inflammatory and dichotomizing rhetoric of a Samuel Parris? How precisely does Lawson's sermon exemplify the spirit of those interpretations? To say his sermon exhibits a preference for naturalistic over supernatural explanations would be plainly anachronistic and circular. In what can the distinction of one from the other consist on the threshold of the modern era? "Lawson's sermon dramatized the political and secular roots of the craze," Jenson writes, "but Parris's sermon depicted it as a battle between real witches (members of the opposing faction) and the rest of the community."[110] This is doubtless true. But the appeal to a distinction between the merely political, therefore secular, explanation and one figuring "real witches" misses the essential point that both Puritan divines see the community's afflictions as the Devil's handiwork. In Lawson's account Satan gains entrance through contentions and rivalry; in Parris's he works through the capitulation of individuals to secret lusts. There is human complicity with diabolical forces in both explanations, but where one isolates and stigmatizes an accused, the other very precisely turns the tables on accusers.

In a world of supernatural explanations, the division of modernity from its past, which must now begin to recede, passing away into an ever more distant night, is struck first here with a move that defies facile essentializations but is at the very least a kind of doubt jammed in the spokes of an otherwise brakeless momentum. The truth of Girard's dictum that we invent science when we have first stopped burning witches is glimpsed in an exemplary moment of the epochal transition under way. The vision of a world dichotomized into saints and devils, echoing with a command to extirpate the latter, is pierced by the suspicion that there is something about the hunt itself—and the hunters—that must be interrogated and withstood: the conflicts in which they and their victims are embroiled owe more to their adversarial outlook than to the existence of real villains, the hunt producing its quarry instead of the other way round. The first datum of science may even be the dangerous credulity of the persecutor—an abject plaything of appearances in all their deceitfulness that with the shadowy figments of his scandalized imagination blindfolds his eyes and drapes him in the mantle of the hunt. His diminishing threshold of suspicion and flailing reprisals, which remain for all that quite deadly, acuminated by the monomania of pursuit and spurred on by a text that admits no middle way, are spent in the blood of real victims. In the path of this juggernaut, a qualm and hesitation intrudes. The newly critical spirit marks the beginning of the end of the age, the expiration of its absolute priorities and categorical divisions. Its proud dogmas must soon give way before a henceforth termless critique—the humility and rivalless power of scientific hypothesis.

For a last exemplary vignette of the age in flight, we should mention that the minister and exorcist Cotton Mather will himself fall victim to persecution for his pioneering use of inoculations to prevent the spread of smallpox.[111] His sponsorship in Boston of a method based on two accounts from the *Transactions* of the Royal Society of London[112] will be greeted with fear, loathing, and finally, homicidal retaliation, years after the end of the Salem trials. In November 1721 someone lobs a bomb "of powder and turpentine" through the window of Mather's house at three in the morning with a note that reads "COTTON MATHER, *You Dog, Dam you; I'l inoculate you with this, with a Pox to you.*"[113] Silverman notes that for Mather

> such massive onslaughts against mankind as epidemics and such obstructions to human progress as attempts to impede scientific knowledge, were characteristic works of evil angels. Believing that only their unwelcome presence could explain the rage against inoculation, he saw Boston benighted by the "Power of Darkness," "Satanic Fury" again astir, the place become "a dismal Picture and Emblem of *Hell*; *Fire* with *Darkness* filling it." Only their presence could explain the "crying Wickedness of this Town (A Town at this time strangely possessed with the Devil,) and the vile Abuse which I do myself suffer from it, for nothing but my instructing our base Physicians, how to save many precious Lives."[114]

Accusations and the State

Much of the history we have just reviewed is marked by the fantastic character of the accusations levied by Puritan writers against their foes and the fearful collapse of stable roles and identities, to say nothing of the fusion of distinct earthly rivals who also carnally embody spiritual evil. Jenson notes laconically that "the tendency to merge and shift characteristics among enemies and to level accusations at those with links to old enemies may be universal"[115]—a fair assessment as far as it goes. Still, if we recall that at stake from the beginning are the Puritan theocratic state and the authority of divines to steer its course, it becomes clear just how much more compellingly Girard's historical account of religion's emergence and collapse explains the persecutors and their texts. Where ordained men kept peace in the fold divinely entrusted to their care by adjudicating all matters civil and religious, the teaching that God reveals himself to all "women as well as men, the uneducated with the educated" could only be greeted as a wolfish intrusion designed to scatter the flock.[116] Puritan theocrats must have seen all too well that "immediate revelation" obviated the need for an ordained ministry and that this was tantamount to anarchy. The democratic character of antinomian and Quaker spirituality brings into focus precisely what is at stake in the climacteric shift, from collective forms of religious life with their dependence on priestly mediation to fully individuated and self-determined expressions of belief and unbelief alike.

That it was a woman in the first case, stepping out of her appointed place and usurping male prerogatives to become the evidently persuasive mouthpiece for this new error, only made matters worse. Hutchinson as teacher exemplified, by teaching, the new freedoms and impunity she enjoined on all. In the scandalized eye of writers like Winthrop, Weld, and Johnson, it is not just the ordinary divisions into accepted roles and stations that are thus obliterated, but more fundamental ones still, without which social conflagration extends into something cosmic and all-destroying. Dyer's baby is exemplary in this regard—the *corpus delicti* abolishing every natural division (human, bird, fish, ape) in itself and one other besides: as bride of the Devil, Dyer begets a child who is fully *preter*natural. Hutchinson's transmogrification is even more exalted and appalling: she becomes in Weld's lurid depiction a nearly mythological being, whose womb pours forth demon offspring like that of a Hindu goddess. These accounts conform themselves to the mythic pattern traced by Girard, who reads the birth of monsters as a signature event marking the crisis of differences. The truth of human rivalry "must somehow be expelled . . . beyond the realm of human activity," he writes.[117] The fantastic accusations serve the "strongly functional nature of the scapegoat operation," which ripens the victim for slaughter, transposing human enmity and conflict "to the realm of the divine, in the form of an inscrutable god."[118] A similar dissolution of boundaries is evident in the accusations that greet the Quaker missionizing of the midcentury with their crying susceptibility to phantasmic superimposition and adversary merger. The crisis at Salem achieves what Girard might call a mythopoeic pitch and intensity; the charges lack nothing in the way of profligate inventiveness and frightful imagery. But, although there will be victims, no real concord obtains. In the swift erosion of public support for the persecutors we find a token of the degree to which the whirling momentum of ever more fantastic accusations and draconian punishments has lost its centripetal force and power of social cohesion. It cannot achieve the peace that it once did.

CHAPTER 10

A Latent History of the Modern World

The Scapegoat King

Among the earliest metaphorical uses of the expression a clear majority appear in the political writing of the period, with its often withering characterizations of politicians and kings. Peter Heylyn uses it in the *Cyprianus anglicus* of 1668 to comment on a tract published "against the Lord Treasurer, who is now made the Scape-Goat, to bear all those faults in Civil Matters which formerly had been imputed to the Duke of *Buckingham*."[1] A similar use is found in a reference to the infamous George Jeffreys, who in 1685 presides over the "Bloody Assizes" following a failed insurrection of the Duke of Monmouth, during which hundreds of rebels are expropriated, tortured, enslaved, and killed. Though he will be promoted to lord chancellor by King James II that same year, Jeffreys is ultimately "censur'd by his Master for his former Services"; in "A New Martyrology . . ." John Tutchin records that just before his abdication of the throne and flight to France, King James admits to one of Jeffrey's victims that "my Lord Chancellor had been a very ill Man, and done very ill things."[2] Sensing "Death was couched in the Words," Jeffreys, whose "*Life would have been like the* Scape Goat" had he remained and "*born all their Crimes, and been beheaded for his own*," escapes to Wapping disguised as a sailor, though he is later apprehended and dies in the Tower of London.[3] This citation compares well with a reference of 1711 to Lieutenant-Colonel Hamilton, another bloodstained fugitive, of whom the Lord Viscount

Dundee wrote that he was persuaded "to abscond for a Time, and then slip over to [King William] in *Flanders*" after his participation at the Massacre of Glencoe, a tactic designed to make him seem "more guilty than the rest."[4] It is thus "he is made the *Scape-goat*," Dundee writes, "and all this Sin laid upon his Head."[5] That these last citations, which are among the earliest in the English record, name war criminals on the lam, men whose escape from justice may itself be played against them by more cynical manipulators of public sympathy, is striking. As in the plague citations above, the emphasis here falls on the deflection of blame or punishment, the first truly political act, however unconscious it remains in the earliest stages of human communal formation. Innocence is hardly the most salient feature of these scapegoats, suggesting the process of deflection is essentially indifferent to ethics. It is a mechanical rather than a moral function.

Finally, we confront a more formidable grouping of references that return us to Frazer's and Girard's speculations on the ritual origins of kingship. In 1694 the metaphor is used to name King James II himself, whose ministers escape punishment "for all those Things that were called Miscarriages during his Reign," when "he whom both the Constitution, and all the Laws of the Land made not only impunible but innocent" was "selected as the *Scape-Goat*, to have all the Offences of the Ministers, and of the subordinate Tools of the Government, transferred and laid upon him, and *drove* away, under the Guilt and Weight of them, into a Wilderness and Land of Oblivion."[6] It is the axiom that "the King could do no wrong," which made him an ideal scapegoat, as King William III may himself one day become, "a sacrifice to expiate" the crimes of his ministers, to suffer "the Reproach, and bear the Punishment of them."[7] John Kettlewell makes a similar comment when he writes in 1719 of King James II's plans to return to power. Every scheme to bring about a counterrevolution "the Wisdom of God saw fit not to prosper, whence they were all dashed to pieces so of a sudden, when they did seem to be best laid, and best Fixt," he says.[8] "And yet while nothing could succeed with him, it is somewhat observable, that all Things should succeed with Those who had been the Principal Advisers and Instruments of what had brought all these Calamities upon him: And that no Evil and Wicked Counsellors ... should be Prosecuted by the Nations Representatives for what they had Traitorously Pushed him upon. So that he was made the *Scape-Goat* to run away, and to carry with him the Sins of the whole Nation."[9] *A Secret History of One Year* attributes a similar comment to King William III, who, deflecting criticism for his leniency toward James's heavily reviled ministers, is quoted as saying "That King *James* had made himself the SCAPEGOAT" and, like "the SCAPEGOAT in the Old Law [who] was to bear the Sins of the People, and be turned into the Wilderness; which Suffering was accepted by Heaven instead of a Punishment upon the People," so "King *James* having suffer'd the Loss of his Crown, and the Dispossessing of his supposed Posterity, and the Banishment of himself and Family from his Dominions, was a sufficient Sacrifice for all those who adhered to him."[10] The logic of this last use is of course regressive, employing the scapegoat in the old apotropaeic way, to avert disaster from others on whom it should justly fall—the kind of political rationalization that becomes increasingly suspect and finally outrageous, although here, in 1712, on the lips of King William and in the way of an excuse for clemency, it may yet pass uncontested. Even so it forms a sharp contrast with the judgment implicit in every other designation of King James II as scapegoat enumerated here.

In at least one later tract, James's predecessor to the throne and brother will be so named: *A Sermon Preached towards the Latter End of the Last Century, on the Anniversary Thanksgiving Day for Putting an End to the Great Rebellion, by the Restitution of the King and Royal Family*, appears anonymously in 1715 decrying the murder of "that Excellent Prince and Christian, King Charles I . . . before his own Palace,"[11] and likening the subsequently exiled Charles II to "a mere Scape Goat . . . [who] after the Sins of the People had been laid on him [was] forced to wander into a strange Country, and not suffered to continue there but hunted like a Partridge upon the Mountains, driven from the kind of Hospitality his Relations and Kindred had afforded him in France, to seek for shelter in a strange Land."[12] The bishop of Carlile, William Nicolson, delivers a sermon at the Collegiate Church of Westminster in 1702 upon "The Anniversary of the Martyrdom of King Charles the First," in which the slain ruler is severally compared to Christ with whom he is said to have shared "*a Crown of Thorns*."[13] Nicolson adds that "this *Lamb* is also *led to the Slaughter, Revil'd*, and *Spit upon*; Nay, and publickly Executed as a Traiterous Rebel, before the Gates of his own Palace, hardly one honest Centurion daring so much as to mutter that he was a Religious Man."[14] Notwithstanding the Messianic allusions, and those specifically taken from Isaiah 53, Nicolson does not designate King Charles I a scapegoat, using the expression to indicate others who may be all too easily blamed for his death: "'Twill be our great Concern," he says, "to Reflect impartially upon the General Guilt of the whole *People of the Land*, without singling out a *Scape-Goat* from any particular Set or *Party of Men*."[15]

Like Cato's letter featuring the "plague" of public corruption, Nicholson's sermon urges against recourse to this facile expedient. The thing to note is that in nearly all these references, and notwithstanding the degree of actual guilt attaching to those called scapegoats—some of whom are unquestionably imbrued in blood and richly culpable—there is no question that being made a scapegoat is something to be avoided, that the making of scapegoats, even when not premeditated, is finally an illegitimate procedure. It tends to let certain malefactors slip away unpunished while others suffer more than their due. The guilty are liable for their own sins. To the extent they are blamed or punished for the sins of others, they are misused and deprived of justice. That among the earliest designees we discover so many kings is striking, given all that Frazer and Girard have written about the institution of kingship and its origins. As with the scapegoat references to plague, the question is that of connections between phenomena so obliterated by time and institutionalization that no concrete recollection of them remains and that suddenly reappear.

We should note one other reference to royalty, in this case to King James's son, the exiled Stuart "Prince of Wales" James Francis Edward, who Charles Leslie says "express'd no Resentment at the cruel Proceedings of the last Parliament, to leave him no Place to flee unto, but to drive him like the Scape-Goat, unto a Land not inhabited, with all the Sins of the Nation upon his Head, to perish in the most miserable manner, *Unpityed, Unrelieved.*"[16] In 1708 this same prince makes an attempt on the throne of England, sailing from France with a fleet to invade Scotland. He is famously driven back by the British admiral George Byng, whose son, John Byng, will be controversially tried and executed some decades later, in what appears to have been a decisive moment for the dissemination of our word into the common tongue.

The Innocent Admiral

By the early 1720s the metaphorical expression appears to have hardened considerably with the values that attend its use today. It is variously employed to designate the proprietors of the South Seas Company and in one source its treasurer, who escapes justice at the height of a major financial scandal and so draws more than his fair share of the ensuing fire. The Treaty of Utrecht (concluding the War of Spanish Succession) is said to be a convenient scapegoat for the failed policies of certain ministers, and in one source the emperor Napoleon is called a scapegoat for all of Europe. Still, metaphorical uses in newspapers and books remain scattered and few. In 1755, England dispatches a fleet under the command of Admiral John Byng to shore up the British base at Minorca, which, when he arrived, was already under siege by the French. Finding himself underprovisioned and outmanned, Byng returns to Gibraltar, leaving the island to the French. Court-martialed under articles of war newly revised to provide for the execution of officers who failed "to do their utmost," Byng is sentenced to die and shot aboard the HMS *Monarch* in March 1757. Voltaire's *Candide* registers the event with a barb: "Mais dans ce pays-ci il est bon de tuer de tems en tems un Amiral pour encourager les autres."[17]

If the fall of Minorca was initially met with anger and calls for Byng's punishment, the tide of popular opinion soon turns against the admiralty, which is widely suspected of having blamed Byng to cover their own mismanagement of the expedition. In 1756, *A Letter to a Member of Parliament in the Country, from his Friend in London, Relative to the Case of Admiral Byng* will allege the accused "may be destined rather a *Martyr* to *private Policy*, than a *Victim* to *public Justice!*"

> Upon the Effects of any fatal Mismanagement, you are sensible, it is no unusual *State-Trick*, for those in Power, to devote some Sacrifice (however innocent) to the popular Resentment, and thus, by a Sort of political *Legerdemain*, divert the public Attention from a *real* to an *ideal* Offender: How successfully this ministerial *Hocus-Pocus* has in former Days been played off, History abundantly evinces; nor is it impossible but our future Annals may afford an Instance of ... an Admiral made a *Scapegoat*, to bear away the Offences of a ***.[18]

A letter to the *Patriot Proclaimer* in the aftermath of his death draws the same conclusion about Byng's use by his accusers to deflect criticism from themselves:

> Honourable had it been for the late ministry and the nation, and perhaps fatal in a far less degree to the unfortunate admiral Bying, if in his evil hour the same spirit of candour had been allowed to operate in his accusers; or rather in those who found it necessary to overcharge his name with opprobrium, that it might thereby attract all the venom of public indignation, and give them an opportunity to skulk into shelter from the storm which their own misconduct had most contributed to raise. He was made to pay, at the hard price of life and reputation, for the iniquities of many: was the scape-goat, the sin-offering for all.[19]

In a letter from the English journalist and politician John Wilkes to Lord Grenville dated October 1756, a few months before Byng's execution, public indignation is said to be rising so that "Byng has now everywhere some warm advocates, from an idea I hope of his innocence, at least a less degree of guilt."[20] Wilkes then observes: "*Poor Byng* is the phrase in every mouth, and then comes the hackneyed simile of the *Scapegoat.*"[21]

The comment tantalizes as much for what it says about the popularity of the expression as what it leaves unsaid. Above all we should like to know if the scapegoat rode the admiral's coattails to ubiquity or was already a cliché when the controversy erupts. The question, which may be finally unanswerable, is that of its circulation in *speech* before 1757. In published matter, its use clearly explodes, so that there are nearly twice as many references in books between 1751 and 1800 as during the first fifty years of the eighteenth century, with a great many more of these metaphorical in the current sense. In the overwhelming majority of references to Byng as a scapegoat, it is precisely his innocence of the charges that counts. The focal point of public scandal is that a loyal officer was made to pay with his life for the criminal misconduct of his accusers.

The Scapegoat in the Period Literature

We shall conclude our research of the earliest English uses with a handful of citations taken from fiction and poetry, but let us do so by way of a further reference to Byng, who appears in Tobias Smollett's *The History of England, from the Revolution to the Death of George the Second* in a now familiar connection. "In a word, he was devoted as the Scape-goat of the ministry," Smollett writes, "to whose supine negligence, ignorance, and misconduct, the loss of that important fortress was undoubtedly owing. Byng's miscarriage was thrown out like a barrel to the whale in order to engage the attention of the people, that it might not be attracted by the real cause of the national misfortune."[22] The image of the whale is recapitulated here from Smollett's 1769 satire, *The History and Adventures of an Atom*, where it is deployed to invoke the deliquescent fury and monstrous formation of the mob.

> In his general consternation, Fok-fi-roku stood up and offered a scheme, which was immediately put in execution. "The multitude, my Lords, (said he) is a many headed monster—it is a Cerberus that must have a sop:—it is a wild beast, so ravenous that nothing but blood will appease its appetite:—it is a whale, that must have a barrel for its amusement:—it is a

dæmon to which we must offer up human sacrifice. Now the question is, who is to be this sop, this barrel, this scapegoat?[23]

The description is of the highest interest because of its resort to myth for a picture of social uproar and differential collapse, of crisis assuaged by the blood of a victim and in no other way. Smollet's risible Japanese characters and his ancient Japan where the action of the novel takes place are a thin guise for eighteenth-century England and its political actors, and though he paints a bleak picture of wicked premeditation at the top, he is also tapping into something about society and its indenture to violence recorded nowhere else but in myth.[24] The next citation is a droll excerpt from a hymn to hard work, included here for its use of the scapegoat to designate a slave in time of slavery—an adumbration, as such, of the use to which the "scapegoat" will be put by the disenfranchised in coming years, as the advantage of declaring victimhood becomes common currency.

FROM "THE DUTY OF EMPLOYING ONE'S SELF"

How many such in Indolence grown old,
With Vigour ne'er do any thing, but scold?
Who Spirits only from Ill-humour get;
Like Wines that die, unless upon the Fret?
Weary'd of flouncing to himself alone,
Acerbus keeps a Man to fret upon.
The Fellow's nothing in the Earth to do,
But to sit quiet, and be scolded to.
Pishes and Oaths, when'er the Master's sour'd,
All largely on the Scape-goat Slave are pour'd.
This drains his Rage; and tho to *John* so rough,
Abroad you'd think him complaisant enough.
As for myself, whom Poverty prevents
From being angry at so great Expense;
Who, should I ever be inclin'd to rage,
For want of Slaves, War with myself must wage;
Must rail, and hear; chastising, be chastiz'd;
Be both the Tyrant, and the Tyranniz'd.[25]

Our final reference, which is also one of the earliest, perhaps *the* earliest in which the modern sense of the expression stands clear, illuminated by the context of its protest against the misogyny of the period, is mercurial in its prescience and self-possession. A poem of heroic couplets written in response to Robert Gould's *Love Given O're: Or, A Satyr Against the Pride, Lust and Inconstancy of Women* (1682), *The Female Advocate* of Sarah Fyge Egerton first came to light in 1686, when its author, the daughter of a London apothecary, was still in her teens.

> A thousand Instances there might be brought,
> (Not far fetch'd, tho' they were dearly bought)
> To prove that Man more false than Woman is,
> More unconstant, nay and more perfidious:
> But these are Crimes which hell, (I'm sure not heaven)
> As they pretend, hath peculiar given
> Unto our Sex, but 'tis as false as they,
> And that's more false than any one can say.
> All Pride and Lust too to our charge they lay,
> As if in sin we all were so sublime
> As to monopolize each hainous crime;
> Nay, *Woman now is made the Scape-goat, and*
> *'Tis she must bear sins of all the land*:
> But I believe there's not a Priest that can
> Make an atonement for one single man,
> Nay, it is well if he himself can bring
> An humble, pious heart for th' offering;
> A thing which ought to be inseparable
> To men o'th' Gown and of the Sacred Table;
> Yet it is sometimes wanting, and they be
> Too often sharers of Impiety:
> But howsoever the strange World now thrives,
> I must not look in my Teachers lives,
> But methinks the World doth seem to be
> Nought but confusion and degeneracy,
> Each Man's so eager of each fatal sin,
> As if he fear'd he should not do't again;
> Yet still his soul is black, he is the same
> At all times, tho' he doth not act all flame,
> Because he opportunity doth want,
> And to him always there's not a grant
> Of Objects for to exercise his will,

And for to shew his great and mighty skill
In all Sciences diabolical.[26]

The scapegoat reference is deployed here with the canny assurance of someone who understands the political advantage of declaring for the weak and
maligned party. That it should appear precisely in the context of a statement
like this, whose witness to the ugly truth pushes past the things men say to
cast a cold eye on what they do, the religious and irreligious alike—as though
there were finally no difference between them—makes it exemplary of the
perspectival shift and critical revolt under way. "If I am defamed at least my
eyes are open," Egerton seems to say. It is thus the victim discovers herself in a
position of strength, in possession of a luminous disillusionment.

The Plowbeam and the Loom

"I wold desire that all women shuld reade the gospel and Paules epistles," writes William Tyndale in his 1529 translation of Erasmus's *Exhortations to the Diligent Study of Scripture*, "and I wold to god they were translated in to the tonges of all men."

> So that they might not only be read and knowne of the scotes and yryshmen But also of the Turkes and sarracenes. Truly it is one degre to good living, yee the first . . . to have a little sight in the scripture, though it be but a grosse knowledge. . . . I wold to god the plowman wold singe a texte of the scripture at his plowbeme, and that the wever at his lowme with this wold drive away the tediousness of tyme. I wold the wayfaringe man with this pastyme wold expelle the weryness of his jorney. And to be shorte I wold that all the communication of the christen shuld be of the scripture.[1]

Tyndale's English translation of the New Testament began circulating in 1525 with a first successful run of 3,000 copies at Worms in Germany. Cheap, portable, and easily smuggled, the Bibles quickly found their way onto English soil, much to the alarm of church authorities, who greeted their unwelcome intrusion with interdictions and book burnings. The bishop Turnstall's tireless efforts to confiscate or buy up every available copy of Tyndale's book culminated in a number of bonfires outside St. Paul's Cross in London, the church from whose pulpit Thomas Bilson would fire the opening volley of the Descensus controversy just a few decades later. Espionage, imprisonments, tortures, and immolations follow. In February 1530, the priest Thomas Hitton is burned at the stake for Bible smuggling and heresy, becoming the English Reformation's first victim. Tyndale's most powerful enemies, men like Thomas More and Cardinal Wolsey, saw his English Bible as an open attack on ecclesiastical authority and with good reason. Schama notes that "the printed vernacular Bible had the potential to turn the 'priesthood of all believers' from a heretical fantasy into a true religion."[2] Unless it was stopped it would usher in "a time when every man or woman, no matter how ignorant, would be presumptuous enough to judge doctrine for themselves."[3] Strikingly clear-eyed and intentional, Tyndale will write in the 1530 *Prologue* to his translation of the Pentateuch: "I perceaved by experyence how that it was impossible to stablysh the laye people in any truth excepte yf scripture were playnly layde before their eyes in their mother tonge that they might se the processe ordre and meninge of the texte."[4] The translation whose populist mandate Tyndale epitomizes is the text that admits the "scapegoat' to the mother tongue. Five years on the scholar will pay for the presumption of bringing the scriptures into English with his life. Kidnapped and imprisoned at Vilvoorde in 1535, Tyndale is burned at the stake the following year (after first being strangled), but the organized effort to stamp out his Bible is of course an abject failure. By 1545, Henry the VIII will be heard complaining that the "most precious jewel, the Word of God, is disputed, rhymed, sung and jangled in every alehouse and tavern."[5]

There is no way Tyndale could have anticipated the linguistic destiny of the "Scapegoat" that, a little over a century after it is coined, abandons the pulpit to become a secular metaphor—a distinctively restricted denominator of human violence. As we have seen, the relationship it expresses is something that takes shape theologically first. If the Calvinist scapegoat typologies include the Father, the Son, and the people as parties to an act of vicarious punishment, they and their soteriological drama are rapidly effaced when the scapegoat enters common speech, where heavy traffic reduces it to a relation of the crowd to its victim.

We see, too, that, almost upon its inception, the metaphor picks up a preferential connotation in favor of the victim it names, an ineradicable bias that is also an implicit judgment of his accusers. These meanings are new and they mark the expression at an early moment in its metaphorical life as already exceeding the neutrality of "vicarious punishment," a sense that terms like *katharma* and *peripsēma* comprise insofar as they designate the Greek ritual victim, if they also acquire connotations of wretchedness thereby, insinuations of misfortune beneath contempt. These, as we have seen, give them currency as popular epithets. The final semantic charge attaching to the metaphor of the scapegoat reverses these judgments. The scapegoat is no longer just a maledicted surrogate—although he is that, too—but a merely expedient victim, and therefore *innocent*. Far from making him an object of contempt, this bestows on him a sympathetic advantage. Between the world that gave us the victim as byword and that which produces our metaphor lies all the distance traversed by the goat that got away who, unlike its pagan counterparts, transcends ritual origins to become a sign of vindication. The benefit of the doubt now goes to the accused; the accusers are henceforth in the dock. As such, the metaphor incorporates the spirit of the age in which it was conceived—newly skeptical of authority, wary of the usual allegations, readily defaulting to the side of the defamed. This predisposition is *no theological legacy*. Because the language of penal substitution sacralizes violence, calling forth the propitiating exchange on which the life of the people has always been said to depend, it remains within the liminal closure of religion. What the history of the scapegoat reveals is the collapse of a metaphysical economy that to varying degrees and in different adaptations structured religious belief from the dawn of the primitive sacred through early modernity. Its long typological itinerary describes a process of cleavage and differential liquidation that ends the heretofore unbroken domination of the religious weltanschauung, ushering in an unprecedented age of scientific discovery and religious indifference or secularism.

Otherwise unaccountable patterns in the first metaphorical references provide oblique and discontinuous but ultimately compelling indications that Frazer and Girard were more instinctually clued in than many contemporary scholars have been willing to admit. In view of the evidence, their divinations into human prehistory are less easily chalked up to mere fantasy, nor ought they be consigned to obsolescence on philosophical scruples alone. Between Frazer's and Girard's diametrically opposed theories of history, as between their views on Jesus' place in "the great army of martyrs" extending past human recollection, the gulf doubtless remains wide and deep. An impartial evaluation of the theoretical elegance and explanatory power of their respective work runs headlong into Frazer's militant atheism at this point, which like Girard's avowed Catholicism threatens to derail it. Both thinkers unleash devastating critiques of religion that insist on its supersession by scientific thought. If Frazer is too datedly positivistic and shrill in his denunciations, Girard, who penned what is perhaps *the* most formidable theory of the death of religion ever ventured, poses an even bigger problem, since he is also a lay member of the church. If we must here circumvent the question of personal faith or its refusal, we remain steadfastly interested in the question of Jesus' world-historical conspicuousness—of the degree to which the story of his death and vindication dominated the ages. What are the calculable effects of its mounting and, finally, inescapable prominence?

This is to ask what toll the Gospels, as paradigmatic biographies of the scapegoat, have taken—on paganism, to be sure, but more precisely on Christianity itself. Do they finally subvert the religion's most deeply constitutive teaching—the story it tells itself about why he came? The latter has, as we have seen, undergone a number of seismic shifts over a millennial history during which the indistinguishably mythic narrative gives way to reveal an ancient ritual procedure, a sacrifice enjoined on all. If each is called to play his part in the supreme act of penitential satisfaction through personal reenactments of its saving quid pro quo, the ritual imperative will eventually narrow its aim to the *one* in whose death the logic of the deed undoes itself. The stages here mirror those in which, religion takes rise, only, run backward into the crucible of violence where everything began. Is the story of Jesus inimical to religion as such and the narrative codifications of theology in particular? Does the irreducibly historical character of the Gospels' reportage defy every mythologizing, ritualizing—in a word—*religious*—homage that could be paid to the redeemer? Could any religion erected upon the death of one whose face was set to die as foretold by the prophets and as the prophets themselves died—victims of *religious* violence—comprehend his historical destiny? If the death of Jesus so closely resembled that of innumerable mythic victims that "secondary and superficial mythological crystallizations"[6] formed inevitably, encrusting its trajectory through time, is there anything in seventeen centuries of Christian thought that ought not be reckoned mere crystalline accretion? What survives the shearing force of history's acceleration from the threshold of modernity through the present apocalyptic turn in the age of science? These and like questions detain us at the close of this study. What the history unquestionably allows us to see is the scapegoat traversing the boundary that divides our world from the dominion of its past, a Christian witness against Christendom.

Katharma and *Peripsēma*
Testimonia

Eupolis, fr. 384 (=117K)

καὶ μὴν ἐγὼ πολλῶν παρόντων οὐκ ἔχω τί λέξω.
οὕτω σφόδρ᾽ ἀλγῶ τὴν πολιτείαν ὁρῶν παρ᾽ ἡμῖν.
ἡμεῖς γὰρ οὐχ οὕτω τέως ᾠκοῦμεν οἱ γέροντες,
ἀλλ᾽ ἦσαν ἡμῖν τῆι πόλει πρῶτον μὲν οἱ στρατηγοὶ
ἐκ τῶν μεγίστων οἰκιῶν, πλούτωι γένει τε πρῶτοι,
οἷς ὡσπερεὶ θεοῖσιν, ηὐχόμεσθα· καὶ γὰρ ἦσαν.
ὥστ᾽ ἀσφαλῶς ἐπράττομεν· νυνὶ δ᾽ ὅπηι τύχοιμεν
στρατευόμεσθ᾽ αἱρούμενοι καθάρματα στρατηγούς¹

And yet with much that I might tell I don't know what to say;
It gives me such a pain to see the plight we're in today.
We old 'uns didn't act like this; the men we chose for leading
Were scions of the noblest houses, first in wealth and breeding.
We worshipped them for Gods on earth, and that is what they were, sir;
And so with them to rule the roost we lived without a care, sir.
Now, we no sooner take the field than we must needs set over us
Rubbish we ought to throw away [*katharmata*]—Oh, anything will
   do for us.²

Scholia on Aristophanes, *Frogs* 733

733a φαρμακοῖσιν// καθάρμασι. τοὺς γὰρ φαύλους καὶ παρὰ τῆς φύσεως ἐπιβεβουλευμένους εἰς ἀπαλλαγὴν αὐχμοῦ ἢ λιμοῦ ἤ τινος τῶν τοιούτων ἔθυον, οὓς ἐκάλουν "καθάρματα."³

733a for scapegoats [*pharmakoisin*] // for offscourings [*katharmasi*]. For they sacrificed [*ethuon*] those who were mistreated by nature to allay a drought or famine or something of that sort; and they called them "offscourings" [*katharmata*].⁴

Aristophanes, *Plutus* 454

Βλεψίδημος
ποίοις ὅπλοισιν ἢ δυνάμει πεποιθότες;
ποῖον γὰρ οὐ θώρακα, ποίαν δ' ἀσπίδα   450
οὐκ ἐνέχυρον τίθησιν ἡ μιαρωτάτη;
Χρεμύλος
θάρρει: μόνος γὰρ ὁ θεὸς οὗτος οἶδ' ὅτι
τροπαῖον ἂν στήσαιτο τῶν ταύτης τρόπων.
Πενία
γρύζειν δὲ καὶ τολμᾶτον ὦ καθάρματε,
ἐπ' αὐτοφώρῳ δεινὰ δρῶντ' εἰλημμένω;   455
Χρεμύλος
σὺ δ' ὦ κάκιστ' ἀπολουμένη τί λοιδορεῖ
ἡμῖν προσελθοῦσ' οὐδ' ὁτιοῦν ἀδικουμένη;⁵

BLEPSIDEMUS: But what weapons have we? Are we in a condition to show fight? Where is the breastplate, the buckler, that this wretch has not pawned?

CHREMYLUS: Be at ease. Plutus will readily triumph over her threats unaided.

POVERTY: Dare you reply, you scoundrels [*katharmate*], you who are caught red-handed at the most horrible crime?

CHREMYLUS: As for you, you cursed jade, you pursue me with your abuse, though I have never done you the slightest harm.⁶

Scholia on Aristophanes, *Plutus* 454

454d. "κάθαρμα" τὸ βδέλυγμα. γίνεται δὲ ἀφ᾽ ἱστορίας τοιαύτης, ὡς [ὅτι] ἐν ταῖς Ἀθήναις ἦν ἔθος τοιοῦτον, ὅτι εἰ [ἐ]συνέβη ἁμαρτῆσαι τὴν πόλιν τι εἰς τοὺς θεούς, εἰς ἐξιλέωσιν τοῦ τοιούτου ἀτοπήματος, ἀφόριζεν (sic) ὁ λαὸς ἕνα ἄνθρωπον ὃς πάντων δυσειδέστατος ἦν. ἔθυον γοῦν αὐτὸν εἰς λύτρον παντός.

"Offscourings" [*katharma*] is abomination. It follows from such a reference, that in Athens there was such a custom, that if it happened that the city committed some offence [*hamartēsai*] against the gods, to atone [*eis exileōsin*] for such an offence [*apopēmatos*], the people separated out [*aphorizen*] one man who was ugliest of everyone. In sum, they sacrificed him [*ethuon*] as a payment [*lutron*] for all.

454e. [. . .] ὅτε γὰρ χρησμὸς περὶ τοιούτου ἐγένετο, εὑρίσκετο δυσειδὴς πάντα ἐκεῖσε ἄνθρωπος. τοῦτον ἔκαιον, "κάθαρμα" ποιοῦντες τῆς πόλεως διά τινα θεομηνίαν. ἁρμένου οὖν τούτου εἰς τὸ καυθῆναι, περιέψων αὐτὸν πάντες, λέγοντες "γενοῦ ἡμῖν ἀπαλλαγὴ κακῶν." ἐκ τούτου ἐλέγετο καὶ "περίψημα."

For when there was an oracle concerning such an event [a disaster or offence against the gods], a thoroughly ugly man was found and brought to that place. They burned him, making him the offscourings [*katharma*] of the city because of divine wrath. Therefore, when he had been selected for burning, everyone wiped him clean [*periepsōn*], saying, "Become a deliverance from evils for us." From this we also have the word *peripsēma*. ["anything wiped off, offscouring," LSJ].

454f. τοὺς φαρμακοὺς τῆς πόλεως καὶ τοὺς γόητας "καθάρματα" ἐκάλουν διὰ αἰτίαν τοιαύτην· πόλις τις ἐδυστύχει, καὶ ἐδόθη αὐτῇ χρησμός, ἵνα ἐκτεφρώσῃ τὸν ἔχθιστον τῆς πόλεως καὶ ἀθλιώτατον, καὶ λάβωσι τὴν τέφραν ἐκείνου πρὸς ἀποτροπιασμὸν τῶν τῆς πόλεως κακῶν. ὃ δὴ καὶ γέγονε. καὶ λαβόντες τὸν δυστυχέστατον τῆς πόλεως, κατὰ μέσην τὴν ἀγορὰν κατέκαυσαν ἀγρίαις συκαῖς. τὴν δὲ τέφραν τούτου λαβόντες, εἰς ἀποσόβησιν τῶν τῆς πόλεως κακῶν ἐκέκτηντο. καὶ ἐντεῦθεν ἐπεκράτησε λέγειν πάντας τοὺς δυστυχεῖς καὶ πένητας καὶ ἀθλίους καὶ γόητας καὶ φαρμακοὺς "καθάρματα."[7]

They would call the scapegoats [*pharmakous*] of the city and the swindlers [*goētas*, "sorceror, wizard, juggler, cheat," LSJ] offscourings [*katharmata*] for this reason. A certain city would undergo a misfortune, and an oracle was given to it, that it should burn to ashes the most hated [*ekhthiston*] and wretched [*athliōtaton*] man of the city, and they should take his ashes as an expiation of the evils of the city. Which indeed was done. And after they taken the most wretched [*dustukhestaton*] man in the city, in the middle of the agora they thoroughly burned him with wild figs. And after they took his ashes, they succeeded in scaring away [*eis aposobēsin*] the city's evils. And from that the practice of calling all the unfortunate and poor and wretched and swindlers and pharmakoi "*katharmata*" came to be in force.[8]

Aristophanes, *Knights* 1136

Χορός
χοὔτω μὲν ἂν εὖ ποιοῖς,
εἴ σοι πυκνότης ἔνεστ᾽
ἐν τῷ τρόπῳ, ὡς λέγεις,
τούτῳ πάνυ πολλή,
εἰ τούσδ᾽ ἐπίτηδες ὥσπερ   1135
δημοσίους τρέφεις
ἐν τῇ πυκνί, κᾆθ᾽ ὅταν
μή σοι τύχῃ ὄψον ὄν,
τούτων ὃς ἂν ᾖ παχύς,
θύσας ἐπιδειπνεῖς.   1140
Δῆμος
σκέψασθε δέ μ᾽, εἰ σοφῶς
αὐτοὺς περιέρχομαι
τοὺς οἰομένους φρονεῖν
κἄμ᾽ ἐξαπατύλλειν.
τηρῶ γὰρ ἑκάστοτ᾽ αὐτοὺς   1145
οὐδὲ δοκῶν ὁρᾶν
κλέπτοντας: ἔπειτ᾽ ἀναγκάζω
πάλιν ἐξεμεῖν
ἅττ᾽ ἂν κεκλόφωσί μου,
κημὸν καταμηλῶν.[9]   1150

CHORUS [*singing*]: What profound wisdom! If it be really so, why! all is for the best. Your ministers, then, are your victims, whom you nourish and feed up [*dēmosious trepheis*] expressly in the Pnyx, so that, the day your dinner is ready, you may immolate the fattest and eat him.

DEMOS [*singing*]: Look, see how I play with them, while all the time they think themselves such adepts at cheating me. I have my eye on them when they thieve, but I do not appear to be seeing them; then I thrust a judgment down their throat as it were a feather, and force them to vomit up all they have robbed from me.[10]

Scholia on Aristophanes, *Knights* 1136c

1136c. δημοσίους λέγει τοὺς λεγομένους φαρμακούς, οἵπερ καθαίρουσι τὰς πόλεις τῷ ἑαυτῶν φόνῳ. ἔτρεφον γάρ τινας Ἀθηναῖοι λίαν ἀγεννεῖς καὶ πένητας καὶ ἀχρήστους, καὶ ἐν καιρῷ συμφορᾶς τινος ἐπελθούσης τῇ πόλει, λιμοῦ λέγω ἢ τοιούτου τινός, ἔθυον τούτους ἕνεκα τοῦ καθαρθῆναι τοῦ μιάσματος καὶ τῆς ἑαυτῶν κακίας, καὶ θεραπείαν εὑρεῖν τοῦ ἐπικειμένου κακοῦ. οὓς καὶ ἐπωνόμαζον καθάρματα.[11]

1136c. By *dēmosious* "those who are public" he means those who are called *pharmakoi,* who cleanse the cities by their death. For the Athenians would nourish some who were exceedingly low-born, penniless, and useless [*akhrēstous*], and when a time of a disaster of some sort came upon the city, I mean a famine or something similar, they would sacrifice these to cleanse the city from the pollution and from their evil, and to find a cure [*therapeian*] for the disaster they were enduring. They also gave the *pharmakoi* the name offscourings [*katharmata*].[12]

Demosthenes, *Against Midias* XXI

[185] οἷον ἔστι μέτριος καὶ φιλάνθρωπός τις ἡμῶν καὶ πολλοὺς ἐλεῶν· τούτῳ ταὐτὸ δίκαιον ὑπάρχειν παρὰ πάντων, ἄν ποτ' εἰς χρείαν καὶ ἀγῶν' ἀφίκηται. ἄλλος οὑτοσί τις ἀναιδὴς καὶ πολλοὺς ὑβρίζων, καὶ τοὺς μὲν πτωχούς, τοὺς δὲ καθάρματα, τοὺς δ' οὐδ' ἀνθρώπους ὑπολαμβάνων· τούτῳ τὰς αὐτὰς δίκαιον ὑπάρχειν φοράς, ἅσπερ αὐτὸς εἰσενήνοχε τοῖς ἄλλοις. ἂν τοίνυν ὑμῖν ἐπίῃ σκοπεῖν, τούτου πληρωτὴν εὑρήσετε Μειδίαν ὄντα τοῦ ἐράνου, καὶ οὐκ ἐκείνου.[13]

[185] For instance, one of us is moderate, kindly disposed and merciful: he deserves to receive an equivalent return from all, if he ever falls into want or distress. Yonder is another, who is shameless and insulting, treating others as

if they were beggars, the scum of the earth [*katharmata*], mere nobodies: he deserves to be paid with the same measure that he has meted to others. If you will consent to look at it in a true light, you will find that this, and not the former, is the kind of contribution that Meidias has made.[14]

Demosthenes, *Against Midias* XXI

[198] ἐμοὶ μὲν νὴ τὸν Δία καὶ τὸν Ἀπόλλω καὶ τὴν Ἀθηνᾶν (εἰρήσεται γάρ, εἴτ᾽ ἄμεινον εἴτε μή,) ὅθ᾽ οὗτος ὡς ἀπήλλαγμαι περιιὼν ἐλογοποίει, ἔνδηλοί τινες ἦσαν ἀχθόμενοι τῶν πάνυ τούτῳ λαλούντων ἡδέως. καὶ νὴ Δί᾽ αὐτοῖς πολλὴ συγγνώμη· οὐ γάρ ἐστι φορητὸς ἄνθρωπος, ἀλλὰ καὶ πλουτεῖ μόνος καὶ λέγειν δύναται μόνος, καὶ πάντες εἰσὶ τούτῳ καθάρματα καὶ πτωχοὶ καὶ οὐδ᾽ ἄνθρωποι.[15]

[198] I swear solemnly by Zeus, by Apollo, and by Athena—for I will speak out, whatever the result may be—for when this man was going about, trumping up the story that I had abandoned the prosecution, I observed signs of disgust even among his ardent supporters. And by heaven! they had some excuse, for there is no putting up with the follow; he claims to be the only rich man and the only man who knows how to speak; all others are in his opinion outcasts [*katharmata*], beggars, below the rank of men.[16]

Lucian, *Dialogues of the Dead* 2.1

ἐπειδὰν ἡμεῖς οἰμώζωμεν καὶ στένωμεν ἐκείνων μεμνημένοι τῶν ἄνω, Μίδας μὲν οὑτοσὶ τοῦ χρυσίου, Σαρδανάπαλλος δὲ τῆς πολλῆς τρυφῆς, ἐγὼ δὲ Κροῖσος τῶν θησαυρῶν, ἐπιγελᾷ καὶ ἐξονειδίζει ἀνδράποδα καὶ καθάρματα ἡμᾶς ἀποκαλῶν, ἐνίοτε δὲ καὶ ᾄδων ἐπιταράττει ἡμῶν τὰς οἰμωγάς, καὶ ὅλως λυπηρός ἐστι.

Whenever we moan and groan at our memories of life above, Midas recalling his gold, Sardanapalus his great luxury, and I, Croesus, my treasures, he [Menippus] mocks and reviles us, calling us slaves and scum [*katharmata*]: sometimes he even disturbs our lamentations by singing. In short, he's a pest.[17]

Plutarch, *Sulla* 33.1–2

ἔξω δὲ τῶν φονικῶν καὶ τὰ λοιπὰ τοὺς ἀνθρώπους ἐλύπει. δικτάτορα μὲν γὰρ ἑαυτὸν ἀνηγόρευσε, δι᾽ ἐτῶν ἑκατὸν εἴκοσι τοῦτο τὸ γένος τῆς ἀρχῆς ἀναλαβών. ἐψηφίσθη δὲ αὐτῷ πάντων ἄδεια τῶν γεγονότων, πρὸς δὲ τὸ μέλλον ἐξουσία θανάτου, δημεύσεως, κληρουχιῶν, κτίσεως, πορθήσεως, ἀφελέσθαι βασιλείαν, καὶ ᾧ βούλοιτο χαρίσασθαι. [2] τὰς δὲ διαπράσεις τῶν δεδημευμένων οἴκων οὕτως ὑπερηφάνως ἐποιεῖτο καὶ δεσποτικῶς ἐπὶ βήματος καθεζόμενος, ὥστε τῶν ἀφαιρέσεων ἐπαχθεστέρας αὐτοῦ τὰς δωρεὰς εἶναι, καὶ γυναιξὶν εὐμόρφοις καὶ λυρῳδοῖς καὶ μίμοις καὶ καθάρμασιν ἐξελευθερικοῖς ἐθνῶν χώρας καὶ πόλεων χαριζομένου προσόδους, ἐνίοις δὲ γάμους ἀκουσίως ζευγνυμένων γυναικῶν.[18]

33. But besides his massacres, the rest of Sulla's proceedings also gave offence. For he proclaimed himself dictator, reviving this particular office after a lapse of a hundred and twenty years. Moreover, an act was passed granting him immunity for all his past acts, and for the future, power of life and death, of confiscation, of colonization, of founding or demolishing cities, and of taking away or bestowing kingdoms at his pleasure. [2] He conducted the sales of confiscated estates in such arrogant and imperious fashion, from the tribunal where he sat, that his gifts excited more odium than his robberies. He bestowed on handsome women, musicians, comic actors, and the lowest of freedmen [*katharmasin*], the territories of nations and the revenues of cities, and women were married against their will to some of his favorites.[19]

Tzetzes, *Chiliades* 8.905–910

Ὁ φαρμακὸς τὸ κάθαρμα τοιόνδε τι ὑπῆρχε·
τὸν πάντων δυσμορφότατον καύσαντες—ὥσπερ εἶπον—
εἰς καθαρμὸν τῆς πόλεως ἐν συμφοραῖς μεγίσταις,
τὴν τέφραν ἔρραινον αὐτοῦ πάσῃ σχεδὸν τῇ πόλει.
Τοῦτο μὲν οὖν τὸ κάθαρμα πρὶν φαρμακὸν ἐκάλουν.
Ὁ φαρμακεὺς ὁ χρώμενος φαρμάκοις εἰς τὸ κτείνειν.[20]

The scapegoat [*pharmakos*] was the purification [*to katharma*] in his fashion.
After they had burnt the ugliest man of all—as I said earlier—for the purification of the city during the greatest disasters,
they sprinkled [*errainon*] his ash throughout nearly the whole city.

Therefore they called this rite purification [*katharma*] before scapegoat
[*pharmakos*].
The poisoner [*pharmakeus*] was he who used drugs to kill.[21]

Photius (s.v. περίψημα)

οὕτως ἐπέλεγον τῷ κατ᾽ ἐνιαυτὸν ἐμβαλλομένῳ τῇ θαλάσσῃ νεανίᾳ ἐπ᾽ ἀπαλλαγῇ
τῶν συνεχόντων κακῶν· περίψημα ἡμῶν γενοῦ· ἤτοι σωτηρία καὶ ἀπολύτρωσις·
καὶ οὕτως ἐνέβαλον τῇ θαλάσσῃ, ὡσανεὶ τῷ Ποσειδῶνι θυσίαν ἀποτιννύντες.[22]

Thus they would say over the youth who was thrown each year into the sea
for the release from the oppressing ills: 'May you be our *peripsēma*.' Either
deliverance or redemption. And thus they would throw him into the sea, as
if paying a sacrifice to Poseidon.[23]

Notes

Preface

1. Bradley McLean, "On the Revision of Scapegoat Terminology," *Numen* 37, no. 2 (1990), 168.

2. McLean, "Revision of Scapegoat Terminology," 169.

3. McLean, "Revision of Scapegoat Terminology," 169.

4. McLean, "Revision of Scapegoat Terminology," 169.

5. McLean, "Revision of Scapegoat Terminology," 169.

6. B. Hudson McLean, *The Cursed Christ: Mediterranean Expulsion Rituals and Pauline Soteriology* (Sheffield, England: Sheffield Academic Press, 1996), 66.

7. McLean, *The Cursed Christ*, 65.

8. McLean, *The Cursed Christ*, 70.

9. Mary Douglas, "The Go-Away Goat," in *The Book of Leviticus: Composition and Reception*, vol. 3, ed. Rolf Rendtorff, Robert A. Kugler, and Sarah Smith Bartel (Leiden, Netherlands: Koninklijke Brill, 2003), 121.

10. Douglas, "The Go-Away Goat," 122.

11. Douglas, "The Go-Away Goat," 124.

12. Douglas, "The Go-Away Goat," 125.

13. Douglas, "The Go-Away Goat," 121.

14. Douglas, "The Go-Away Goat," 121.

15. Douglas, "The Go-Away Goat," 124.

16. D. J. Stökl is even more combative. Like McLean and Douglas, he deplores the term's generalized use, and he is similarly no fan of Girard's: "The sacrificial theory of René Girard, presented in his books *La violence et le sacré* and *Le bouc émissaire*, has been a focus of attention, whether one agrees with his main theory, an amplification of the Freudian myth, or not. He surveys various

rituals in various places and at various times that treat a victim similar to the Levitical scapegoat and with a similar atoning function. In the book of Leviticus, however, it is very clear that the ritual refers not to a human being but to an animal, a goat. Strangely enough, most of Girard's scapegoats are not animals but *human* beings. Girard might have supposed that the appellation 'scapegoat' would be more easily understood by a modern Western audience than for example the Greek term *pharmakos*, which *is* concerned with human victims. He could be reasonably sure that the subsumption of human sacrifices under the scapegoat ritual would be acceptable to his readers, because 'scapegoat' has become a fixed term in Western thought. But since when? Given that Girard's central chapter talks about Jesus as scapegoat, one would expect that the analogy between the death of a human being (Jesus) and the scapegoat ritual was first drawn in the New Testament and through this entered the Western *imaginaire*, its collective repertoire of motifs. However, as is well known, the Christian canon does *not* refer to Jesus as scapegoat. When and how did the scapegoat enter the Western *imaginaire* as a category connoting a type of *human* atonement sacrifice, if not in the New Testament?" "The Christian Exegesis of the Scapegoat between Jews and Christians," in *Sacrifice in Religious Experience*, ed. Albert I. Baumgarten (Leiden, Netherlands: Koninklijke Brill, 2002), 208. This assessment is clearly more astute and Stökl deserves credit for seeing that Girard is only the inheritor of a term whose semantic field was staked out long before he began theorizing. He is, moreover, asking the highly pertinent question: when indeed and how did the term first acquire its generalized usage? The real culprits, according to Stökl, are the early Christian writers who, motivated by rivalry with Jewish tradition, pulled the "scapegoat" up by its biblical roots and bequeathed it to modern theorists in all its henceforth flaccid referentiality. It is "because of the Church Fathers," he says, "[that] we consider in a single category the different phenomena *pharmakos*, Jesus' self-sacrifice, and scapegoat rituals." The tendency of religious studies people to compare these phenomena "without referring to the crucial difference between goat and man" begins with them. If the term "scapegoat" is widely deployed today to denote "a type of *human* atonement sacrifice," Girard comes by this usage honestly enough. "*Pharmakos* would have been a more reasonable title for Girard's book," Stökl offers, "were not the 'scapegoat' the central term in our—i.e. the modern Western—*imaginaire* as a result of the Church Fathers' propaganda." Stökl's formidable dissertation furnishes a compendious list of early Christian exegetes writing on the scapegoat, but the article from which the above comments were taken seriously overstates their influence on the word's meaning and use today, something only a careful analysis of the relevant texts will allow us to see. Stökl, "Christian Exegesis of the Scapegoat," 228.

17. David L. Jeffrey, *A Dictionary of Biblical Tradition in English Literature* (Grand Rapids, MI: Eerdmans, 1992), 684.

18. Abbe Raynal, *A Philosophical and Political History of the Settlements and Trade of the Europeans in the East and West Indies. Revised, Augmented, and Published, in Ten Volumes, by the Abbé Raynal. Newly Translated from the French, by J. O. Justamond, F.R.S. with a New Set of Maps Adapted to the Work, and a Copious Index. in Eight Volumes*, vol. 1 (London, 1783), 86.

19. René Girard, *The Scapegoat*, trans. Yvonne Freccero (Baltimore, MD: Johns Hopkins University Press, 1986), 40.

20. Girard, *The Scapegoat*, 40.

21. Girard, *The Scapegoat*, 41.

22. Girard, *The Scapegoat*, 41.

23. René Girard, Jean-Michel Oughourlian, Guy Lefort, Stephen Bann, and Michael Leigh Metteer, *Things Hidden since the Foundation of the World* (Stanford, CA: Stanford University Press, 1987), 131–132.

24. Girard, *The Scapegoat*, 120.

25. We should note here the first in a number of conceptual oppositions (deliberate/rigidly

formalized—spontaneous/unconscious) by which the secret action of the scapegoat as a constitutive principle may be glimpsed. A structuralist intuition for the antinomies it generates (which recall Lévi-Strauss's *mana* and Derrida's *pharmakon*) proves helpful for making sense of the long history under review in this monograph.

26. René Girard and Michael Hardin, *Reading the Bible with René Girard: Conversations with Steven E. Berry* (Unpublished manuscript, 2011), 42.

27. Girard et al., *Things Hidden*, 132.

28. Theodore Adorno, 1950, quoted in the *Oxford English Dictionary* (1989), 582.

29. Zhufeng Luo, "Han yu da ci dian bian ji wei yuan hui" and "Han yu da ci dian bian zuan chu," in *Hanyu Da Cidian*, 1st ban ed., vol. 8 (Shanghai: Cishu chubanshe, 1990), 755.

30. Jan N. Bremmer, *Greek Religion and Culture, the Bible, and the Ancient Near East* (Leiden, Netherlands: Koninklijke Brill, 2008), 175.

Chapter 1. Rites of Riddance and Substitution

1. William Tyndale, [*The Pentateuch*] (Malborow in the lande of Hesse [i.e., Antwerp]: By me Hans Luft [i.e. Johan Hoochstraten], 1530), 29.

2. Aron Pinker, "A Goat to Go to Azazel," *Journal of Hebrew Scriptures* 7 (2007): 12.

3. Erhard Gerstenberger, *Leviticus: A Commentary*, 1st American ed. (Louisville, KY: Westminster John Knox Press, 1996), 219–220. The official placement of the goat recalls the prescriptions for stolen goods recovered (Josh. 7:23), and a wife suspected of infidelity (Num. 5:16).

4. Gordon J. Wenham, *The Book of Leviticus*, vol. 3 (Grand Rapids, MI: Eerdmans, 1979), 233. Wright notes that if the immolated goat "remove[s] impurity from the sanctuary, the scapegoat rite serves to eliminate the transgressions of the people." The relationship "of these two evils to one another is observed in the Priestly conception that the sin of an Israelite causes impurity to become attached to the sanctuary. . . . The blood rite removes the impurities caused by the people's sins, and the scapegoat rite removes the sins themselves—the cause of the impurity." David P. Wright, *The Disposal of Impurity: Elimination Rites in the Bible and in Hittite and Mesopotamian Literature* (Atlanta, GA: Scholars Press, 1987), 18–19.

5. Jacob Neusner, *The Mishnah: A New Translation* (New Haven, CT: Yale University Press, 1988), 275. Grabbe translates a relevant portion of the Targum Pseudo-Jonahthan: "And he shall send (the goat) by a man previously appointed, to lead (it) to the rugged wilderness which is Bet Haduri. . . . And the goat will ascend the mountains of Bet Haduri . . . and a blast of wind from before the Lord will blow it down so that it dies." Lester L. Grabbe, "The Scapegoat Tradition: A Study in Early Jewish Interpretation," *Journal for the Study of Judaism in the Persian, Hellenistic and Roman Period* 18, no. 2 (1987): 159.

6. Wright, *The Disposal of Impurity*, 50–51.

7. Bremmer, *Greek Religion and Culture*, 171–172.

8. Wright, *The Disposal of Impurity*, 49.

9. Wright, *The Disposal of Impurity*, 49.

10. Wright, *The Disposal of Impurity*, 153.

11. Jacob Milgrom, *Leviticus: A Book of Ritual and Ethics; A Continental Commentary* (Minneapolis: Fortress Press, 2004), 166.

12. Milgrom, *Leviticus: A Book of Ritual*, 168. Wright notes that "Azazel should be viewed as a demon, as the etymology of the name suggests, but perhaps as an inactive one with no real role to play in the rite except to indicate the place to which the sins are dispatched. This view of Azazel is

corroborated by the fact that the scapegoat is not an offering to him ... the goat is not sacrificed to Azazel; it is merely sent to him." Wright, *The Disposal of Impurity*, 24.

13. Milgrom, *Leviticus: A Book of Ritual*, 168–169.

14. In a few late Jewish commentators the scapegoat is plainly a tribute paid to induce the Accuser of Israel to speak favorably instead (see *Pirke De-Rabbi Eliezer*). Nachmanides (Rambam) writes, "Now the Torah has absolutely forbidden to accept them (angels) as deities, or to worship them in any manner. However, the Holy One, blessed be He, commands us that on the Day of Atonement we should let loose a goat in the wilderness, to that 'prince,' which rules over wastelands, and this (goat) is fitting for it because he is its master, and destruction and waste emanate from his power, which in turn is the cause of the stars of the sword, wars, quarrels, wounds, plagues, division and destruction.... Also in his portion are the devils called 'destroyers' in the language of our Rabbis, and in the language of our Scriptures 'satyrs (demons).'" Pinker, "A Goat to Azazel," 6. Pinker notes that "in Nachmanides' view Azazel is the angel Samael or Satan, one of God's servants, to whom God commands to give a portion of God's own sacrifice. Samael gets a bribe ... that he might not annul the effect of Israel's offerings." Pinker, "A Goat to Azazel," 6. The Zohar makes the scapegoat a figure of he "whose office it is to spy out the earth for those who transgress the commands of the law" and under whose control are "many demons": "When that he-goat reaches the rock (of Azazel) there is great rejoicing and the emissary who went forth to accuse returns and declares the praises of Israel, the accuser becoming the defender." Harry Sperling, Maurice Simon, and Paul P. Levertoff, *The Zohar*, 2nd ed., vol. 5 (New York: Soncino Press, 1984), 51.

15. Milgrom, *Leviticus: A Book of Ritual*, 168.

16. Milgrom, *Leviticus: A Book of Ritual*, 169.

17. David P. Wright, "The Gesture of Hand Placement in the Hebrew Bible and in Hittite Literature," *Journal of the American Oriental Society* 106 (1986): 436.

18. Wright, "Gesture of Hand Placement," 434.

19. Wright, "The Gesture of Hand Placement," 434.

20. Wright, "The Gesture of Hand Placement," 436.

21. Wright, "The Gesture of Hand Placement," 436.

22. Pinker, "A Goat to Go to Azazel," 9.

23. Wenham, *The Book of Leviticus*, 234–235.

24. Pinker, "A Goat to Azazel," 9.

25. Pinker, "A Goat to Azazel," 6.

26. Pinker, "A Goat to Azazel," 6.

27. Jacob Milgrom, *Leviticus 1–16: A New Translation with Introduction and Commentary* (New York: Doubleday, 1991), 1020.

28. 1 Enoch 6:1–2, in Matthew Black, James C. VanderKam, and O. Neugebauer, *The Book of Enoch, Or, I Enoch: A New English Edition with Commentary and Textual Notes* (Leiden, Netherlands: E. J. Brill, 1985), 28.

29. Genesis 6:1–8: "Now it came about, when men began to multiply on the face of the land, and daughters were born to them, that the sons of God saw that the daughters of men were beautiful; and they took wives for themselves, whomever they chose. Then the Lord said, 'My Spirit shall not strive with man forever, because he also is flesh; nevertheless his days shall be one hundred and twenty years.' The Nephilim were on the earth in those days, and also afterward, when the sons of God came in to the daughters of men, and they bore *children* to them. Those were the mighty men who *were* of old, men of renown. Then the Lord saw that the wickedness of man was great on the

earth, and that every intent of the thoughts of his heart was only evil continually. And the Lord was sorry that He had made man on the earth, and He was grieved in His heart. And the Lord said, "I will blot out man whom I have created from the face of the land, from man to animals to creeping things and to birds of the sky; for I am sorry that I have made them.' But Noah found favor in the eyes of the Lord."

30. 1 Enoch 9:8–9, in Black, VanderKam, and Neugebauer, *The Book of Enoch*, 30.

31. 1 Enoch 7:2–5, in Black, VanderKam, and Neugebauer, *The Book of Enoch*, 28.

32. 1 Enoch 10:2, in Black, VanderKam, and Neugebauer, *The Book of Enoch*, 30.

33. 1 Enoch 10:4, in Black, VanderKam, and Neugebauer, *The Book of Enoch*, 30.

34. Grabbe notes: "The name Asael . . . is of course not the same as Azazel . . . of Lev. 16, 8.10.26. However, there are a number of parallels between the Asael narrative in 1 Enoch and the wording of Leviticus 16 which ancient interpreters were not likely to overlook: the similarity of the names Asael, and Azazel; the punishment in the desert; the placing of sin on Asael/Azazel; the resultant healing of the land." Grabbe, "The Scapegoat Tradition," 153.

35. 1 Enoch 8:1–2, in Black, VanderKam, and Neugebauer, *The Book of Enoch*, 28–29.

36. 1 Enoch 10:4, in Black, VanderKam, and Neugebauer, *The Book of Enoch*, 30.

37. 1 Enoch 10:5, in Black, VanderKam, and Neugebauer, *The Book of Enoch*, 30.

38. Milgrom, *Leviticus 1–16*, 1021.

39. 1 Enoch 10:5–6, in Black, VanderKam, and Neugebauer, *The Book of Enoch*, 30.

40. 1 Enoch 10:8, in Black, VanderKam, and Neugebauer, *The Book of Enoch*, 30.

41. G. H. Box and J. I. Landsman, *The Apocalypse of Abraham* (New York: Macmillan, 1919), 51. The passage reworks the covenant sacrifice of Genesis 15:10–21.

42. See also Isaiah 13:21, Baruch 4:35, Tobit 8:3, Matthew 12:34, Luke 11:24, and Revelation 18:12.

43. W. F. Albright, "The High Place in Ancient Palestine," *Vetus Testamentum Supplement* 4 (1956): 246n.

44. Ida Zatelli, "The Origin of the Biblical Scapegoat Ritual: The Evidence of Two Eblaite Texts," *Vetus Testamentum* 48, no. 2 (1998): 262–263. Milgrom notes that the scapegoat "is in reality returning evil to its source, the netherworld." Milgrom, *Leviticus 1–16*, 1021.

45. Daniel Stökl Ben Ezra, *The Impact of Yom Kippur on Early Christianity: The Day of Atonement from Second Temple Judaism to the Fifth Century* (Tübingen, Germany: Mohr Siebeck, 2003), 89.

46. Grabbe, "The Scapegoat Tradition," 167.

47. "The scapegoat must remain in the wilderness, dead or alive; under no circumstances is it permitted to return to the human society that has sent it out. Later generations saw to it that the scapegoat was guaranteed not to return; they had a non-Jew, if possible, push the animal into a ravine, where it broke its neck" (Gerstenberger, *Leviticus*, 221).

Chapter 2. Ancient Types and Soteriologies

1. Eleonore Stump, *Aquinas* (New York: Routledge, 2003), 427.

2. See also, Acts 26:17b–18: "I am sending you, to open their eyes so that they may turn from darkness to light and from the dominion of Satan to God, in order that they may receive forgiveness of sins and an inheritance among those who have been sanctified by faith in Me."

3. Paul puts the same expression in close proximity to the juridical language of Romans 3, where sinners are "justified as a gift by His grace through the redemption (*apolutrōsis*) which is in Christ

Jesus" (3:24) and the author of Hebrews gives the metaphor a cultic inflection when he writes that Jesus "is the mediator of a new covenant, in order that since a death has taken place for the redemption (*apolutrōsis*) of the transgressions that were committed under the first covenant, those who have been called may receive the promise of the eternal inheritance" (9:15).

4. The nineteenth-century historiographies failed to register this; Pelikan notes: "so great was [the emphasis on the saving significance of the resurrection of Christ] in the soteriology of many church fathers that the definition of salvation through Christ's victory over man's enemies has been called 'the classic' theory of the atonement. To be sure, other ways of speaking about the atonement were too widespread even among the Greek fathers to permit us to ascribe exclusive or even primary force to any one theory, but Christ as victor was more important in orthodox expositions of salvation and reconciliation than Western dogmatics has recognized." Jaroslav Pelikan, *The Christian Tradition: A History of the Development of Doctrine* (Chicago: University of Chicago Press, 1971), 1:149.

5. *Second Apology* 5, in Alexander Roberts, James Donaldson, and A. Cleveland Coxe, *The Ante-Nicene Fathers: Translations of the Writings of the Fathers Down to A.D. 325*, reprint of the Edinburgh ed. (Grand Rapids, MI: Eerdmanns, 1986), 1:190.

6. Justin Martyr, *Second Apology* 5, in Roberts, Donaldson, and Coxe, *The Ante-Nicene Fathers*, 1:190.

7. Justin Martyr, *Second Apology* 5, in Roberts, Donaldson, and Coxe, *The Ante-Nicene Fathers*, 1:190.

8. Justin Martyr, *Second Apology* 5, in Roberts, Donaldson, and Coxe, *The Ante-Nicene Fathers*, 1:190.

9. Justin Martyr, *Second Apology* 13, in Roberts, Donaldson, and Coxe, *The Ante-Nicene Fathers*, 1:193.

10. Justin Martyr, *Dialogue with Trypho*, in Roberts, Donaldson, and Coxe, *The Ante-Nicene Fathers*, 1:134. To this he adds that Christ "rose from the dead . . . the chief of another race regenerated by Himself" (138). Irenaeus will push the implications of Justin's language, developing the first fully-fledged Christian theory of the atonement according to which "the only true and steadfast Teacher, the Word of God, our Lord Jesus Christ . . . did, through his transcendent love, become what we are, that He might bring us to be even what He is Himself." Irenaeus, *Against Heresies* V, pref., in Roberts, Donaldson, and Coxe, *The Ante-Nicene Fathers*, 1:527. Another Eastern father—Athanasius—would say rather more famously: "For He was made man that we might be made God," "On the Incarnation of the Word," in *A Select Library of Nicene and Post-Nicene Fathers of the Christian Church*, 2nd series, ed. Philip Schaff and Henry Wace (Grand Rapids, MI: Eerdmanns, 1978), 4:65. Irenaeus writes that Christ as the second Adam "recapitulated in Himself the long sequence of mankind," restoring through his obedience all that humankind lost in Adam's rebellion. Irenaeus, *Against Heresies* 3, 22, 2, quoted in J. N. D. Kelly, *Early Christian Doctrines*, 5th ed. (San Francisco: Harper & Row, 1978), 173. "For doing away with [the effects of] that disobedience of man which had taken place at the beginning by the occasion of a tree, 'He became obedient unto death, even the death of the cross' [Phil. 2:8]; rectifying that disobedience which had occurred by reason of a tree, through that obedience which was [wrought out] upon the tree [of the cross]." Irenaeus, *Against Heresies* 5, 16, 3, in Roberts, Donaldson, and Coxe, *The Ante-Nicene Fathers*, 1:544. In consenting to be born, live, and die Christ sanctifies every stage of human life, "perfecting man after the image and likeness of God." Irenaeus, *Against Heresies* 5, 21, 2, in Roberts, Donaldson, and Coxe, *The Ante-Nicene Fathers*, 1:549; His resurrection from the dead makes immortal all who live through him. Irenaeus writes: "And then, again, this Word was manifested when the Word of God was made man, assimilating Himself to man, and man to Himself, so that by means of his resemblance to the Son, man might become precious to the Father. For in times long past, it was *said* that man was created after the image of God, but it was not [actually] *shown*; for the Word was as yet invisible, after whose image man was created. Wherefore also he did easily lose the similitude. When, however, the Word of God became flesh, He confirmed both these: for He both showed forth the image truly, since He became Himself

what was His image; and He re-established the similitude after a sure manner, by assimilating man to the invisible Father through means of the visible Word. Irenaeus, *Against Heresies* 5, 16, 2, in Roberts, Donaldson, and Coxe, *The Ante-Nicene Fathers*, 1:544.

11. Irenaeus, *Against Heresies* 5, 21, 3, in Roberts, Donaldson, and Coxe, *The Ante-Nicene Fathers*, 1:550.

12. Irenaeus, *Against Heresies* 5, 1, 1, in Roberts, Donaldson, and Coxe, *The Ante-Nicene Fathers*, 1:527; Pelikan notes that "Because of the prominence of demonology in Christian piety and theology, the Christian thinkers who dealt with the idea of ransom usually took it to be a ransom paid to the devil to set man free. Irenaeus does not seem to have had this conception in mind in his exposition of the idea of ransom, but Origen clearly did." Pelikan, *The Christian Tradition*, 1:148.

13. Pelikan, *The Christian Tradition*, 1:147.

14. Henry Scowcroft Bettenson, *The Later Christian Fathers: A Selection from the Writings of the Fathers from St. Cyril of Jerusalem to St. Leo the Great* (New York: Oxford University Press, 1970), 141–142.

15. Irenaeus, *Against Heresies* 5, 1, 3, in Roberts, Donaldson, and Coxe, *The Ante-Nicene Fathers*, 1:527.

16. Gregory of Nyssa, in Bettenson, *The Later Christian Fathers*, 141.

17. Gregory of Nyssa, *The Great Catechism*, 23, in Schaff and Wace, *Select Library*, 2nd series, 5:493.

18. Augustine, *On the Holy Trinity* 13.13.17, in *A Select Library of the Nicene and Post-Nicene Fathers of the Christian Church*, 1st series, ed. Philip Schaff (Grand Rapids, MI: Eerdmanns, 1978), 3:176.

19. Gregory of Nyssa, in Bettenson, *The Later Christian Fathers*, 141.

20. Gregory of Nyssa, in Bettenson, *The Later Christian Fathers*, 142.

21. Aulén notes, "The fact that these descriptions in the Fathers of an orderly, legal process alternate so strangely with those of the devil's deception is enough to show that there is no intention of comprehending the Divine action within a legal scheme . . . in the *Fathers* the essential idea which the legal language is intended to express is that God's dealings even with the powers of evil have the character of 'fair play.'" Gustaf Aulén, *Christus Victor: An Historical Study of the Three Main Types of the Idea of Atonement*, trans. A. G. Hebert (New York: Macmillan, 1951), 54.

22. Gregory of Nyssa, in Bettenson, *The Later Christian Fathers*, 141–142.

23. Ambrose on Psalm 56:7 ("they have fallen into the pit they dug for me"): "This trick had to be practiced on the Devil, by the taking of a body by the Lord Jesus; and the taking of a body that was corruptible and weak; so that it might be crucified, because of its weakness." *Exposition of the Gospel of Luke* 4:12, in Bettenson, *The Later Christian Fathers*, 180–181.

24. Cyril of Alexandria, *Exposition from the Gospel of John* 1:29, in Bettenson, *The Later Christian Fathers*, 264.

25. Aulén, *Christus Victor*, 4–5.

26. Aulén, *Christus Victor*, 56.

27. Aulén, *Christus Victor*, 58.

28. "A passage which is perhaps more often quoted by the Fathers than any other New Testament text." Aulén, *Christus Victor*, 74.

29. Aulén, *Christus Victor*, 59.

30. Aulén, *Christus Victor*, 78.

31. Cyril of Alexandria, *On Worship in Spirit and Truth*, 3, in Bettenson, *The Later Christian Fathers*, 265.

32. Peter's first epistle incorporates its language: "For you have been called for this purpose, since

Christ also suffered for you, leaving you an example for you to follow in His steps, who committed no sin, nor was any deceit found in His mouth; and while being reviled, He did not revile in return; while suffering, He uttered no threats, but kept entrusting Himself to Him who judges righteously; and He Himself bore our sins in His body on the cross, that we might die to sin and live to righteousness; for by His wounds you were healed. For you were continually straying like sheep, but now you have returned to the Shepherd and Guardian of your souls" (2:21–25).

33. Zodhiates defines *chāphēts*: "to find pleasure in, to take delight in, to be pleased with, to have an affection for, to desire, to choose, to bend, to bow. The main meaning is to feel a strong positive attraction for something. Unlike other synonyms for this emotion, this word connotes subjective involvement. . . . It means to like someone or something very, very much." Spiros Zodhiates, *The Hebrew-Greek Key Study Bible: King James Version, the Old Testament, the New Testament: Zodhiates' Original and Complete System of Bible Study* (Iowa Falls, IA: World Bible Publishers; Chattanooga, TN: AMG Publishers, 1984), 1727.

34. Pelikan notes that "Tertullian's doctrine of 'satisfaction' may have come from Roman private law, where it referred to the amends one made to another for failing to discharge an obligation, or from Roman public law, which enabled the term to be interpreted as a form of punishment." Pelikan, *The Christian Tradition*, 1:147.

35. Tertullian, *On Penitence* 5, in Roberts, Donaldson, and Coxe, *The Ante-Nicene Fathers*, 3:660.

36. Tertullian, *On Penitence* 6, Roberts, Donaldson, and Coxe, *The Ante-Nicene Fathers*, 3:661.

37. Mark J. Boda and Gordon T. Smith, *Repentance in Christian Theology* (Collegeville, MN: Liturgical Press, 2006), 159–160. "In his approach to penance Tertullian availed himself of the basic principles of the theory of recapitulation advanced by Irenaeus of Lyons . . . [and] conceived of the death of Christ as a way of obtaining remission of the sins of Adam and of all subsequent human beings by means of compensation. In Tertullian's view the sinner owed satisfaction to God's justice. Repentance was to become the mechanism that achieved the effect of compensation. Tertullian conceived of the death of Christ as a way of obtaining remission of the sins of Adam and of all subsequent human beings by means of compensation. Boda and Smith, *Repentance in Christian Theology*, 159.

38. Tertullian, *On Penitence* 9, in *Treatises on Penance: On Penitence and on Purity*, trans. William P. Le Saint (Westminster, MD: Newman Press, 1959), 31.

39. Tertullian, *On Penitence* 9, in *Treatises on Penance*, 31.

40. Tertuallian, *On Penitence* 9, in *Treatises on Penance*, 31–32.

41. Tertullian, *On Penitence* 2, in *Treatises on Penance*, 17.

42. Tertullian, *On Penitance* 2, in *Treatises on Penance*, 17.

43. Tertullian, *On Exhortation to Chastity* 2, in Roberts, Donaldson, and Coxe, *The Ante-Nicene Fathers*, 4:51. Then again, "unless you [pursue that which He *more* wills] you savour of contrariety to His *superior* volition; and you rather offend than merit reward, by doing what He wills indeed and rejecting what He *more* wills. Partly, you sin; partly, if you sin not, still you deserve no reward. Moreover, is not even the unwillingness to deserve reward a sin?" Tertuallian, *On Exhortation to Chastity* 2, in Roberts, Donaldson and Coxe, *The Ante-Nicene Fathers*, 4:51.

44. Tertullian, *On Exhortation to Chastity* 2, in Roberts, Donaldson, and Coxe, *The Ante-Nicene Fathers*, 4:51–52.

45. One of the issues of Cyprian's day was the readmission of Christians who lapsed during persecution, some of whom obtained "certificates" (*libellus pacis*) from the martyrs urging mercy. "We believe, indeed, that the merits of martyrs and the works of the righteous are of great avail with the Judge," Cyprian writes. Cyprian, *On the Lapsed* 17, in Roberts, Donaldson, and Coxe, *The*

Ante-Nicene Fathers, 5:442. He must, however, beseech "the martyrs and confessors who sought that peace should be granted to the lapsed" to "designate those by name to whom you desire that peace should be granted" in order to prevent abuses whereby vaguely worded certificates might like blank checks be misused to readmit others: "For it opens a wide door to say, 'Such a one with his friends': and twenty or thirty or more, may be presented to us, who may be asserted to be neighbours and connections, and freedmen and servants, of the man who receives the certificate." Cyprian, *Epistle 10*, 4, in Roberts, Donaldson, and Coxe, *The Ante-Nicene Fathers*, 5:291. He instructs the clergy "that they who have received a certificate from the martyrs and can be assisted by their help with the Lord in respect of their sins . . . should be remitted to the Lord with the peace promised to them by the martyrs," whereas "others who, without having received any certificate from the martyrs . . . must wait, in dependence on the protection of the Lord, for the public peace of the Church itself." Cyprian, *Epistle 13*, 2, in Roberts, Donaldson, and Coxe, *The Ante-Nicene Fathers*, 5:293–294.

46. "According to Catholic doctrine, God chooses to reward acts of supererogation with the gift of greater merit than the agent requires for salvation. This surplus merit is stored in the 'Treasury of the Saints,' owned by the Church, and available to be drawn on by others. This notion of 'congruent merit' or freely-given and transferable reward provided the theological underpinnings for, among other things, the practice of granting indulgences, or the cancelling of another's punishment for some or all of their sins." Edward Craig, ed., *Routledge Encyclopedia of Philosophy* (New York: Routledge, 1998), 1:232.

47. Aulén, *Christus Victor*, 128.

48. Kelly, *Early Christian Doctrines*, 71.

49. James Carleton Paget, "The Epistle of Barnabas," *Expository Times* 117, no. 11 (2006): 442–443.

50. *Epistle of Barnabas*, 7 in *Early Christian Writings: The Apostolic Fathers*, trans. Maxwell Staniforth (New York: Dorset Press, 1986), 167–168. This portion is prefaced by mention of a goat whose "inwards, unwashed with vinegar" were to be eaten by the priests, signifying the flesh of Christ offered for the sins of the people—a possibly confused reference to "a third goat offered for a sin-offering the portions of which were not to be eaten on the fast day but in the evening after its completion"; Grabbe, "The Scapegoat Tradition," 163. Grabbe mentions Numbers 29:11, and the Mishnah Yoma in this connection. See also Mishnah Menahoth 11:7, which states: "If the Day of Atonement fell on a Sabbath the loaves were shared out at evening. If it fell on a Friday the he-goat of the Day of Atonement was consumed at evening. The Babylonians used to eat it raw since they were not squeamish." Herbert Danby, trans., *The Mishnah* (Oxford: Clarendon Press, 1933), 509.

51. Justin Martyr, *Dialogue with Trypho*, 40, in *The Proof from Prophecy: A Study in Justin Martyr's Proof-Text Tradition: Text-Type, Provenance, Theological Profile*, ed. Oskar Skarsaune (Leiden, Netherlands: E. J. Brill, 1987), 310.

52. Justin Martyr, *Dialogue with Trypho*, 40, in *The Proof from Prophecy*, 310. Stökl notes: "Justin explicitly interprets the theological implications of the sacrificial goat typology of Christ as a vicarious atonement for all sinners. This is somewhat strange considering the association of the scapegoat, not the sacrificial goat, with the Passion." Stökl Ben Ezra, *The Impact of Yom Kippur on Early Christianity: The Day of Atonement from Second Temple Judaism to the Fifth Century*, 156.

53. Tertullian, *Against Marcion*, 3.7, in Roberts, Donaldson and Coxe, *The Ante-Nicene Fathers*, 3:327. Tertullian's *Against the Jews* contains a nearly identical passage.

54. Jennifer K. Berenson Maclean, "Barabbas, the Scapegoat Ritual, and the Development of the Passion Narrative," *Harvard Theological Review* 100, no. 3 (2007): 318–319.

55. Maclean, "Barabbas," 319; Tertullian develops the type of the immolated goat as consumed by the church for an image of the Second Parousia as eschatological feast. But this reading more nearly

interprets that third goat consumed by the priests of the temple, with which the immolated goat has obviously been conflated.

56. A fragment in the Catenae on Proverbs with Hippolytus's interpretation of Proverbs 30:3 assimilates the two goats: "*And a goat as leader of the flock* / Since, it says, this is / who was slaughtered for the sins of the world / and offered as a sacrifice / and sent away to the Gentiles as in the desert / and crowned with scarlet wool on the head by the unbelievers / and made to be a ransom for the humans / and manifested as life for all" (Stökl Ben Ezra, *Impact of Yom Kippur*, 158). It is striking that the one extrabiblical detail retained by Hippolytus—in which both Barnabas and Tertullian recognized a sign of Christ's Passion—becomes a type of Christ's coronation by the Gentiles. A wide variety of later sources interpret the scapegoat in a similarly triumphal mode. Many more exploit the pecuniary metaphor of Christ's "ransom for all," which, however, tends henceforth to be tied with the immolated goat.

Chapter 3. The Sulfurous and Sublime

1. Origen, *Against Celsus* V, 43 in Roberts, Donaldson, and Coxe, *The Ante-Nicene Fathers*, 4:592–593.

2. Origen, *Against Celsus* V, 43, in Roberts, Donaldson, and Coxe, *The Ante-Nicene Fathers*, 4:592–593. What Origen has in mind by "an expiatory sacrifice" is hardly clear given the scapegoat's identification with the Devil as perhaps here too with his followers. But in another typology taken from his ninth homily on Leviticus he explains that "if all the people of God were holy and all were blessed, there would not be two lots for the he-goats, one lot to be sent 'into the wilderness,' the other offered to God, but there would be one lot and one offering to the Lord alone." He adds that all those found in "the lot of the scapegoat" are sent "into the wilderness," taking "upon their heads the sins of those who have repented," having "made themselves worthy of such a ministry." This sin-bearing in behalf of the repented by the carnal is even referred to Christ's words in Luke 19: 26—"I tell you, to everyone who has will be given more; but anyone who has not will be deprived even of what he has"—the usual sense of which has been neatly inverted. The immolated goat is likened to those deemed worthy to die as martyrs, whereas he who belongs to the scapegoat's lot is "not worthy . . . to be slain at the altar of God nor is his blood fit to be poured out 'at the base of the altar." It is striking that these first extended claims about the scapegoat's errand feature the vicarious sin-bearing of bad Christians whose "end . . . is 'the wilderness,' that is, a desolate place—desolate of virtues, desolate of God, desolate of justice, desolate of Christ, desolate of all good." Origen, *Homilies on Leviticus: 1–16*, trans. Gary Wayne Barkley (Washington, DC: Catholic University of America Press, 1990), 181–182.

3. Origen, *Homilies on Leviticus*, 184.

4. Origen, *Homilies on Leviticus*, 185; "How the Devil was crucified on two-fold wood is worth the trouble to learn. The cross of our Lord Jesus Christ was twofold. Perhaps to you it seems an astonishing and novel word that I say, 'The cross was twofold,' that is, it is twofold and for a double reason. For the Son of God was indeed visibly crucified in the flesh, but invisibly on that cross the Devil 'with his principalities and authorities was affixed to the cross' [Col. 2:14–15]. . . . Therefore, there is a double reason for the cross of the Lord: the one, by which the apostle Peter says that Christ crucified leaves behind an example for us [1 Pet. 2:21], and this second one, by which the cross was a token of victory over the Devil, on which he was both crucified and triumphed. Origen, *Homilies on Joshua*, trans. Barbara J. Bruce and ed. Cynthia White (Washington, DC: Catholic University of America Press, 2002), 87–88.

5. "Let us also now attempt to add something to what was said long ago to the best of our ability, that we may show how 'as a type of things to come' this one he-goat was sacrificed to the Lord as an offering and the other one was sent away 'living.' Hear in the Gospels what Pilate said to the

priests and the Jewish people: 'Which of these two do you want me to send out to you, Jesus, who is called the Christ, or Barabbas?' Then all the people cried out to release Barabbas but to hand Jesus over to be killed. Behold, you have a he-goat who was sent 'living into the wilderness,' bearing with him the sins of the people who cried out and said, 'Crucify, crucify.' Therefore, the former is a he-goat sent 'living into the wilderness' and the latter is the he-goat which was offered to God as an offering to atone for sins and he made a true atonement for those people who believe in him. But if you ask who it is who led this he-goat 'into the wilderness' to verify that he also was washed and made clean, Pilate himself can be taken as 'a prepared man.'" Origen, *Homilies on Leviticus*, 204–205.

6. Origen, *Homilies on Leviticus*, 187.

7. Origen, *Commentary on Matthew*, 14, 19, in Roberts, Donaldson, and Coxe, *The Ante-Nicene Fathers*, 9:508.

8. Jerome, *Homilies of Saint Jerome*, trans. Marie Liguori Ewald (Washington, DC: Catholic University of America Press, 1966), 249.

9. Ambrose, *Letter to Simplicianus* 13, in *A Library of Fathers of the Holy Catholic Church Anterior to the Division of the East and West* (Oxford: John Henry Parker, 1881), 408.

10. Ambrose, *Letter to Simplicianus* 13–14, 408.

11. PL91:351B. All translations from *Patrologia Latina* courtesy of Ian Lockey.

12. PL91:351B.

13. "But the man, who leads out the goat, can be called Pilate, by whose opinion he is sent out, the one who is said to have been cleaned. And once the water has been received, he washes his hands in front of all the people saying: I am innocent because of the blood of this just one." PL91:351C.

14. PL113:344B; the *Glossa Ordinaria* was probably compiled by the Laon school.

15. PL113:344B.

16. PL 164:437A–439B.

17. PL 164:438C.

18. PL 164:439A.

19. William of Auvergne, Bishop of Paris, *Guilielmi Alverni Episcopi Parisiensis, Mathematici Perfectissimi, Eximii Philosophi, Ac Theologi Praestantissimi, Opera Omnia, Quae Hactenus Reperiri Potuerunt, Reconditissimam Rerum Humanarum, Ac Divinarum Doctrinam Abundè Complectentia, Ac Proinde Bonarum Artium Ac Scientiarum Studiosis, Maximè Verò Theologis, Ac Divini Verbi Concionatoribus Apprimè Necessaria: Nunc Demùm in Hac Novissima Editione Ab Innumeris Errorum Chiliadibus Expurgata, Instaurata, Elucidata, Atque Sermonibus & Variis Tractatibus Aucta Ex m.Ss. Codd. Ut Et Praefationibus Ad Lectorem Apertius Intelligetur: Quorum Catalogum Proxima Post Praefationes Pagina Indicabit Cum Indicibus Locupletissimis Rerum Notabilium* (Orléans: ex typographia F. Hotot; London: Robertum Scott, bibliopolam, 1674), 39. Translation courtesy of Ian Lockey.

20. William of Auvergne, *Opera Omnia*, 39.

21. William of Auvergne, *Opera Omnia*, 26.

22. Thomas Aquinas and John Henry Newman, *Catena Aurea: Commentary on the Four Gospels Collected Out of the Works of the Fathers by Saint Thomas Aquinas* (New York: Cosimo Classics, 2007), 313.

23. Jeremiah Burroughs, *The Eighth Book of Mr Jeremiah Burroughs. being a Treatise of the Evil of Evils, Or the Exceeding Sinfulness of Sin. Wherein is Shewed, 1 there is More Evil in the Least Sin, than there is in the Greatest Affliction. 2 Sin is most Opposite to God. 3 Sin is most Opposite to Mans*

Good. 4 Sin is Opposite to all Good in General. 5 Sin is the Poyson, Or Evil of all Other Evils. 6 Sin Hath a Kind of Infiniteness in it. 7 Sin Makes a Man Conformable to the Devil. all these several Heads are Branched Out into very Many Particulars. / Published by Thomas Goodwyn, William Bridge, Sydrach Sympson, William Adderly, [Double Brace] William Greenhil, Philip Nye, John Yates, ed. Thomas Goodwin (London: Printed by Peter Cole in Leaden-Hall, and are to be sold at his shop at the sign of the Printing-Press in Cornhil, neer the Royal Exchange, 1654), 460–461.

24. Robert L. Wilken, "The Jews and Christian Apologetics after Theodosius I Cunctos Populos," *Harvard Theological Review* 73, nos. 3–4 (1980): 455.

25. "And now observe again how much Moses says about the deities that avert evil: 'And he shall take two he-goats of the goats for a sin-offering . . . and present them before the Lord at the door of the tabernacle of the covenant. And Aaron shall cast lots upon the two goats; one lot for the Lord and the other lot for the scapegoat' so as to send him forth, says Moses, as a scape-goat, and let him loose in the wilderness. Thus then is sent forth the goat that is sent for a scape-goat, and of the second goat Moses says: 'Then shall he kill the goat of the sin-offering that is for the people before the Lord, and bring his blood within the veil, and shall sprinkle the blood upon the altar-step, and shall make an atonement for the holy place, because of the uncleanness of the children of Israel and because of their transgression in all their sins.' Accordingly it is evident from what has been said, that Moses knew the various methods of sacrifice." *The Works of the Emperor Julian*, trans. Wilmer Cave Wright, vol. 3, (Cambridge: Harvard University Press, 1954), 403–405.

26. *Against Julian* 9, in Roberts, Donaldson, and Coxe, *The Ante-Nicene Fathers*, 3:327 n. 1.

27. *St. Cyril of Alexandria: Letters*, trans. John I. McEnerney, vol. 1 (Washington, DC: Catholic University of America Press, 1987), 170.

28. Cyril of Alexandria, *Letters*, 170.

29. Cyril of Alexandria, *Letters*, 172.

30. Cyril of Alexandria, *Letters*, 172–173.

31. Cyril of Alexandria, *Letters*, 174.

32. Cyril of Alexandria, *Letters*, 175.

33. Cyril of Alexandria, *Letters*, 175–176; toward the end of the letter Cyril recapitulates: "Accordingly, the law was a picture and, in the law, the types of things were fertile with the truth, with the result that even if the precept introduced two goats to illustrate the mystery of Christ . . . he in both was one, both in suffering and beyond suffering, and in death and over death and ascending in the heavens, the first-fruits of humanity, as it were, thereafter restored unto incorruption." Cyril of Alexandria, *Letters*, 181.

34. *Glaphyrorum in Leviticum liber*, PG 587D. All translations from *Patrologia Graeca* courtesy of Ian Lockey.

35. PG 93:989D–990A.

36. PG 93:992A.

37. PG 93:992B.

38. Note the *Glossa ordinaria* here: "Christ, sacrificing himself through the living goat, sends himself prepared by men, that is his own virtue, as a living goat, into solitude, of course immortal solitude, and insensible divinity to places which cannot be crossed by us, and deserted of all evil. From where: All knowing Jesus, because the Father gave him everything, and because he arose from God, also crosses to God." PL 113:344A.

39. Theodoret, *Eranistes*, *The Fathers of the Church: A New Translation*, trans. Gérard H. Ettlinger (Washington, DC: Catholic University of America Press, 2003), 202.

40. Theodoret, *Eranistes*, 202. Quoting Gregory of Nazianzus, Orthodoxos explains that "the phrase, 'The Word became flesh,' can mean the same as the statements that he became sin [2 Cor. 5:21] and a curse [Gal. 3:13]—not that the Lord changed into them, for that is impossible, but that by accepting them he assumed our transgressions and bore our sicknesses [Isa. 53:4]." Theodoret *Eranistes*, 63. See also: "[The goats] represent Christ our Lord in such a way that these two animals are received not on behalf of two personas, but on behalf of two natures. For since the mortality and immortality of Christ our Lord could not be sketched out easily through one goat (for the goat is only mortal), by necessity he ordered two to be offered: thereby the one that is slaughtered represents the passible nature of the flesh, and the one that is released indicates the impassible nature of divinity." *Quaestiones in Leviticum*, PG 80:330A.

41. Though the popularity of this interpretation among English commentators will exceed that of the dualistic typologies we have considered thus far we should note that Cyril advances one such typology of his own that adroitly deflects the polytheistic implications of the others in its class and is then variously repeated by a minority of commentators. In his *Commentary on the Gospel of Luke* Cyril says of the two goats that "one of these was called 'the lord'; and the other, the 'sent-away,'" the first of which figures the Word who "though He was God, was in our likeness, and took the form of us sinners as far as the nature of the flesh was concerned" that "we might be *sent away* from death and destruction." Cyril of Alexandria, *Commentary on the Gospel of Luke*, Sermon LIII, in *Cyril of Alexandria, The Early Church Fathers*, ed. Norman Russell (New York: Routledge, 2000); emphasis added. The typology reappears in a sermon of the seventeenth-century English divine John Stoughton, where the scapegoat is a type of sinners absolved and set free: "Sweet was the figure of the two *Goates*," says Stoughton, who offers two "escape" typologies as viable alternatives: "either because *Christ* was slaine that we might escape, or because *Christ* the same *was dead and is alive,* as the *Revelation* speakes." John Stoughton, *XI. Choice Sermons Preached upon Selected Occasions, in Cambridge. Viz. I. the Preachers Dignity, and Duty: In Five Sermons, upon 2. Corinth. 5. 20. II. Christ Crucified, the Tree of Life: In Six Sermons, on 1. Corinth. 2. 2. by John Stoughton, Doctor in Divinity, Sometimes Fellow of Immanuel Colledge in Cambridge, Late Preacher of Aldermanburie, London. According to the Originall Copie, which was Left Perfected by the Authour before His Death.*, ed. Anthony Burgess (London: Printed by R. B[adger] for Iohn Bellamie, Henry Overton, Iohn Rothwell, and Ralph Smith, 1640), 52–53. Samuel Clarke is of the same opinion: "The two Goats . . . expresse Christ in a double respect, either because he was slaine that we might escape: or because Christ was dead and is alive . . . he dying for our sinnes, and rising again for our justification." Samuel Clarke, *Medulla Theologiae, Or, the Marrow of Divinity Contained in Sundry Questions and Cases of Conscience, both Speculative and Practical: The Greatest Part of them Collected Out of the Works of our most Judicious, Experienced and Orthodox English Divines, the Rest are Supplied by the Authour / by Sa. Clarke . . .* (London: Printed by Thomas Ratcliff for Thomas Underhill, 1659), 298. The only other mention of the view that "we like the scape-Goat must go free upon [Christ's] performance" is purely derisory: "Were it not glad tidings, a Gospel indeed" writes Dr. Walter Raleigh, "that we might be Feasting, Carousing, Swearing, Drinking, and yet under the eye of God at the same instant, as if we were Watching, Fasting, Praying, Weeping even with Christ himself in the Garden. As though God beheld Men through Christ, as Men do other things, by a perspective, which representeth them to the Eye not in their own colours, but in the colour of the glass they pass through." Walter Raleigh, *Reliquiae Raleighanae being Discourses and Sermons on several Subjects / by the Reverend Dr. Walter Raleigh* (London: Printed by J. Macock for Joseph Hindmarsh, 1679), 79–80.

42. Heinrich Bullinger, *Fiftie Godlie and Learned Sermons Diuided into Fiue Decades, Conteyning the Chiefe and Principall Pointes of Christian Religion, Written in Three Seuerall Tomes Or Sections, by Henrie Bullinger Minister of the Churche of Tigure in Swicerlande. Whereunto is Adioyned a Triple Or Three-Folde Table Verie Fruitefull and Necessarie. Translated Out of Latine into English by H.I.*

Student in Diuinitie (London: By [Henry Middleton for] Ralphe Newberrie, dwelling in Fleet-streate a little aboue the Conduite, 1577), 373.

43. In the "Christians Bulwarke Against Satans Battery," Henry Burton writes, "Hee is the truth of the type of those two goates . . . the one slaine, the other let goe. figuring the humanity the slaine Goate, and the diuinity of Christ, the scape Goate." Henry Burton, *The Christians Bulvvarke, Against Satans Battery. Or, the Doctrine of Iustification so Plainely and Pithily Layd Out in the Severall Maine Branches of it as the Fruits Thereof may be to the Faithfull, as so Many Preservatives Against the Poysonous Heresies and Prevailing Iniquities of these Last Times. by H.B. Pastor of S. Mathevvs Friday-Street* (London: [By R. Young] for Henry Taunton, and are to be sold at his shop in Saint Dunstans Church-yard, 1632), 68–69. Edward Reynolds calls the scapegoat "a signe of Christ our Sacrifice as risen and living againe." Edward Reynolds, *Israels Prayer in Time of Trouble with Gods Gracious Answer Thereunto, Or, an Explication of the 14th Chapter of the Prophet Hosea in Seven Sermons Preached upon so Many Days of Solemn Humiliation / by Edward Reynolds* (London: Printed by Thomas Newcomb for Robert Bostock, 1645 [i.e., 1649]), 17. Cyril of Alexandria is duly named by Thomas Walkington as calling Christ "the *scape Goat* according to his divinity, as hee is the *Goat* for oblation according to his humanity." Thomas Walkington, *Rabboni Mary Magdalens Teares, of Sorrow, Solace. the One for Her Lord being Lost. the Other for Him being found. in Way of Questioning. Wondring. Reioycing. . . . Preached at S. Pauls Crosse, After the Rehearsall, and Newly Reuised and Enlarged: By Thomas Walkington, Doctor in Diuinity, and Minister of the Word at Fulham.* (London: Printed by Edw. Griffin, for Richard Whitakers, and are to bee sold in Pauls Church-yard at the signe of the Kings Head, 1620), 105. R. Gove elaborates: the immolated goat "which (say Divines) prefigured the *Humane Nature of Christ . . . was* crucified and killed," whereas the scapegoat which prefigured his divine nature "though it gave vertue, value, and efficacy of merit to his *Human Nature*, and to the sufferings thereof, yet suffered not with it but like the scape-goat, escaped them, and was free of them." R. Gove, *The Saints Hony-Comb, Full of Divine Truths, Touching both Christian Belief, and a Christians Life, in Two Centuries. by Richard Gove* (London: Printed for Richard Royston at the Angel in Ivy-lane, 1652), 73. Thomas Taylor reproduces the type more plainly: "The two goates, one slaine for sinne, the other a scape goat," are said to shadow "Christ both slaine for sinne, and yet escaping." Thomas Taylor, *Iaphets First Publique Perswasion into Sems Tents, Or, Peters Sermon which was the First Generall Calling of the Gentiles Preached before Cornelius / Expounded in Cambridge by Thomas Taylor, and Now Published for the further use of the Church of God* ([Cambridge?] Printed by Cantrell Legge, printer to the Vniversitie of Cambridge, and are to be sold by Raph Mab at the signe of the Angel in Pauls Churchyard, 1612), 160.

44. Henoch Clapham, *The Discription of a True Visible Christian Right Confortable & Profitable for all such as are Distressed in Sowle about Present Controversies in the Churche. Dravven by He. Cl. but Published by Occasion (as Will Appeare in the Epistle) by Io. I.*, ed. John Joope ([Amsterdam?] 1599), 13.

45. William Guild makes the scapegoat a type of "his impassible Diety" who "rose againe triumphantly" after "bear[ing] all the sinnes both great and small of his elect . . . *the iniquities of his Chosen* . . . vnto death." William Guild, *Moses Vnuailed: Or those Figures which Serued Vnto the Patterne and Shaddow of Heauenly Things, Pointing Out the Messiah Christ Iesus, Briefly Explained Wherevnto is Added the Harmony of all the Prophets, Breathing with One Mouth the Mysterie of His Comming, and of that Redemption which by His Death He was to Accomplish . . . by William Guild, Minister of Gods Word at King-Edward in Scotland* (London: Printed by G[eorge] P[urslowe] for Iohn Budge: and are to be sold at his shop in Pauls Churchyard, at the signe of the Greene Dragon, 1620), 139. Francis Roberts draws the same widely attested connection between the scapegoat and "Christs reviving and Resurrection from the dead bearing our sins far away." Francis Roberts, *Mysterium & Medulla Bibliorum the Mysterie and Marrow of the Bible, Viz. God's*

Covenant with Man in the First Adam before the Fall, and in the Last Adam, Iesvs Christ, After the Fall, from the Beginning to the End of the World: Unfolded & Illustrated in Positive Aphorisms & their Explanation . . . / by Francis Roberts (London: Printed by R. W. for George Calvert, 1657), 784. William Gouge writes, "over the scape goat (which also typified Christ, who by his divine nature, had victory over death) sin was confessed, and that goat is said to *bear all their sins.* Expresly was this foretold...and it is most cleerly revealed to be accomplished." William Gouge, *A Learned and very Useful Commentary on the Whole Epistle to the Hebrews Wherein Every Word and Particle in the Original is Explained . . . : Being the Substance of Thirty Years Wednesdayes Lectures at Black-Fryers, London / by that Holy and Learned Divine Wiliam Gouge . . . : Before which is Prefixed a Narrative of His Life and Death: Whereunto is Added Two Alphabeticall Tables . . .* , (London: Printed by A. M., T. W. and S. G. for Joshua Kirton, 1655), 408. Edward Reynolds sounds a like note: The scapegoat as a sign of the risen Christ "is said to carry the sinnes of the People into the wildernesse, Levit. 16.22. Thereby signifying Christs taking our sinnes from us." Reynolds, *Israels Prayer,* 17.

46. John Preston, with Thomas Goodwin and George Glover, *The Golden Scepter Held Forth to the Humble VVith the Churches Dignitie by Her Marriage. and the Churches Dutie in Her Carriage. in Three Treatises. the Former Delivered in Sundry Sermons in Cambridge, for the Weekely Fasts, 1625. the Two Latter in Lincolnes Inne. by the Late Learned and Reverend Divine, Iohn Preston, Dr. in Divinity, Chaplaine in Ordinary to His Maiesty, Mr. of Emanuel Colledge in Cambridge, and Somtime Preacher at Lincolnes Inne* (London: Printed by R. Badger for N. Bourne at the Royall Exchange, and R. Harford at the gilt Bible in Queenes-head Alley in Pater-noster Row, and by F. Eglesfield at the Marigold in Pauls Church-yard, 1638), 121.

47. Edward Leigh, *A Systeme Or Body of Divinity Consisting of Ten Books: Wherein the Fundamentals and Main Grounds of Religion are Opened, the Contrary Errours Refuted, most of the Controversies between Us, the Papists, Arminians, and Socinians Discussed and Handled, several Scriptures Explained and Vindicated from Corrupt Glosses: A Work Seasonable for these Times, Wherein so Many Articles of our Faith are Questioned, and so Many Gross Errours Daily Published / by Edward Leigh* (London: Printed by A. M. for William Lee, 1654), 317. We should note one other small but variously attested tradition among seventeenth-century commentators according to which the scapegoat is "a true prognostique" of Jesus, who after his baptism is led "into the Wildernes by the Spirit to be tempted by the Divell." Thomas Jackson, *Christs Ansvver Vnto Iohns Question: Or, an Introduction to the Knowledge of Iesus Christ, and Him Crucified Deliuered in Certaine Sermons in the Famous Towne of New-Castle Vpon Tine. by Thomas Iackson, Dr. of Diuinitie, Vicar of Saint Nicolas Church there, and Fellow of Corpus Christi Colledge in Oxford* (London: Printed by G[eorge] P[urslowe] for Iohn Clarke, and are to be sold at his shop vnder Saint Peters Church in Corne-hill, 1625), 139. John Trapp's 1647 Commentary on the Gospels and Acts is a good example of this, linking the pneumatic impetus in Mark 1:12—"the spirit driveth him... into the wildernesse"—to the sending of "that legall scape-Goat" who accordingly becomes a type of Christ's temptation. John Trapp, *A Commentary Or Exposition upon the Four Evangelists, and the Acts of the Apostles: Wherein the Text is Explained, some Controversies are Discussed, Divers Common Places are Handled, and Many Remarkable Matters Hinted, that had by Former Interpreters been Pretermitted. Besides, Divers Other Texts of Scripture which Occasionally Occur are Fully Opened, and the Whole so Intermixed with Pertinent Histories, as Will Yeeld both Pleasure and Profit to the Judicious Reader. / by John Trapp M. A. Pastour of Weston upon Avon in Gloucestershire* (London: Printed by A. M. for John Bellamie, at the sign of the three golden-Lions near the Royall-Exchange, 1647), 3. This minority tradition also develops the motif of sin-bearing as forgiveness or absolution. One adaptation of the latter argues that "one speciall end" of Jesus' departure "into the Wildernesse, was to carry thither the sinnes of all that came vnto *Johns* baptisme." Jackson, *Christs Ansvver,* 141. Another declares the scapegoat a type "most punctually agreeing . . . with our Redeemers going into the Desert . . . led *by the* holy Spirit, as by the hands of

a fit man, into the midst of the *Wilderness*," deploying John's confession of "*the Lamb of God which taketh away the sins of the world*" to specify the moment when "the *burden* of our *iniquities*" is fully "laid upon his *head.*" Peter Heylyn, *Theologia Veterum, Or, the Summe of Christian Theologie, Positive, Polemical, and Philological, Contained in the Apostles Creed, Or Reducible to it According to the Tendries of the Antients both Greeks and Latines : In Three Books / by Peter Heylyn* (London: Printed by E. Cotes for Henry Seile, 1654), 160.

48. Nathanael Culverwell, *An Elegant and Learned Discourse of the Light of Nature, with several Other Treatises . . .* , ed. William Dillingham (London: Printed by T. R. and E. M. for John Rothwell, 1652), 36.

49. Henry Jessey, *The Exceeding Riches of Grace Advanced by the Spirit of Grace, in an Empty Nothing Creature, Viz. Mrs. Sarah Wight Lately Hopeles and Restles, Her Soule Dwelling Far from Peace Or Hopes Thereof: Now Hopefull, and Joyfull in the Lord, that Hath Caused Light to Shine Out of Darknes . . . / Published for the Refreshing of Poor Souls, by an Eye and Ear-Witness of a Good Part Thereof, Henry Jesse* (London: Printed by Matthew Simmons for Henry Overton, and Hannah Allen, and are to be sold at their shops, 1647), 67. Daily notes that "When she was fifteen, the self-evident signs of [Wight's] reprobation were pathetically juvenile, but serious enough in the Calvinistic scheme of things. Once she disobeyed the instructions of a 'superior.' Another time she lied to her mother about a lost hood which she said was at her grandmother's house. . . . Sarah Wight became convinced of her damnation, refused all food (except ale), was suicidal, self-abusive and physically wasted away to flesh and bones. She appears to have been in a catatonic state for eight days: her body rigid, fists clenched, lips pursed, and eyes squeezed tightly shut." She eventually emerges from this trance, reborn after her "death to the world" as "an empty nothing creature" with a renewed capacity to be filled with "grace." Barbara Ritter Dailey, "The Visitation of Sarah Wight: Holy Carnival and the Revolution of the Saints in Civil War London," *Church History* 55, no. 4 (1986): 444.

50. Richard Coppin, *A Blow at the Serpent; Or a Gentle Answer from Madiston Prison to Appease Wrath Advancing it Self Against Truth and Peace at Rochester. Together with the Work of Four Daies Disputes, in the Cathedral of Rochester, in the Countie of Kent, Betweene several Ministers, and Richard Coppin, Preacher there, to Whom very Many People Frequentlie Came to Hear, and Much Rejoyced at the Way of Truth and Peace He Preached, at the Same Whereof the Ministers in those Parts Began to Ring in their Pulpits, Saying, this Man Blasphemeth, . . . Whereupon Arose the Disputes, at which were some Magistrates, some Officers, and Souldiers, Peaceable and Well-Minded, and very Many People from all Parts Adjacent, before Whom the Truth was Confirm'd and Maintained. the Whole Matter Written by the Hearers, on both Sides. Published for the Confirmation and Comfort of all such as Receive the Truth in the Love of it. by Richard Coppin, Now in Maidston Prison for the Witness of Jesus. Twenty Five Articles since Brought Against Him by the Ministers, as Blasphemie, and His Answers to them, how He was* (London: printed by Philip Wattleworth, and are to be sold by William Larnar at the Black-moor neer Fleet-Bridge, 1656), 13. The most ample statement of the idea that "pardon of sin is expressed in Scripture, by not remembring of sin" is given by Christopher Love, who reads Jeremiah 31: 34 ("I will forgive their iniquity; and I will remember their sin no more") as "an allusion to the Scape-goat, which was to bear the sins of the people on his head, to carry them into the land of forgetfulnesse; Thus the Lord that remembers all things, that God is said graciously not to remember the sins of his people, not to remember them so, as to damn them for them; he will forget your iniquities and remember them no more." Christopher Love, *The Penitent Pardoned a Treatise Wherein is Handled the Duty of Confession of Sin and the Priviledge of the Pardon of Sin: Together with a Discourse of Christs Ascension into Heaven and of His Coming again from Heaven: Wherein the Opinion of the Chiliasts is Considered and Solidly Confuted / being the Sum and Substance of several Sermons Preached by*

that Faithful Servant of Christ, Mr. Christopher Love (London: Printed for John Rothwell . . . and for Nathanael Brooks, 1657), 35.

Chapter 4. Economies of Blood

1. 2.19, Anselm, *The Major Works*, ed. Brian Davies and G. R. Evans (New York: Oxford University Press, 1998), 354.

2. Pelikan, *The Christian Tradition*, 3:143.

3. 1.13, Anselm, *The Major Works*, 287.

4. 1.19, Anselm, *The Major Works*, 302.

5. 2.6, Anselm, *Why God Became Man, and the Virgin Conception and Original Sin* (Albany, NY: Magi Books, 1969), 124.

6. 2.18, Anselm, *The Major Works*, 350.

7. 2.18, Anselm, *The Major Works*, 350.

8. But what do you give someone who literally has everything? Because "all things which belonged to the Father belonged to him," there is strictly no recompense possible. Because it is "permissible for the Son to give what is his own, and it is only to someone else that the Father can give what he owes," the inevitable beneficiary is the human race; 2.19, Anselm, *The Major Works*, 353.

9. 1.9, Anselm, *The Major Works*, 278–279.

10. 1.9, Anselm, *The Major Works*, 279.

11. 1.8, Anselm, *The Major Works*, 275.

12. 1.8, Anselm, *The Major Works*, 275.

13. Gary A. Anderson, *Sin: A History* (New Haven, CT: Yale University Press, 2009), 196.

14. Anderson, *Sin*, 195–196.

15. Anderson, *Sin*, 196.

16. Anderson, *Sin*, 197.

17. Anderson, *Sin*, 197.

18. 2.4, Anselm, *The Major Works*, 319.

19. 2.4, Anselm, *The Major Works*, 319.

20. Aulén, *Christus Victor*, 93–94.

21. Aulén, *Christus Victor*, 58–59.

22. Anderson calls Aulén to account for insisting that the doctrine of satisfaction begins with Tertullian and so partakes of a "uniquely Latin (read, Catholic) construal of the human condition" that "puts too much emphasis on the human contribution to atonement." According to Anderson the roots of the doctrine run far deeper into the biblical record than Aulén believed. Like "the concept of sin and debt" with which it is "inextricably linked," the idea of making satisfaction for sins has a number of earlier—Hebrew Bible, Second Temple, Qumran, and New Testament—antecedents. Anderson, *Sin*, 44. This is doubtless correct. Still, Anselm's doctrine of the atonement turns on the possibility of a meritorious surplus and its vicarious transfer. This idea, which pervaded religious and secular life in the Middle Ages, structured his understanding of how Christ saves.

23. James R. Ginther, *The Westminster Handbook to Medieval Theology* (Louisville, KY: Westminster John Knox Press, 2009), 143.

24. J. van Herwaarden, *Between Saint James and Erasmus: Studies in Late-Medieval Religious Life: Devotion and Pilgrimage in the Netherlands* (Boston: Brill, 2003), 96.

25. This appears most clearly in the emphasis Anselm places on penance as a means of appropriating the remittance of sins that Christ's death makes available to the worthily disposed: "So that man redeemed all others in that what he freely gave to God paid for the debtors what they owed. By this price man was not only redeemed from blame but whenever he returns with genuine penitence he is received, though that penitence is not promised to sinners. Because of that which was done on the cross, by the cross our Christ has redeemed us. Then whosoever wills to come to this grace with the love it deserves, will be saved. And those who despise it are justly damned, because they do not pay the debt they owe." Anselm, *The Major Works*, 234.

26. Pelikan, *The Christian Tradition*, 3:143.

27. *Summa Theologica*, trans. Fathers of the English Dominican Province, 1st complete American ed. (New York: Benziger, 1948), III, 48, A4, Rp. 2.

28. *Summa Theologica*, III, 48, A4, Rp. 2.

29. *Summa Theologica*, III 48, A4, Rp. 2.

30. *Summa Theologica*, III, 46, A 3, Rp. 3.

31. *Summa Theologica*, III, 46, A2, Rp. 3.

32. *Summa Theologica*, III, 47, A3, Rp. 1.

33. *Summa Theologica*, I–II, 87, A6, Body Para. 1/2.

34. *Summa Theologica*, Supp., 13, A1, Rp. 5.

35. Philip L. Quinn, "Aquinas on Atonement," in *Trinity, Incarnation, and Atonement: Philosophical and Theological Essays*, vol. 1, ed. Ronald Jay Feenstra and Cornelius Plantinga (Notre Dame, IN: University of Notre Dame Press, 1989), 163.

36. *Summa Theologica*, I–II, 87, A6, Body Para. 2/2.

37. *Summa Theologica*, I, 49, A4, Body.

38. *Summa Theologica*, III, 49, A4, Body.

39. *Summa Theologica*, III, I, A2, Rp. 2.

40. *Summa Theologica*, III, I, A2, Rp. 2.

41. *Summa Theologica*, III, 47, A3, Body.

42. *Summa Theologica*, III, 47, A3, Body.

43. *Summa Theologica*, III, 48, A5, Rp. 1 and 2.

44. Pelikan notes that although Anselm never explains the death of Christ as substitutionary, *Cur Deus homo* "was in fact an effort 'to discover the reason why Jesus' death could justly be counted by God as vicarious.'" Pelikan, *The Christian Tradition*, 3:144.

45. *Summa Theologica*, III, 49, A1, Rp. 3.

46. "Now in Baptism man shares the Power of Christ's Passion fully, since by water and the Spirit of Christ, he dies with Him to sin, and is born again in Him to a new life, so that, in Baptism, man receives the remission of all debt of punishment. In Penance, on the other hand, man shares in the power of Christ's Passion according to the measure of his own acts." *Summa Theologica*, II, 86, A4, Rp. 3. By these he applies the satisfaction that Christ's Passion makes to sins committed after he is baptized.

47. *Summa Theologica*, III 49, A1, Rp. 5.

48. *Summa Theologica*, Supp., 13, A1, OTV Para. 3/3.

49. *Summa Theologica*, III, 52, A1, Rp. 2.

50. "Christ's descent into hell had its effect of deliverance on them only who through faith and charity were united to Christ's Passion, in virtue whereof Christ's descent into hell was one of deliverance. But the children who had died in original sin were in no way united to Christ's Passion by faith and love: for, not having the use of free will, they could have no faith of their own; nor were they cleansed from original sin either by their parents' faith or by any sacrament of faith. Consequently, Christ's descent into hell did not deliver the children from thence." *Summa Theologica*, III, 52, A7, Body.

51. *Summa Theologica*, Supp., 13, A2, Body. "As regards the payment of the debt, one man can satisfy for another, provided he be in a state of charity, so that his works may avail for satisfaction. Nor is it necessary that he who satisfies for another should undergo a greater punishment than the principal would have to undergo (as some maintain, who argue that a man profits more by his own punishment than by another's), because punishment derives its power of satisfaction chiefly from charity whereby man bears it. And since greater charity is evidenced by a man satisfying for another than for himself, less punishment is required of him who satisfies for another, than of the principal: wherefore we read in the *Lives of the Fathers* (v, 5) of one who for love of his brother did penance for a sin which his brother had not committed, and that on account of his charity his brother was released from a sin which he had committed. Nor is it necessary that the one for whom satisfaction is made should be unable to make satisfaction himself, for even if he were able, he would be released from his debt when the other satisfied in his stead. But this is necessary in so far as the satisfactory punishment is medicinal: so that a man is not to be allowed to do penance for another, unless there be evidence of some defect in the penitent, either bodily, so that he is unable to bear it, or spiritual, so that he is not ready to undergo it." *Summa Theologica*, Supp., 13, A2, Body.

52. Quinn, "Aquinas on Atonement," 171.

53. Quinn, "Aquinas on Atonement," 171–172.

54. John Thomas McNeill and Helena M. Gamer, *Medieval Handbooks of Penance: A Translation of the Principal "Libri Poenitentiales" and Selections from Related Documents* (New York: Columbia University Press, 1990), 48.

55. *Summa Theologica*, Supp., 25, A1, Body Para. 2/3–3/3.

56. Damian, *Opusculum 43* (Letter 161), chapter 6 (PL 145, col. 686; ed. Reindel, 4:144). Cited in Rachel Fulton, *From Judgment to Passion: Devotion to Christ and the Virgin Mary, 800–1200* (New York: Columbia University Press, 2002), 103–104.

57. John of Salisbury, *Policraticus: Of the Frivolities of Courtiers and the Footprints of Philosophers*, trans. Cary J. Nederman (New York: Cambridge University Press, 1990), 170–171.

58. *Summa Theologica*, I–II, A5, Rp. 6, Para. 1/3.

59. Aquinas also mentions that the scapegoat "was to bear the sins of the people" because "the forgiveness of the people's sins was signified by its being let loose." *Summa Theologica*, I-II, 102, A5, Rp. 6, Para. 1/3.

60. Ishodad gives his own typology: "by the goat which is immolated, [God] represents to them the divine reconciliation, and by the other which is burdened with sins, the total repudiation of their iniquity by the offering of confession, to the effect of stimulating them to hasten, to know, by thought and action, to obtain the divine reconciliation, so that their iniquity is removed from sight." Ishodad of Merv, *Commentaire d'Ishodad de Merv sur l'Ancien Testament. II Exode-Deutéronome*, ed. Ceslas van den Eynde (Louvain, Belgium: Secrétariat du Corpus SCO, 1958), 105–106.

61. *Summa Theologica*, I–II, 102, A5, Rp. 6, Para. 2/3.

62. *Summa Theologica*, I–II, 102, A5, Rp. 6, Para. 2/3.

63. *Summa Theologica*, I–II, 102, A5, Rp. 6, Para. 2/3.

64. Stanislas Lyonnet and Leopold Sabourin, *Sin, Redemption, and Sacrifice: A Biblical and Patristic Study* (Rome: Biblical Institute, 1970), 283.

65. Lyonnet and Sabourin, *Sin, Redemption, and Sacrifice*, 283.

66. Jean Calvin, *Commentaries on the Four Last Books of Moses: Arranged in the Form of a Harmony*, vol. 2 (Edinburgh: Printed for the Calvin Translation Society, 1855), 316. The relevant portion in the original Latin follows: "Duplex hîc ponitur expiationis forma: nam ex duobus hircis alter more legali oblatus fuit in victimam, alter emissus, ut esset κάθαρμα *vel* περίψημα. Utriusque autem figuræ veritas in Christo fuit exhibita, quia & agnus Dei fuit (cuius immolatio delevit peccata mundi), & ut κάθαρμα esset, extinctus fuit in eo decor, & reiectus fuit ab hominibus. Posset quidem afferri magis arguta speculatio, nempe postquam oblatus erat hircus, emissionem eius fuisse resurrectionis Christi figuram: acsi immolatio unius hirci testata esset, in morte Christi satisfactionem pro peccatis quærendam esse: alterius autem vita & discessus ostédisset, Christum ex quo pro peccatis oblatus est, & maledictionem hominum sustinuit, vivum tamen manere & superstitem. Ego verò quod simplicius est & certius amplector, eóque sum contentus: hircum qui vivus & liber abibat, vice piaculi fuisse, ut ex illius discessu & fuga certior fieret populus peccata sua procul abacta euanuisse. Atque hoc folum in Lege fuit piaculare sacrificiú absque sanguine. Neque id Apostoli sentétiæ repugnant: ná quú hirci duo cõiunctim oblati fuerint, satis fuit alterius cædé intercedere, & sanguinem fundi in expiationem. Sors enim non iaciebatur donec ad ostium tabernaculi uterque hircus adductus esset. Ita quanuis unum vivum sisteret sacerdos ad recóciliationem, quemadmodum verbis Mosis exprimitur, non tamen placatus fuit Deus absque sanguine, quia vis expiationis à sacrificio alterius hirci pendebat." Jean Calvin, *Mosis libri V : cum Iohannis Caluini commentariis ; Genesis seorsum, reliqui quatuor in formam harmoniae digesti* (Geneva: Excud. Henr. Stephanus, 1563), 279. Calvin's French translation (published posthumously in 1564) reads: "Il est ici parlé de deux façons de reconcilier: car de deux boucs que le peuple presentoit, l'un estoit offert en hostie à la façon de la Loy, l'autre estoit lasché pour estre comme en detestation ou malediction. Or la verité de ces deux figures a este manifestee en Jesus Christ, d'autant qu'il a este l'agneau de Dieu, duquel l'oblation effaçoit les pechez du monde, & d'autre part il a este desfiguré & reietté des hommes, iusques à leur estre en horreur, afin d'estre fuiet à malediction pour nous. On pourroit bien amener une speculation plus subtile, c'est que quand on laissoit eschapper le bouc, la liberté qu'on luy donnoit estoit figure de la resurrectiõ de Jesus Christ: comme si l'oblation de l'un des boucs eust tesmoigné, qu'on deuoit cercher satisfaction pour ses pechez en la mort de Jesus Christ: mais que la vie & le departement de l'autre, signifioit que Jesus Christ apres auoir este offert pour les pechez, & pour la malediction des hommes, demeure neantmoins vif & en son entier. Mais ie pren ce qui est le plus simple & plus certain, & m'en contente: assauoir que le bouc qui s'en alloit vif, estoit comme une beste maudite, afin que par son eslongnement & sa fuite, le peuple fust asseuré que ses pechez estoyentiettez au loin pour s'efuanouir. Il n'y a eu que ce sacrifice satisfactoire en la Loy sans effusion de sang. Et cela ne contreuient point au dire de l'Apostre: car puis qu'on offroit deux boucs ensemble & conioinctement, c'estoit assez que la mort de l'un entreueint, afin que le sang fust espádu ensaitisfactiõ. Car on ne iettoit point le fort, iusques à ce que tous les deux boucs fussent amenez à la porte du tabernacle. Ainsi combien que le Sacrificateur en presentast l'un vif pour reconciliation, selon que Moyse l'exprime, toutesfois Dieu n'a point este appaisé sans effusion de sang, veu que la vertu de reconcilier prouenoit de la mort de l'hostie." Jean Calvin, *Commentaires de M. Jean Calvin, sur les cinq livres de Moyse. Genese est mis à part, les autres quatre livres sont disposez en forme d'Harmonie: avec cinq indices, dont les deux contenans les passages alleguez et exposez par læautheur, sont adjoustez de nouveau en ceste traduction* (Geneva: Imprimé par François Estienne, 1564), 503.

67. Jean Calvin, *Commentaries*, vol. 20 (Grand Rapids, MI: Baker Book House, 1984), 1 Cor. 4:13.

68. Calvin, *Commentaries*, 1 Cor. 4:13.

69. Calvin, *Commentaries*, 1 Cor. 4:13.

70. Henry Hammond, *A Paraphrase and Annotations upon all the Books of the New Testament Briefly Explaining all the Difficult Places Thereof / by H. Hammond* (London: Printed by J. Flesher for Richard Davis, 1659), 520–521.

71. Hammond, *A Paraphrase and Annotations*, 521.

72. Calvin, *Four Last Books of Moses*, 316.

73. Calvin, *Four Last Books of Moses*, 316.

Chapter 5. The Damnation of Christ's Soul

1. Dewey D. Wallace Jr., "Puritan and Anglican: The Interpretation of Christ's Descent into Hell in Elizabethan Theology," *Archiv Für Reformationsgeschichte* 69 (1978): 248.

2. Thomas Bilson, *The Effect of Certaine Sermons Touching the Full Redemption of Mankind by the Death and Bloud of Christ Iesus Wherein Besides the Merite of Christs Suffering, the Manner of His Offering, the Power of His Death, the Comfort of His Crosse, the Glorie of His Resurrection, are Handled, what Paines Christ Suffered in His Soule on the Crosse: Together, with the Place and Purpose of His Descent to Hel After Death: Preached at Paules Crosse and Else Where in London, by the Right Reuerend Father Thomas Bilson Bishop of Winchester. with a Conclusion to the Reader for the Cleering of Certaine Obiections made Against Said Doctrine* (London: By Peter Short for Walter Burre, and are to be sold in Paules Churchyard at the signe of the Flower deluce, 1599), A2r.

3. John Calvin, *Institutes of the Christian Religion*, ed. John Thomas McNeill and trans. Ford Lewis Battles (Philadelphia: Westminster Press, 1960), vol. 2, 2.16, 508–509.

4. Calvin, *Institutes*, vol. 2, 2.16, 509–510.

5. Calvin, *Institutes*, vol. 2, 2.17, 533.

6. Calvin, *Institutes*, vol. 2, 2.16, 516.

7. Calvin, *Institutes*, vol. 2, 2.16, 504.

8. Calvin, *Institutes*, vol. 2, 2.16, 517.

9. Calvin, *Institutes*, vol. 2, 2.16, 517.

10. Calvin, *Institutes*, vol. 2, 2.16, 515–516.

11. Calvin, *Institutes*, vol. 2, 2.16, 519.

12. Calvin, *Institutes*, vol. 2, 2.16, 519.

13. Calvin, *Institutes*, vol. 2, 2.16, 519.

14. Calvin, *Institutes*, vol. 2, 2.16, 516.

15. Calvin, *Institutes*, vol. 2, 2.16, 516.

16. Calvin's repeated references to the Suffering Servant are finally emboldened with all the strong ontological scriptures we read in Cyril's and Theodoret's typologies of the immolated goat along with a few others: "The apostle testifies to this more openly when he teaches: 'For our sake he who knew no sin was made sin by the Father, so that in him we might be made the righteousness of God' [2 Cor. 5:21]. The Son of God, utterly clean of all fault, nevertheless took upon himself the shame and reproach of our iniquities, and in return clothed us with his purity. It seems that Paul meant the same thing when he says of sin, 'He condemned sin in his flesh' [Rom. 8:3 p.]. The Father destroyed the force of sin when the curse of sin was transferred to Christ's flesh. Here, then, is the meaning of this saying: Christ was offered to the Father in death as an expiatory sacrifice

that when he discharged all satisfaction through his sacrifice, we might cease to be afraid of God's wrath. Now it is clear what the prophet's utterance means: 'The Lord has laid on him the iniquity of us all' [Isa. 53:6]. That is, he who was about to cleanse the filth of those iniquities was covered with them by transferred imputation. The cross, to which he was nailed, was a symbol of this, as the apostle testifies: 'Christ redeemed us from the curse of the law, when he became a curse for us. For it is written, "Cursed be every one who hangs on a tree," that in Christ the blessing of Abraham might come upon the Gentiles' [Gal. 3:13–14; Deut. 21:23]. Peter means the same thing when he teaches: 'He himself bore our sins . . . on the tree' [1 Pet. 2:24], because from the very symbol of the curse we more clearly understand that the burden with which we had been oppressed was laid upon him." Calvin, *Institutes*, vol. 2, 2.16, 510–511.

17. From *The Necessity of Reforming the Church Presented to the Imperial Diet at Spires, A.D. 1544, in the Name of All Who Wish Christ to Reign*, in *Tracts and Treatises*, trans. Henry Beveridge (Grand Rapids, MI: Eerdmans, 1958), 163.

18. Calvin, *Tracts and Treatises*, 163.

19. Calvin, *Institutes*, vol. 2, 2.16, 507.

20. Wallace, "Puritan and Anglican," 275.

21. Henry Jacob, *A Treatise of the Sufferings and Victory of Christ, in the Work of our Redemption* (Middelburg, Netherlands: Printed by Richard Schilders, 1598), 16. Wallace notes that "Jacob's argument is profoundly theological, based upon the importance to himself and his fellow Puritans of a particular understanding of the atonement: for Christ to redeem the whole man, he must assume the whole man, body and soul, and suffer the penalty due to the body and soul of man, thus expiating man's sin by suffering on the cross the very pains of hell." Wallace, "Puritan and Anglican," 274.

22. Jacob, *Treatise*, 16.

23. Jacob, *Treatise*, 12.

24. Jacob, *Treatise*, 33.

25. Jacob, *Treatise*, 33.

26. Jacob, *Treatise*, 34.

27. Jacob, *Treatise*, 39.

28. Jacob, *Treatise*, 14.

29. Jacob, *Treatise*, 34–35.

30. Henry Jacob, *A Defence of a Treatise Touching the Sufferings and Victorie of Christ in the Worke of our Redemption* (Middelburg, Netherlands: R. Schilders, 1600), 11.

31. Jacob, *Defence*, 11. At times this "peculiar and *extraordinary way*" of suffering "belonging onely to Christ," by which sin is merely imputed but in such a way that Christ may be identified with it, appears to depend on his possessing two natures, as when Jacob writes that "not the body onely, but also the Soule of Christ, euen euery whitt, of his humanitie" is "burnt and consumed in the fier of affliction" as "a whole burnt offering for our sinnes." Jacob, *Treatise*, 13. "The immortall Soule of Christ", though it too suffers and is itself "a sinne offering," survives the ordeal: "If any saye, This *scape-goate* suffered not as the *slayne goate* did, but was *sent away* free and vntouched. Thus then the Soule of Christ must scape and not suffer when his body suffered. I aunswere. The *scaping* of this Goate may signifie the *Soules* immortalitie, whiche died not when the body dyed." Jacob, *Defence*, 11–13.

32. Jacob, *Treatise*, 37.

33. Jacob, *Defence*, 11.

34. Jacob, *Defense*, 7.

35. Jacob, *Defense*, 11–12.

36. Jacob, *Treatise*, 6.

37. Jacob, *Treatise*, 7.

38. Jacob, *Treatise*, 7.

39. Jacob, *Defence*, 11.

40. Jacob, *Defence*, 7.

41. "The cause why he went thither . . . was to overthrow & destroy the kingdom & might of Satan in the place of his greatest strength, even in hel, and as our head to free all his members from daunger and feare of comming thither: the sorrowes and terrors whereof he loosed with his presence, treading them underneath his feete, and rose againe into a blessed and immortall life, leading captivity captive, and taking from hell and Satan all power to prevaile against his elect." Bilson, *Effect of Certaine Sermons*, A4r.

42. Bilson, *Effect of Certaine Sermons*, A2v.

43. "I do not exclude the torments on the crosse imparted to the soule of Christ," Bilson adds, "but onelie the paines of hell which were neuer figured by anie sacrifice, nor scaped by anie Sacrament of the old or new testament." Bilson, *Effect of Certaine Sermons*, 238. The scriptures are moreover "plaine and pregnant that Christ DIED: *for our sinnes,* and by his DEATH, *destroied him that had power of death, euen the Diuell, and reconciled vs, when we were strangers and enemies,* IN THE BODIE OF HIS FLESH THROVGH DEATH, (for wee are *reconciled to God, by the* DEATH *of his sonne, and sanctified by* THE OFFERING OF THE BODIE OF *Iesus Christ* once, who *himselfe bare our sinnes in his* BODIE *on the Tree:* where hee *was put to death concerning the* FLESH." Bilson, *Effect of Certaine Sermons*, A3r.

44. Bilson, *Effect of Certaine Sermons*, A3r.

45. Thomas Bilson, *The Suruey of Christs Sufferings for Mans Redemption and of His Descent to Hades Or Hel for our Deliuerance: By Thomas Bilson Bishop of Winchester. the Contents Whereof may be Seene in Certaine Resolutions before the Booke, in the Titles Ouer the Pages, and in a Table made to that End. Perused and Allowed by Publike Authoritie* (London: Printed by Melchisedech Bradwood for Iohn Bill, 1604), 108–109. See also: Bilson, *Effect of Certaine Sermons*, 235.

46. Bilson, *Suruey of Christs Sufferings*, 110.

47. Bilson, *Suruey of Christs Sufferings*, 108.

48. Bilson, *Suruey of Christs Sufferings*, 109.

49. Bilson, *Suruey of Christs Sufferings*, 108.

50. Bilson, *Suruey of Christs Sufferings*, 109.

51. Bilson, *Suruey of Christs Sufferings*, 109.

52. Bilson, *Suruey of Christs Sufferings*, 107.

53. Bilson, *Suruey of Christs Sufferings*, 106.

54. Wallace, "Puritan and Anglican," 283.

55. Calvin, *Institutes of the Christian Religion*, vol. 2, 2.16, 516.

56. George Abbot, *An Exposition Vpon the Prophet Ionah Contained in Certaine Sermons, Preached in S. Maries Church in Oxford. by George Abbot Professor of Diuinitie, and Maister of Vniuersitie Colledge* (London: Imprinted by Richard Field, and are to be sold by Richard Garbrand, 1600), 164.

57. John Jackson, *Ecclesiastes the Worthy Church-Man, Or the Faithfull Minister of Iesvs Christ. Described by Polishing the Twelve Stones in the High-Priests Pectorall, as they were First Glossed and Scholyed on in a Synod-Sermon; and After Enlarged by Way of Discourse, to His Two Brethren. by Iohn Iackson Parson of Marske in Richmond-Shire* (London: Printed [by M. Flesher] for Richard More, and are to be sold at his shop in Saint Dunstanes Church-yard in Fleetstreet, 1628), 26. *The City of God* contains a passing reference to the belief that diamond "is so hard that it can be wrought neither by iron nor fire, nor they say, by anything at all except goat's blood," although Augustine mentions neither Christ nor the scapegoat in this connection. Augustine of Hippo, *The City of God*, Book XXI, 4 in Schaff, *Select Library*, 1st series, 2:455.

58. Jackson, *Ecclesiastes*, 26.

59. Edmund Calamy, *Englands Looking-Glasse Presented in a Sermon Preached before the Honorable House of Commons at their Late Solemne Fast, December 22, 1641 / by Edmund Calamy* (London: Printed by I. Raworth for Chr. Meredith, 1642), 27. Italics added.

60. Sir Richard Baker, *Meditations and Disquisitions upon the One and Fiftieth Psalme of Dauid Miserere Mei Deus. by Sr. Richard Baker, Knight* (London: Printed by Edward Griffin, for Anne Bouler, and are to be sold at the Marigold, in Pauls Church-yard, 1638), 70–71.

61. Sir Thomas Browne, *Pseudodoxia Epidemica, Or, Enquiries into very Many Received Tenents and Commonly Presumed Truths by Thomas Browne* (London: Printed by T. H. for E. Dod, 1646), 83.

62. Browne, *Pseudodoxia Epidemica*, 83.

63. "But this I perceive is easier affirmed than proved. For Lapidaries, and such as professe the art of cutting this stone, doe generally deny it." The source of the error is found with "the holy Fathers" who "without further enquiry did take it for granted, and rested on the authorities of the first deliverers." Of these "Albertus . . . promiseth this effect but conditionally, that is not except the Goat drinke wine, and be fed with *Siler montanum, petroselinnum,* and such herbes as are conceived of power to breake stone in the bladder. But the words of Pliny, from whom most likely the rest at first derived it, if strictly considered, doe rather overthrow then any way advantage this effect. His words are these . . . 'broken with Goat's bloud but not [except] it bee fresh and warme, and that not without many blows; and then also it will breake the best anvills and hammers of Iron.' And answerable hereto is the assertion of Isidore and Solinus. By which account, a Diamond, steeped in Goat's bloud, rather encreaseth in hardnesse then acquireth any softnesse by the infusion; for the best we have are comminuible without it; and are so far from breaking hammers that they submit unto pistillation and resist not an ordinary pestle. Upon this conceit arose, perhaps the discovery of another, that is that the bloud of a Goat, was soverigne for the [kidney] stone, as it stands commended by many good Writers, and brings up the composition in the powder of Nicolaus or rather because it was found an excellent medicine for the stone, and its ability commended by some to dissolve the hardest thereof; it might be conceived by amplifying apprehensions, to be able to break a Diamond, and so it came to be ordered that the Goat should be fed with saxifragous herbes, and such as are conceived of power to breake the stone. However it were as the effect is false in the one, so is it surely very doubtfull in the other. For although inwardly received it may be very diuretick, and expulse the stone in the kidnyes; yet how it should dissolve or breake that in the bladder, will require a further dispute, and perhaps would be more reasonably tryed by a warme injection thereof, then as it is commonly used." Browne, *Pseudodoxia Epidemica*, 83–84.

64. Browne, *Pseudodoxia Epidemica*, 84.

65. Abbot, *Exposition*, 164.

66. Abbot, *Exposition*, 164–165.

67. Abbot, *Exposition*, 165.

68. John Owen, *Of Communion with God the Father, Sonne, and Holy Ghost, each Person Distinctly*

in Love, Grace, and Consolation, Or, the Saints Fellowship with the Father, Sonne, and Holy Ghost, Unfolded by John Owen (Oxford: Printed by A. Lichfield . . . for Tho. Robinson, 1657), 102.

69. Burton, *Christians Bulvvarke*, 68–69.

70. The most unlikely scapegoat exegete here is the English philosopher Thomas Hobbes, whose *Leviathan* contains a similarly indifferent formulation: "Thus is the Lamb of God equivalent to both those Goates; sacrificed, in that he dyed; and escaping, in his Ressurection; being raised opportunely by his Father." To this he adds that the goat led into the wilderness carries "away with him the iniquities of the people." Hobbes continues: 'To the *Office* of a *Redeemer*, that is, of one that payeth the Ransome of Sin, (which Ransome is Death,) it appertaineth, that he was Sacrificed, and thereby bare upon his own head, and carried away from us our iniquities, in such sort as God had required. . . . As the Sacrifice of the one Goat was a sufficient (because an acceptable) price for the Ransome of all Israel; so the death of the Messiah, is a sufficient price, for the Sins of all mankind, because there was no more required. Our Saviour Christs sufferings seem to be here figured, as cleerly; as in the oblation of Isaac, or in any other type of him in the Old Testament: He was both the sacrificed Goat, and the Scape Goat; *Hee was oppressed, and he was afflicted* (Esay 53.7); *he opened not his mouth; he is brought as a lamb to the slaughter, and as a sheep is dumbe before the shearer, so he opened not his mouth:* Here he is the *sacrificed Goat. He hath born our Griefs,* (ver. 4) *and carried our sorrows:* And again, (ver.6) *the Lord hath laid upon him the iniquities of us all:* And so he is the *Scape Goat. He was cut off from the land of the living* (ver. 8) *for the transgression of my People:* There again he is the *sacrificed Goat.* And again, (ver. 11) *he shall bear their sins:* Hee is the *Scape Goat.*" The passage is striking for its very deliberateness, the orderly intercalation of lines depicting the Suffering Servant imparting to the figure of the immolated goat new sacrificial resonances, but not without turning what it means to bear sins down a sunless *via* of its own; in Hobbes's reading the scapegoat as a bearer of griefs and sorrows becomes like its immolated fellow an image of "our Saviour Christs sufferings." This militates against the triumphalism by which the scapegoat as type of Christ's resurrection is ordinarily marked. Isaiah's language is so dark and life from the dead so joylessly adduced that the passage all but turns the escape motif on its head. The bleak implications of what it means to bear sins overwhelm the dual-nature typology, which then seems perfunctory and misplaced. Thomas Hobbes, *Leviathan, Or, the Matter, Forme, and Power of a Common Wealth, Ecclesiasticall and Civil by Thomas Hobbes* (London: Printed for Andrew Crooke, 1651), 261–262.

71. Burton, *Christians Bulvvarke*, 69. The typology is recapitulated from an earlier work. See: Henry Burton, *Truth's Triumph Ouer Trent: Or, the Great Gulfe Betweene Sion and Babylon that is, the Vnreconcileable Opposition Betweene the Apostolicke Church of Christ, and the Apostate Synagogue of Antichrist, in the Maine and Fundamentall Doctrine of Iustification, for which the Church of England Christs Spouse, Hath Iustly, through Gods Mercie, for these Manie Yeares, According to Christs Voyce, Separated Her Selfe from Babylon, with Whom from Henceforth She must Hold no Communion. by H.B. Rector of S. Mathews Friday-Street* (London: Printed [by Robert Young] for Mich. Sparke, 1629), 69.

72. Anthony Burgess, *CXLV Expository Sermons upon the Whole 17th Chapter of the Gospel According to St. John, Or, Christs Prayer before His Passion Explicated, and both Practically and Polemically Improved by Anthony Burgess* (London: Printed by Abraham Miller for Thomas Underhill, 1656), 507.

73. Burgess, *Expository Sermons*, 507.

74. Burgess, *Expository Sermons*, 507.

75. Robert Southey, *Southey's Common-Place Book*, series 2, ed. John Wood Warter (London: Longman, Brown, Green and Longmans, 1850), 151.

76. Jackson, *Ecclesiastes*, 26–27.

77. Jackson, *Ecclesiastes*, 27.

78. Jackson, *Ecclesiastes*, 27.

79. Richard Steward, *Catholique Divinity: Or, the most Solid and Sententious Expressions of the Primitive Doctors of the Church. with Other Ecclesiastical, and Civil Authors: Dilated upon, and Fitted to the Explication of the most Doctrinal Texts of Scripture, in a Choice Way both for the Matter, and the Language; and very Useful for the Pulpit, and these Times. / by Dr. Stuart, Dean of St. Pauls, Afterwards Dean of Westminster, and Clerk of the Closet to the Late K. Charles* (London: Printed for H. M. and are to bee sold by Timo. Smart at his shop in the Great Old-Bayly near the Sessions-house, 1657), 272–273.

80. George Downame, *A Treatise of Iustification. by George Dovvname, Doctor of Divinity and Bishop of Dery* (London: Printed by Felix Kyngston for Nicolas Bourne, and are to be sold at his shop, at the south entrance of the Royall Exchange, 1633), 90.

81. Samuel Purchas, *Purchas His Pilgrimage. Or Relations of the VVorld and the Religions Obserued in all Ages and Places Discouered, from the Creation Vnto this Present in Foure Partes. this First Containeth a Theologicall and Geographicall Historie of Asia, Africa, and America, with the Ilands Adiacent. Declaring the Ancient Religions before the Floud . . . with Briefe Descriptions of the Countries, Nations, States, Discoueries, Priuate and Publike Customes, and the most Remarkable Rarities of Nature, Or Humane Industrie, in the Same. by Samuel Purchas, Minister at Estwood in Essex* (London: Printed by William Stansby for Henrie Fetherstone, and are to be sold at his shoppe in Pauls Church-yard at the signe of the Rose, 1613), 107.

82. George Stradling, with James Harrington, *Sermons and Discourses upon several Occasions by G. Stradling . . . ; Together with an Account of the Author* (London: Printed by J.H. for Thomas Bennet, 1692), 53–54.

Chapter 6. Anthropologies of the Scapegoat

1. Robert Fraser, *The Making of "The Golden Bough": The Origins and Growth of an Argument* (Basingstoke, Hampshire, UK: Macmillan Press, 1990), 142.

2. James George Frazer, *The Golden Bough: A Study in Magic and Religion*, 3rd ed., vol. 6 (London: Macmillan, 1913), preface.

3. Frazer, *The Golden Bough*, 407–408.

4. Frazer, *The Golden Bough*, 422.

5. Frazer, *The Golden Bough*, 422. The citations in this section identifying the king with deity and positing his actual death at the hands of his worshippers describe just one of two scenarios of nascent monarchy in Frazer's writing. In the other, the king merely plays the part of the god of vegetation, enacting its death and rebirth, thus magically inducing the god and by extension, the crops, to follow suit. There is no expulsion, no blood shed at all in this scenario; for reasons that will become evident, Frazer's vision of the king's actual immolation as a living embodiment of divinity interests Girard far more, but even this, we should remember, is not strictly a matter of persecution according to Frazer, as though the king were an object of communal hatred. In the early societies that Frazer speculates about, there is no malevolence on the part of the community toward its 'victim' who is killed to revive the vegetation and refecundate the women and livestock. The sacred king, whose immolation Frazer saw as congenital to all religion, is not therefore a "scapegoat" in the strict sense. His killing is a purely magical device. Noting inconsistencies in Frazer's writing on the relationship of Myth and Ritual (cf. note 380)—to which his views on kingship are related—Ackerman complains of Frazer's "seeming indifference to self-contradiction," concluding that "the strength of Frazer's mind lay in its power to synthesize vast amounts of data into manageable categories" and that he "lacked the analytic rigor" for "a sweeping investigation

into the deepest springs of human behavior." Robert Ackerman, "Frazer on Myth and Ritual," *Journal of the History of Ideas* 36, no. 1 (1975), 130.

6. Frazer, *The Golden Bough*, 408.

7. Frazer, *The Golden Bough*, 408.

8. The superimposition of the ethical could for example be observed in rites during which a divine animal was heaped with apologies before being slain in what Frazer saw as an attempt to expiate guilt. The Apis bull was another, slightly different case in point. Lucian's account of its sacrifice by the Egyptians mentioned the self-tonsuring of worshippers and lavish displays of grief which Frazer interpreted as purely magical gestures attributable to their belief in the bull's divinity. But Herodotus had mentioned its offering by decapitation, after which a curse was laid on its head. The cursed head was then hustled off to market and sold to the Greeks or, barring that, unceremoniously dumped into the river. In Frazer's view the inconsistency of these gestures pointed to a change in the meaning of the sacrifice. At some point the death of the sacred beast had come to be seen as "an opportunity to heap all kinds of noxious influences—moral culpability, disease—on his unfortunate head." Fraser, *Making*, 140. This too was a form of expiation and the rite had thus acquired a religious signification: "In so far as Apis died to release his strength into another and fitter bull, his slaughter was magical. In so far as he was laden with curses, however, it was religious. In this second capacity, and this capacity alone, Apis died as a scapegoat." Fraser, *Making*, 140.

9. Frazer, *The Golden Bough*, 411.

10. Fraser, *Making*, 150.

11. Frazer, *The Golden Bough*, 355.

12. Fraser, *Making*, 154.

13. Fraser, *Making*, 142.

14. Frazer, *The Golden Bough*, 422–423.

15. Girard et al., *Things Hidden*, 132.

16. Walter Burkert, René Girard, and Jonathan Z. Smith, *Violent Origins* (Stanford, CA: Stanford University Press, 1987), 76.

17. Girard et al., *Things Hidden*, 32.

18. René Girard, *Violence and the Sacred*, trans. Patrick Gregory (Baltimore: Johns Hopkins University Press, 1977), 317–318.

19. Frazer, *The Golden Bough*, 422.

20. René Girard, *Deceit, Desire, and the Novel: Self and Other in Literary Structure* (Baltimore: Johns Hopkins University Press, 1976), 18.

21. Girard, *Violence and the Sacred*, 14–15.

22. Girard, *The Scapegoat*, 317.

23. Jean-Michel Oughourlian and Guy Lefort, "Psychotic Structure and Girard's Doubles," "Special Issue on the Work of Rene Girard," *Diacritics* 8, no. 1 (1978): 72.

24. Richard Joseph Golsan, *René Girard and Myth: An Introduction* (New York: Garland, 1993), 140.

25. Girard et al., *Things Hidden*, 102.

26. Girard et al., *Things Hidden*, 102.

27. Girard et al., *Things Hidden*, 102.

28. Girard et al., *Things Hidden*, 102.

29. Girard et al., *Things Hidden*, 94.

30. The structuralist preoccupation with the problematic of nature and culture is replaced by the evolutionary question of the passage from animal to human: "I think that Lévi-Strauss and his followers are wrong when they say that ethology teaches us nothing relevant to humanity. That's why mimetic theory interests me so much: you can start with it at the animal level and trace it across the threshold of hominization right into human culture. That threshold is when the victim becomes the conscious object of attention by members of the community. The behavior is no longer purely instinctual. You can take as many eons as you want to get to that point, but at least you've got something that takes into account the animality of man without making it triumph. You have cultural specificity, a break between animal and man." Thomas F. Bertonneau, "The Logic of the Undecideable: An Interview with René Girard," *Paroles Gelées* 5 (1987): 22.

31. Girard, *Violence and the Sacred*, 93.

32. Girard, *Violence and the Sacred*, 93.

33. René Girard and James G. Williams, "The Anthropology of the Cross: A Conversation with René Girard," in *The Girard Reader*, ed. James G. Williams (New York: Crossroad, 1996), 269.

34. Girard, *Violence and the Sacred*, 7.

35. For a discussion of "two sorts of substitution" in sacrifice see *Violence and the Sacred*, 74–76, where Jacob's deception of Isaac furnishes Girard with an instance of their misleading superimposition, a defining feature of the "sacrificial system" as such.

36. Wright, *The Disposal of Impurity*, 51.

37. Girard et al., *Things Hidden*, 51.

38. Girard et al., *Things Hidden*, 51.

39. Girard et al., *Things Hidden*, 52.

40. Girard et al., *Things Hidden*, 42.

41. Rebecca Adams and René Girard, "Violence, Difference, Sacrifice: A Conversation with René Girard," in "Violence, Difference, Sacrifice: Conversations on Myth and Culture in Theology and Literature," special issue, *Religion & Literature* 25, no. 2 (1993): 18.

42. Burkert, Girard, and Smith, *Violent Origins*, 88.

43. Girard, *Violence and the Sacred*, 56.

44. Girard et al., *Things Hidden*, 147.

45. Girard et al., *Things Hidden*, 147–148.

46. Girard, *Violence and the Sacred*, 93.

47. Girard, *Violence and the Sacred*, 93.

48. Ackerman notes: "On no matter did [Frazer] change his mind more often than on the nature and origin of myth and its relation to ritual. One can find, strewn through the several editions and many volumes of *The Golden Bough*, statements by Frazer supporting at least three different and incompatible theories concerning myth: euhemerism, cognitionism, and ritualism. The first is a hardy perennial dating back to ancient times and much embraced by Enlightenment *philosophes*: that myths are based (however loosely) on real events in the lives of real heroes and kings, who are the originals of the gods. . . . The second, cognitionism, is Tylor's doctrine that myths arise from the attempt made by primitive man to racionate. The results are etiological tales that explain how the world came to be the way it is; myths are thus mistaken efforts at scientific explanation. The third, ritualism, begins with two assumptions. The first is Frazer's notion . . . that religion originated in man's attempts to control the world by coercing the gods to do his bidding magically (that is, by means of ritual). The second, derived from Frazer's two early

mentors Robertson Smith and Mannhardt, asserts that man worshipping is first (and foremost) an actor. He *does* something to cause his gods to shine their countenances upon him; he may sing or chant and he will certainly dance. When he moves he acts out what he wants the gods to do for him: assure him a plentiful catch or a good hunt, cause his enemies to fall before him, make his women or his fields or his cattle bear. Myth arises when, for some reason—a religious reform, or the passage of time that brings with it simple forgetfulness and/or misunderstanding—the ritual falls into disuse, with the result that the words, which had been only (or mainly) accompaniment to the essential ceremonial actions, now take on an independent life of their own. What do these words say? They originally came into being as a description of what the performers or dancers were doing as they imitated the gods enacting something desirable; they now become the stories of the god's actions themselves—myths. Thus behind the myth is the archaic, superseded ritual, and it is the ritual that permits us to examine how primitive man truly thought of himself in relation to the universe." Ackerman, "Frazer on Myth and Ritual," 123–125. Ackerman observes that euhemerism, the "affirmation of historical originals behind the gods, becomes increasingly important through the third edition [of *The Golden Bough*]." Robert Ackerman, *J. G. Frazer: His Life and Work* (New York: Cambridge University Press, 1987), 239.

49. Girard, *Violence and the Sacred*, 8.

50. Girard, *Violence and the Sacred*, 8.

51. Girard, *Violence and the Sacred*, 3.

52. Girard, *The Scapegoat*, 200.

53. In the Hebrew Bible glimpses of the victim as scapegoat, of his mistreatment or death at the hands of the community, shine through here and there. Although so structurally similar as to be easily mistaken for ordinary myths, they make up a countervailing tradition in Girard's view, one that stands with victims and represents the reconciled community as guilty of murder. They tell stories strikingly like those in myth but with small changes that allow the emphasis to fall on the victim's persecution and so stymie all sacred representations of his status as divine. The story of Cain and Abel contrasts tellingly with that of Romulus and Remus in this regard. Both feature rivalrous doubles. Both end in fratricide and the founding of cities. But where Remus is finally guilty of trespassing "the ideal limit traced by Romulus between the inside and the outside of the city," Abel is innocent and his blood cries out to God from the ground. Romulus kills his brother at a moment when there is as yet no city, because "in order for the city to exist, no one can be allowed to flout with impunity the rules it prescribes." The sacrifice of Remus is therefore a constitutive act that resolves the crisis of doubles and founds Rome, turning Romulus into the incarnation of Roman power. Cain, too, is a founder of cities, but the Bible casts him as a "vulgar murderer," wholly unexcused by the fact that his brother's death "precipitates the first cultural development of the human race." Girard et al., *Things Hidden*, 146–147.

54. Girard, *The Scapegoat*, 101.

55. Girard, *The Scapegoat*, 101.

56. Girard, *The Scapegoat*, 111. In this connection Girard frequently mentions Peter's speech in Acts 3: "Now I know, brothers, that neither you nor your leaders had any idea what you were really doing; but this was the way God carried out what he had foretold, when he said through all his prophets that his Christ would suffer. Now you must repent and turn to God, so that your sins may be wiped out." Acts 3:17–19a.

57. Girard, *The Scapegoat*, 111.

58. Girard , *The Girard Reader*, 282.

59. René Girard and Benoît Chantre, *Battling to the End* (East Lansing: Michigan State University Press, 2010), 20.

Chapter 7. The Goat and the Idol

1. Robin Lane Fox, *Pagans and Christians* (London: Viking, 1986), 31.

2. Fox, *Pagans and Christians*, 31.

3. Fox, *Pagans and Christians*, 37–38.

4. Girard, *The Scapegoat*, 200.

5. Girard, *Violence and the Sacred*, 93.

6. Fulton, *From Judgment to Passion*, 105.

7. Girard et al., *Things Hidden*, 102

8. Girard et al., *Things Hidden*, 102.

Chapter 8. A Figure in Flux

1. Girard, *Things Hidden*, 132.

2. See Preface, note 16.

3. John Norden, *A Christian Familiar Comfort and Incouragement Vnto all English Subiects, Not to Dismaie at the Spanish Threats Whereunto is Added an Admonition to all English Papists, Who Openly Or Couertly Couet a Change. with Requisite Praiers to Almightie God for the Preseruation of our Queene and Countrie. by the most Vnworthie I.N.* (London: [By T. Scarlet and J. Orwin] for J. B[rome], 1596), 9–10.

4. Nathaniel Pownall, with Giles Fletcher, *The Young Divines Apologie for His Continuance in the Vniuersitie with Certaine Meditations, Ritten by Nathaniel Povvnoll, Late Student of Christ-Church in Oxford* ([London]: Printed by Cantrell Legge printer to the Vniuersitie of Cambridge, 1612. And are to be sold in Pauls Churchyard: by Matthevv Lovvnes at the signe of the Bishops head, 1612), 1.

5. Pownall, *The Young Divines Apologie*, 141–142.

6. In the game the community "has perceived and retained the role of chance in the liberating decision"; though the game preserves the "arbitrary nature of the violent resolution" that saves the group, its outcome will nevertheless be treated as divinely predestined. Girard, *Violence and the Sacred*, 312. Thus the casting of lots straddles the line dividing the sacred from its inception in a reflexive act of violence.

7. Jean Barrin, *The Monk Unvail'd: Or, A Facetious Dialogue, Discovering the several Intrigues, and Subtil Practises, Together with the Lewd and Scandalous Lives of Monks, Fryers, and Other Pretended Religious Votaries of the Church of Rome. Written by an Eminent Papist in French. Faithfully Translated by C.V. Gent* (London: Printed for Jonathan Edwin, at the Three Roses in Ludgate-street, 1678),40–41. The Abbé Jean Barrin's infamous *Venus dans le cloitre ou la religieuse en chemise* distinguishes itself sometime around 1680 as "the first French libertine novel set in the convent." The book takes the form of a "sexual initiation dialogue" between two nuns. It will be the occasion of the first common-law conviction for obscene libel upon its translation into English and publication by Edward Curll in 1724. Christopher Rivers, "Safe Sex: The Prophylactic Walls of the Cloister in the French Libertine Convent Novel of the Eighteenth Century," *Journal of the History of Sexuality* 5, no. 3 (1995): 383.

8. Edward Ward, *The Pleasures of Matrimony, Intermix'd with Variety of Merry and Delightful Stories. Containing the Charms and Contentments of Wooing and Wedlock, in all its Enjoyments,*

Recreations, and Divertisements (London: Printed for H. Rhodes at the Star, the corner of Bride-lane, in Fleetstreet, 1703), 147.

9. The *Oxford English Dictionary* gives 1809 as the earliest use for "scapegrace," 1782 for "scamp."

10. J. S., *City and Country Recreation: Or, Wit and Merriment Rightly Calculated, for the Pleasure and Advantage of either Sex. in Two Parts. Part I. Containing the Pleasures of Courtship and Address; Or, the Whole Art of Making Love. Directions for Making a Suitable Choice. A Description of True Love in all its Changes. how to Express Love's Silent Language. to Know if a Party be in Love. Instructions for Courting a Maid Or Widow: And how the Female Sex may make Love Known, without any Injury to a Modest and Vertuous Behaviour; and how to Dive into the Secret Thoughts of their Lovers. the Comforts of Marriage in all its Circumstances; and how a Good Wife may Reclaim a Bad Husband, and the Like of a Husband by a Wife. the Whole Art of Fortune-Telling, Shewing what Good Or Bad Fortune is Assigned You in Affairs of Love, Business, &c. A Collection of Choice Poems, by the most Celebrated Wits of the Age. Part II. Containing all the Cunning Intreagues of the Beaus, Sharpers, Bullies, and Female-Decoys, to Deceive and Ruin Gentlemen, Tradesmen, &c. with their Lively Characters, and a Plain Discription of their several Practices, to Prevent their Future Designs. the Town Miss; Or, London Jilt, in all Her Humours, Shifts, and Intreagues; Set Forth, as a Looking-Glass, for the Unthinking Beaus; Keeping Squires, Foolish Tradesmen, and Others, to See their Folly in. to which is Added, the Misery of Gaming: Or, the Art of Keeping Ready Money in One's Pocket at all Times: With Other Useful Matters, Never before made Publick* (London: Printed by W.O. for P. Parker, at the Leg and Star in Cornhil, 1705), 168–169.

11. J. S., *City and Country*, 169.

12. J. S., *City and Country*, 148.

13. J. S., *City and Country*, 150–151.

14. The *Dispensary Transvers'd: Or, the Consult of Physicians. A Poem. in Six Canto's. Occasion'd by the Death of His Late H. the D. of G-r.* (London: Printed for John Nutt, near Stationers-Hall, 1701), preface.

15. The *Dispensary Transvers'd*, preface.

16. The *Examiners for the Year 1711. to which is Prefix'd, A Letter to the Examiner*, vol. 2 (London, 1712), 311.

17. The *Prophecies, and Predictions, for London's Deliverance with the Conjunction, Effects, and Influences of the Superiour Planets, the Causes Thereof, and the Probability of the Happy Abatement of the Present Dismal Pestilence, (According to Natural Causes the Ti[m]e when, and the we[e]Ks and Moneths Fore-Told, when the City of London [sic] Wil[l] be Freed and Acquitted from the Violent Raging of this Destructive Enemy. The Appearance of which Great Pest was Predicted by the Learned Mr. Lilly. Mr. Booker, Mr. Gadbury, Mr. Trigge, and Mr. Andrews* ([London]: Printed for Tho. Brooks, and are to be sold near the Royal Exchange, 1665), 4.

18. *Prophecies, and Predictions*, 4.

19. *Prophecies, and Predictions*, 5.

20. *Prophecies, and Predictions*, 3.

21. Marseilles Chambre du Conseil de l'Hôtel, de Ville, *An Historical Account of the Plague at Marseilles. Giving a Particular Relation of all the Different Occurrences that Happen'd during the Visitation in that City. Publish'd by Authority at Paris, and Faithfully Translated from the Original French. by a Physician. to which is Added, a Letter from Monsier Pons, Physician of the Faculty of Montpelier, Wrote from Marseilles (while He Resided there by Order of the Regent) to Monsieur De Bon Chevalier, First President of the Court of Aids and Finances of Montpelier; Discovering the Nature and Cause of the Pestilence, its Symptoms, and the Methods and Medicines used for the*

Recovery of the Infected (London: Printed for M. Billingsley under the Royal-Exchange; A. Dodd, without Temple-Bar, and J. Fox in Westminster-Hall, 1721), 116.

22. *Prophecies, and Predictions*, 5.

23. *Prophecies, and Predictions*, 10.

24. John Trenchard, *Cato's Letters: Or, Essays on Liberty, Civil and Religious, and Other Important Subjects. in Four Volumes*, 4th ed., vol. 1 (London: Printed for W. Wilkins, T. Woodward, J. Walthoe, and J. Peele, 1737), 142–143.

Chapter 9. Early Modern Texts of Persecution

1. From *Judgment of the King of Navarre* by Guillaume de Machaut, in Girard, *The Scapegoat*, 2.

2. Machaut, *Judgment*, in Girard, *The Scapegoat*, 4.

3. Girard, *The Scapegoat*, 39.

4. Girard, *The Scapegoat*, 38.

5. Girard, *The Scapegoat*, 41.

6. Girard, *The Scapegoat*, 204.

7. Girard, *The Scapegoat*, 204.

8. George Bishop, *New England Judged, Not by Man's, but the Spirit of the Lord: And the Summe Sealed Up of New-England's Persecutions being a Brief Relation of the Sufferings of the People Called Quakers in those Parts of America from the Beginning of the Fifth Moneth 1656 (the Time of their First Arrival at Boston from England) to the Later End of the Tenth Moneth, 1660 . . . / by George Bishope* (London: Printed for Robert Wilson, 1661), 89.

9. "In 1659 the court sentenced to death Marmaduke Stephenson, a Yorkshire farmer, William Robinson, a young London resident, and Rhode Islander Mary Dyer, a former Boston resident and staunch supporter of Anne Hutchinson. On the intercession of her merchant husband and son, Dyer was reprieved, although she was made to accompany her companions to the place of execution and to stand with a halter around her neck as they were hanged. Dyer then left the colony, but continuing to feel called to witness there, returned to meet her death in 1660." Carla Gardina Pestana, "The Quaker Executions as Myth and History," *Journal of American History* 80, no. 2 (1993): 441.

10. John Winthrop, *The Journal of John Winthrop, 1630–1649*, ed. Richard S. Dunn, James Savage, and Laetitia Yeandle (Cambridge: Harvard University Press, 1996), 253.

11. Thomas Weld, preface to *A Short Story of the Rise, Reign, and Ruin of the Antinomians Familists & Libertines that Infected the Churches of Nevv-England and how they were Confuted by the Assembly of Ministers there, as also of the Magistrates Proceedings in Court Against them: Together with Gods Strange and Remarkable Judgements from Heaven upon some of the Chief Fomenters of these Opinions, and the Lamentable Death of Ms. Hutchison: Very Fit for these Times, here being the Same Errours Amongst Us and Acted by the Same Spirit / Published at the Instant Request of Sundry, by One that was an Eye and Eare-Witnesse of the Carriage of Matters there*, by John Winthrop (London: Printed for Ralph Smith, 1644).

12. Winthrop, *Journal of John Winthrop*, 290.

13. John Winthrop, *Winthrop's Journal, "History of New England," 1630–1649*, ed. James Kendall Hosmer (New York: C. Scribner's Sons, 1908), 1:331.

14. Edward Johnson, *Johnson's Wonder-Working Providence, 1628–1651*, ed. J. Franklin Jameson (New York: C. Scribner's Sons, 1910), 132.

15. Lyle Koehler, "The Case of the American Jezebels: Anne Hutchinson and Female Agitation during the Years of Antinomian Turmoil, 1636–1640," *William and Mary Quarterly* 31, no. 1 (1974): 64.

16. John Winthrop, *A Short Story of the Rise, Reign, and Ruin of the Antinomians, Familists, and Libertines that Infected the Churches of Nevv-England and how they were Confuted by the Assembly of Ministers there as also of the Magistrates Proceedings in Court Against them: Together with God's Strange Remarkable Judgements from Heaven upon some of the Chief Fomenters of these Opinions: And the Lamentable Death of Ms. Hutchison. Very Fit for these Times, here being the Same Errors Amongst Us, and Acted by the Same Spirit: Published at the Instant Request of Sundry, by One That Was an Eye and Eare-Witness of the Carriage of Matters There* (London: Printed for Ralph Smith, 1644), 24.

17. Winthrop, *Short Story*, 66.

18. Winthrop, *Journal of John Winthrop*, 362.

19. Perry Miller, *The New England Mind: The Seventeenth Century* (Cambridge: Harvard University Press, 1963), 391.

20. Winthrop, *Journal of John Winthrop*, 255.

21. Winthrop, *Short Story*, 44.

22. Winthrop, *Journal of John Winthrop*, 255.

23. Johnson, *Johnson's Wonder-Working Providence*, 132.

24. Winthrop, *Journal of John Winthrop*, 255.

25. Winthrop, *Short Story*, 44.

26. Winthrop, *Short Story*, 45.

27. Wintrop, *Short Story*, 44.

28. Winthrop, *Journal of John Winthrop*, 255.

29. Carol F. Karlsen, *The Devil in the Shape of a Woman: Witchcraft in Colonial New England* (New York: Norton, 1987), 17.

30. Weld, preface to Winthrop, *Short Story* (1644).

31. Weld, preface to Winthrop, *Short Story* (1644).

32. Weld, preface to Winthrop, *Short Story* (1644).

33. Weld, preface to Winthrop, *Short Story* (1644).

34. John Wheelwright, *Mercurius Americanus, Mr. Welds His Antitype, Or, Massachusetts Great Apologie Examined, being Observations upon a Paper Styled, A Short Story of the Rise, Reign, and Ruine of the Familists, Libertines, &c. which Infected the Churches of New-England, &c. Wherein some Parties Therein Concerned are Vindicated, and the Truth Generally Cleared. by John Wheelvvright Junior. Philalethes* (London: Printed, and are to be sold at the Bull near the Castle-Tavern in Cornhill, 1645), 6.

35. Wheelwright, *Mercurius Americanus*, 6–7.

36. Karlsen, *Devil*, 122.

37. Pestana notes that on Palm Sunday 1656, Quaker leader James Nayler "re-created Christ's entry into Jerusalem by riding into Bristol on an ass." Pestana, "Quaker Executions," 442. Schama notes that Nayler was "tried for blasphemy by parliament and the Council of State in the late autumn of 1656." His crime "had been to ride through Bristol in imitation of the Saviour (pretending that he *was* Christ, said his prosecutors), his few disciples crying hosanna as he trotted through the rain-soaked streets. For his deranged temerity Nayler was pilloried for two hours, his forehead branded

with a 'B' for blasphemer, his tongue bored through with a hot iron, flogged through the streets
of London—and then taken to Bristol to be flogged all over again before being incarcerated.
He endured the excruciating torment with astonishing fortitude, but died four years later still
suffering from its after-effects." Simon Schama, *A History of Britain: The British Wars, 1603–1776*
(London: BBC, 2001), 241.

38. Anne G. Myles, "From Monster to Martyr: Re-Presenting Mary Dyer," *Early American Literature*
    36, no. 1 (2001), 5.

39. Cotton Mather, *Magnalia Christi Americana: Or, the Ecclesiastical History of New-England, from
    its First Planting, in the Year 1620, Unto the Year of our Lord 1698 . . .* , vol. 2 (Hartford: S. Andrus
    & son, 1853), 527.

40. Mather, *Magnalia Christi Americana*, 527.

41. John Norton, *The Heart of New-England Rent at the Blasphemies of the Present Generation. Or a
    Brief Tractate, Concerning the Doctrine of the Quakers, Demonstrating the Destructive Nature Thereof,
    to Religion, the Churches, and the State; with Consideration of the Remedy Against it. Occasional
    Satisfaction to Objections, and Confirmation of the Contrary Truth. / by John Norton, Teacher of
    the Church [of] Christ at Boston. Who was Appointed Thereunto, by the Order of the General Court*
    (London: Printed by John Allen at the Rising-Sunne in St. Pauls Church-yard, 1660), 8.

42. Norton, *Heart of New-England*, 8.

43. Norton, *Heart of New-England*, 8.

44. Mather, *Magnalia Christi Americana*, 525. "Now, I know not whether the sect which hath
    appeared in our days under the name of Quakers, be not upon many accounts the worst of
    hereticks; for in Quakerism, which has by some been called, the 'sink of all heresies,' we see
    the *vomit* cast out in the by-past ages by who[l]e *kennels* of seducers, lick'd up again for a *new
    digestion*, and once more exposed for the *poisoning* of mankind; though it pretends unto *light*, yet
    by the means of that very pretence it leaves the bewildered souls of men 'in chains unto darkness,'
    and gives them up to the conduct of an *Ignis Fatuus*: but this I know, they have been the most
    venomous of all to the churches in America." Mather, *Magnalia Christi Americana*, 522.

45. Mather, *Magnalia Christi Americana*, 523.

46. Thomas Maule, *Nevv-England Pesecutors* [sic] *Mauled VVith their Own VVeapons Giving some
    Account of the Bloody Laws made at Boston Against the Kings Subjects that Dissented from their Way
    of Worship: Together with a Brief Account of the Imprisonment and Tryal of Thomas Maule of Salem,
    for Publishing a Book Entituled Truth Held Forth and Maintained, &c. / by Tho. Philathes* (New
    York: William Bradford, 1697), 42.

47. ". . . that extraordinary Quaker Ark which crossed the Atlantic without chart or compass and with
    no sailing directions except those vouchsafed by the Holy Spirit." Frederick B. Tolles, "A Quaker's
    Curse: Humphrey Norton to John Endecott, 1658," *Huntington Library Quarterly* 14, no. 4 (1951):
    416.

48. Tolles, "A Quaker's Curse," 416.

49. Humphrey Norton, John Rous, and John Copeland, *New-England's Ensigne it being the Account
    of Cruelty, the Professors Pride, and the Articles of their Faith, Signified in Characters Written in
    Blood, Wickedly Begun, Barbarously Continued, and Inhumanly Finished (so Far as they have Gone)
    by the Present Power of Darkness Possest in the Priests and Rulers in New-England . . . : This being
    an Account of the Sufferings Sustained by us in New-England (with the Dutch) the most Part of it in
    these Two Last Yeers, 1657, 1658: With a Letter to Iohn Indicot, Iohn Norton, Governor, and Chief
    Priest of Boston, and another to the Town of Boston: Also, the several Late Conditions of a Friend
    upon the Road-Iland, before, in, and After Distraction: With some Quaeries Unto all Sorts of People,
    Who Want that which we have, &c. / VVritten at Sea, by Us Whom the VVicked in Scorn Calls*

Quakers, in the Second Month of the Yeer 1659 ; this being a Confirmation of so Much as Francis Howgill Truly Published in His Book Titled, the Popish Inquisition Newly Erected in New-England, &c. (London: Printed by T.L. for G. Calvert, at the Black-Spread Eagle neer the West-end of Pauls, 1659), 60.

50. Joseph Besse, *A Collection of the Sufferings of the People Called Quakers, for the Testimony of a Good Conscience, from the Time of their being First Distinguished by that Name in the Year 1650, to the Time of the Act, Commonly Called the Act of Toleration, Granted to Protestant Dissenters in the First Year of the Reign of King William the Third and Queen Mary, in the Year 1689. Taken from Original Record and Other Authentick Accounts, by Joseph Besse,* vol. 2 (London, 1753), 183.

51. Norton, *New-England's Ensigne,* 61.

52. Kai Erikson, *Wayward Puritans: A Study in the Sociology of Deviance* (New York: Wiley, 1966), 116–117.

53. Tolles, "A Quaker's Curse," 418.

54. Bishop, *New England Judged,* 75.

55. Bishop, *New England Judged,* 75.

56. Bishop, *New England Judged,* 76.

57. Bishop, *New England Judged,* 76.

58. Norton, *New-England's Ensigne,* 62 (italics added).

59. Jones's history contains the following account of Quaker Edward Burrough's interview with the King: "He said to the King, 'There is a vein of innocent blood opened in thy dominions which will run over all, if it is not stopped.' To which the King at once replied, 'but I will stop that vein.' 'Then stop it speedily,' said Burrough, 'for we know not how many may soon be put to death.' 'As speedily as you will. Call the Secretary and I will do it presently.' The secretary came and a mandamus was prepared on the spot. Edward Burrough pressed that it be despatched with haste. 'But I have no occasion at present to send a ship thither,' answered the King. "If *you* care to send one you may do it," and he gave Burrough the privilege of naming the messenger to carry the mandamus. Burrough at once named Samuel Shattuck, the Salem Quaker who had been banished from the Colony on pain of death! and the King appointed him as his royal messenger." Rufus Matthew Jones, Isaac Sharpless, and Amelia M. Gummere, *The Quakers in the American Colonies* (London: Macmillan, 1923), 94.

60. Jones, Sharpless, and Gummere, *Quakers in the American Colonies,* 102.

61. Jones, Sharpless, and Gummere, *Quakers in the American Colonies,* 102.

62. Writing on the period of the "Great Persecution," Cragg notes that "For a generation—from the end of the exile of Charles II [1660] till the beginning of the exile of his brother [1688]—the persecution of non-conformists was the official policy of England's rulers. On the morrow of the Restoration the Puritans began to discover that they had little protection against the malice of their foes.... Legislation against nonconformity was still on the books; the local authorities busied themselves enforcing it. In due course, new laws ... provided an instrument of repression so flexible in character and so inclusive in scope that those who persisted in dissent had little prospect of escape ... persecution pressed with cruel weight upon its victims. Though not enforced with sufficient ruthlessness to achieve its avowed objectives, it caused incalculable suffering to thousands of earnest men and women." Gerald R. Cragg, *Puritanism in the Period of the Great Persecution, 1660–1688* (Cambridge.: University Press, 1957), 248.

63. Cragg, *Great Persecution,* 247.

64. Voltaire, *Philosophical Letters: Letters Concerning the English Nation,* trans. Ernest Dilworth (Mineola, NY: Dover, 2003), 23.

65. Martin Greig, "Heresy Hunt: Gilbert Burnet and the Convocation Controversy of 1701," *Historical Journal* 37, no. 3 (1994), 571.

66. Greig, "Heresy Hunt," 574.

67. Francis Atterbury, *The Epistolary Correspondence, Visitation Charges, Speeches, and Miscellanies, of the Right Reverend Francis Atterbury, D.D. Lord Bishop of Rochester*, vol. 2 (London, 1783–87), 317.

68. Atterbury, *Epistolary Correspondence*, 335–336.

69. Atterbury, *Epistolary Correspondence*, 329.

70. Atterbury, *Epistolary correspondence*, 332.

71. Atterbury, *Epistolary correspondence*, 325.

72. Church of England, Province of Canterbury, *Brief Remarks on the Late Representation of the Lower House of Convocation; as the Same Respects the Quakers Only* (London, 1711), 3–4 (italics added).

73. Gary F. Jensen, *The Path of the Devil: Early Modern Witch Hunts* (Lanham, MD: Rowman & Littlefield, 2007), 157. "By appointing a royal governor, establishing a franchise based on freehold tenure rather than church membership, and mandating religious toleration" the Massachusetts Charter of 1691 abolished the "theocratic state" under Puritan leadership. Bruce Tucker, "The Reinvention of New England, 1691–1770," *New England Quarterly* 59, no. 3 (1986), 317.

74. Christine Leigh Heyrman, "Dissent and the Devil in Essex County," in *Saints and Revolutionaries: Essays on Early American History*, ed. David D. Hall, John M. Murrin, and Thad W. Tate (New York: Norton, 1984), 53.

75. Mather adds that "Their *Quakerism* was the *proper Effect* of their *Possession*; and not an *unconcern'd Consequent*"; Cotton Mather, *Memorable Providences Relating to Witchcrafts and Possessions a Faithful Account of Many Wonderful and Surprising Things that have Befallen several Bewitched and Possessed Person in New-England, Particularly a Narrative of the Marvellous Trouble and Releef Experienced by a Pious Family in Boston, very Lately and Sadly Molested with Evil Spirits: Whereunto is Added a Discourse Delivered Unto a Congregation in Boston on the Occasion of that Illustrious Providence: As also a Discourse Delivered Unto the Same Congregation on the Occasion of an Horrible Self-Murder Committed in the Town: With an Appendix in Vindication of a Chapter in a Late Book of Remarkable Providences from the Calumnies of a Quaker at Pen-Silvania / Written by Cotton Mather . . . and Recommended by the Ministers of Boston and Charleston* (Boston: By R. P., sold by Joseph Brunning, at his Shop at the Corner of the Prison-Lane next the Exchange, 1689), appendix, 6–7.

76. The girl's father, John Goodwin, praises Mather, whose "bowels so yearned towards us in this sad condition that he not only *pray's* with us, and for us, but he taketh one of my Children home to his own house; which indeed was but a troublesome *guest*, for such an one that had so much work lying upon his hands and heart: He took much pains in this great Service, to pull *this Child*, and her Brother and Sister out of the hand of the *Devil*." Mather, *Memorable Providences*, 50. During the Salem trials Mather would make a similar offer to take those afflicted into his home: "In this Evil-Time, I offered, at the beginning, that if the *possessed* People, might bee scattered far asunder, I would singly provide for six of them; and wee would see whether without more bitter methods, *Prayer* with *Fasting* would not putt an End unto these heavy Trials: But my offer (which none of my Revilers, would have been so courageous or so charitable, as to have made) was not accepted." Cotton Mather, *Diary of Cotton Mather, 1681–1724*, vols. 7–8 (Boston: The Society, 1911), 151–152.

77. "A *popish Book* also she could endure *very well*." Mather, *Memorable Providences*, 20–22.

78. Mather, *Memorable Providences*, 43.

79. Mather, *Memorable Providences*, appendix, 1; See also Christine Heyrman's "Dissent and the Devil," 30.

80. Thomas Maule, *Truth Held Forth and Maintained According to the Testimony of the Holy Prophets, Christ and His Apostles Recorded in the Holy Scriptures with some Account of the Judgments of the Lord Lately Inflicted upon New-England by Witchcraft: To which is Added, Something Concerning the Fall of Adam, His State in the Fall, and Way of Restoration to God again, with Many Other Weighty Things . . . / Written in True Love to the Souls of My Neighbours and all Men, which Includeth that Love to them and Myself, by Thomas Maule.* ([New York]: Printed [by William Bradford], 1695), 206.

81. Jensen, *Path of the Devil*, 157.

82. Cotton Mather, *Decennium Luctuosum an History of Remarkable Occurrences, in the Long War, which New-England Hath had with the Indian Salvages, from the Year, 1688. to the Year 1698. Faithfully Composed and Improved* (Boston: Printed by B. Green, and J. Allen, for Samuel Phillips, at the brick shop near the Old-Meeting-House, 1699), 162.

83. Norton, *Heart of New-England*, 8.

84. Richard Godbeer, *The Devil's Dominion: Magic and Religion in Early New England* (New York: Cambridge University Press, 1992), 192.

85. Godbeer, *The Devil's Dominion*, 192.

86. Cotton Mather, *The Wonders of the Invisible World Observations as Well Historical as Theological upon the Nature, the Number and the Operations of the Devils: Accompany'd with I. some Accounts of the Greievous [sic] Molestations by Daemons and Witchcrafts . . . and the Trials of some Eminent Malefactors . . . II. some Councils Directing a due Improvement of the Terrible Things Lately done by the Unusual and Amazing Range of Evil Spirits . . . III. some Conjectures upon the Great Events Likely to Befall the World in General and New England in Particular . . . IV. A Short Narrative of a Late Outrage Committed by a Knot of Witches in Swedeland . . . V. the Devil Discovered, in a Brief Discourse upon those Temptations which are the More Ordinary Devices of the Wicked One / by Cotton Mather* (Boston: Printed and sold by Benjamin Harris, 1693), 20.

87. Mather, *Wonders of the Invisible World*, 9.

88. Mather, *Wonders of the Invisible World*, B1r.

89. Mather, *Wonders of the Invisible World*, B8r.

90. Mather, *Wonders of the Invisible World*, A8v-B1r.

91. Mather, *Wonders of the Invisible World*, 48.

92. Mather, *Wonders of the Invisible World*, 53.

93. Jensen, *Path of the Devil*, 186. In one account this appears to have involved the observation of raw egg whites in water that congealed into shapes, foretelling "the occupation of future spouses." As the girls watched, the egg allegedly "took the shape of a coffin." Jensen, *Path of the Devil*, 186.

94. Jensen, *Path of the Devil*, 188.

95. Jensen, *Path of the Devil*, 188.

96. Claude Moore Fuess, "Witches at Andover," *Proceedings of the Massachusetts Historical Society* 70 (Oct. 1950—May 1953): 17.

97. Fuess, "Witches at Andover," 18.

98. Jensen, *The Path of the Devil*, 218.

99. Jensen, *Path of the Devil*, 222.

100. Jensen, *Path of the Devil*, 221. For his part, Cotton Mather would play an instrumental role in

abetting the bloodshed as a close ally of the court. In his damning retort to Mather's *Wonders of the Invisible World*, Robert Calef records the execution of the minister George Burroughs, who "was carried in a Cart with the others, through the Streets of Salem to Execution; when he was upon the Ladder, he made a Speech for the clearing of his Innocency, with such Solemn and Serious Expressions, as were to the Admiration of all present; his Prayer (which he concluded by repeating the Lord's Prayer) was so well worded and uttered with such composedness, and such (at least seeming) fervency of Spirit, as was very affecting, and drew Tears from many (so that it seemed to some, that the Spectators would hinder the Execution) . . . as soon as he was turned off, Mr. Cotton Mather, being mounted upon a Horse, addressed himself to the People, partly to declare, that he was no ordained Minister, and partly to possess the People of his guilt; saying, That the Devil has often been transformed into an Angel of Light; and this did somewhat appease the People, and the Executions went on; when he was cut down, he was dragged by the Halter to a Hole, or Grave, between the Rocks, about two Foot deep, his Shirt and Breeches being pulled off, and an old pair of Trousers of one Executed, put on his lower parts, he was so put in, together with Willard and Carryer, one of his Hands and his Chin, and a Foot of one them being left uncovered." Robert Calef, *More Wonders of the Invisible World, Or, the Wonders of the Invisible World Display'd in Five Parts . . . : To which is Added a Postscript Relating to a Book Intitled, the Life of Sir William Phips / Collected by Robert Calef, Merchant of Boston in New England* (London: Printed for Nath. Hillar . . . and Joseph Collyer, 1700), 103–104.

101. Deodat Lawson, *Christ's Fidelity the Only Shield Against Satans Malignity. Asserted in a Sermon Delivered at Salem-Village, the 24th of March, 1692. being Lecture-Day there, and a Time of Public Examination, of some Suspected for Witchcraft. by Deodat Lawson, Formerly Preacher of the Gospel there. [Six Lines of Scripture Texts]* (Boston: Printed, by B. Harris, & sold by Nicholas Buttolph, next to Guttridg's coffee-house, 1693), 66.

102. Lawson, *Christ's Fidelity*, 61.

103. Lawson, *Christ's Fidelity*, 51.

104. Lawson, *Christ's Fidelity*, 51.

105. Lawson, *Christ's Fidelity*, 51.

106. Frances Hill, *The Salem Witch Trials Reader* (Cambridge, MA: Da Capo Press, 2000), 125–126.

107. Hill, *Salem Witch Trials Reader*, 126.

108. Hill, *Salem Witch Trials Reader*, 127.

109. Jensen, *Path of the Devil*, 217.

110. Jensen, *Path of the Devil*, 217.

111. Silverman: Mather's friend "Dr. Zabdiel Boylston graphically described some of its hideous effects: "Purple Spots, the bloody and parchment Pox, Hemorahages of Blood at the Mouth, Nose, Fundament, and Privities; Ravings and Deliriums; Convulsions, and other Fits; violent inflamations and Swellings in the Eyes and Throat; so that they cannot see, or scarcely breathe, or swallow anything, to keep them from starving. Some looking as black as the Stock, others as white as a Sheet; in some, the Pock runs into Blisters, and the Skin stripping off, leaves the Flesh raw. . . . Some have been fill'd with loathsome Ulcers; others have had deep, and fistulous Ulcers in their Bodies, or in their Limbs or Joints, with Rottenness of the Ligaments and Bones: Some who live are Cripples, others Idiots, and many blind all their Days." Kenneth Silverman, *The Life and Times of Cotton Mather* (New York: Harper & Row, 1984), 337–338.

112. One of them sent by Constantinople physician Emanuel Timonius advised that inoculations be given "at the beginning of winter or spring, using as healthy a young person as can be found who is stricken with smallpox. Twelve or thirteen days into the illness, some of the youth's larger pustules are pricked with a needle, the matter being pressed out into a washed vessel and carried

without delay to the inoculee in a stopped bottle, kept warm in the bosom of the messenger. The inoculation is performed in a warm room. First, several small cuts are made with a needle or lancet in the patients arm muscles. Then on each cut is placed a drop of the matter, or "variole," which is mixed well with flowing blood. The wound is covered by a concave object, such as a walnut shell, and bound so that the arm is not rubbed by garments. Usually, according to Timonius, ten or twenty pustules break out on the inoculee, who stays at home, keeping warm and on a light diet. The incision runs with pus several days, but in a short time the pocks dry and fall off, rarely pitting." Silverman, *Life and Times*, 339–340.

113. Silverman, *Life and Times*, 350.

114. Silverman, *Life and Times*, 345.

115. Jensen, *Path of the Devil*, 157.

116. Karlsen, *Devil*, 122.

117. Girard, *Violence and the Sacred*, 275.

118. Girard, *Violence and the Sacred*, 276.

Chapter 10. A Latent History of the Modern World

1. Peter Heylyn, *Cyprianus Anglicus, Or, the History of the Life and Death of the most Reverend and Renowned Prelate William, by Divine Providence Lord Archbishop of Canterbury . . . Containing also the Ecclesiastical History of the Three Kingdoms of England, Scotland, and Ireland from His First Rising Till His Death / by P. Heylyn* (London: Printed for A. Seile, 1668), 198.

2. John Tutchin, *A New Martyrology, Or, the Bloody Assizes Now Exactly Methodizing in One Volume Comprehending a Compleat History of the Lives, Actions, Trials, Sufferings, Dying Speeches, Letters, and Prayers of all those Eminent Protestants Who Fell in the West of England and Elsewhere from the Year 1678 . . . : With an Alphabetical Table . . . / Written by Thomas Pitts* (London: Printed [according to the original copies] for John Dunton, 1693), 62.

3. Tutchin, *A New Martyrology*, 62.

4. *Memoirs of the Lord Viscount Dundee, the Highland-Clans, and the Massacre of Glenco: With an Account of Dundee's Officers, After they Went to France. by an Officer of the Army* (London, 1711), 51.

5. *Memoirs of Lord Viscount Dundee*, 51. Compare: "Colonel Hill was in like Manner clear'd, Nemine contradicente; but Lieutenant Colonel Hamilton not appearing, either perhaps because he was not in the Country, or that he was to be made the Scape-Goat, they voted that he was not clear of the Murder." Charles Hornby, *A Third Part of the Caveat Against the Whiggs, in A Short Historical Account of their Transactions since the Revolution* (London, 1712), 75.

6. Robert Ferguson, A Letter to Mr. Secretary T[renchard], Discovering a Conspiracy against the Laws and ancient Constitution of England: With Reflections on the present Pretended Plot, in *A Choice Collection of Papers Relating to State Affairs; during the Late Revolution. some Whereof were Never before Printed*, vol. 1 (London, 1703), 361. Many of the same phrases will be applied to King Charles I by the Sir Richard Bulstrode, who writes that the king's ministers "should have been pitched upon to answer criminally for all those things which were then called Miscarriages; the Law having mark'd them out as Offenders, and as Offerings of Atonement for the King's Faults (were he guilty of any) but instead of this, the King (whom all the Laws of the Land and the Constitution it self, hold not only unpunishable, but innocent) was elected as the Scape-Goat, to have the Offences of his Ministers, and the subordinate Tools of the Government, transmitted and laid upon him." Sir Richard Bulstrode, *Memoirs and Reflections upon the Reign and Government of King Charles the Ist. and K. Charles the IId. Containing an Account of several Remarkable Facts Not Mentioned by Other Historians of those Times: Wherein the Character of the Royal Martyr, and of King Charles II.*

are Vindicated from Fanatical Aspersions. Written by Sir Richard Bulstrode, Resident at Brussels to the Court of Spain, from King Charles II. and Envoy from King James II. Till the Revolution 1688. Now First Published from His Original Manuscript (London, 1721), 7.

7. *Choice Collection of Papers*, 361.

8. John Kettlewell, *A Compleat Collection of the Works of the Reverend and Learned John Kettlewell, B. D. Formerly Vicar of Coles-Hill in Warwick-Shire. in Two Volumes. the several Treatises Printed from Copies Revis'd and Improv'd by the Author, a Little before His Death. . . . to which is Prefix'd, the Life of the Author. Wherein are Contained Many Remarkable Transactions of His Time; Compiled from the Collections of George Hickes, D.D. and Robert Nelson, Esq; and Compleated by a Friend of the Author at the Desire both of Dr. Hickes and Mr. Nelson. with an Appendix of several Original Papers*, vol. 1 (London: Printed for D. Browne, A. Churchhill, J. Knapton, T. Horn, R. Knaplock, 1719), 111.

9. Kettlewell, *A Compleat Collection*, 111.

10. *A Secret History of One Year* (London, Sold by A. Dodd at the Peacock, without Temple-Bar, 1714), 37.

11. *A Sermon Preached Towards the Latter End of the Last Century, on the Anniversary Thanksgiving Day for Putting an End to the Great [sic] Rebellion, by the Restitution of the King and Royal Family, and the Restoration of the Government, in the Church and State, After Many Years Interruption* (Cambridge: 1715), 8.

12. *Sermon Preached Towards the Latter End*, 12.

13. William Nicolson, *A Sermon Preach'd before the Rt Honble the Lords . . . in the Collegiate Church of Westminster, on Saturday, the Thirtieth Day of January, MDCCII. Being The Anniversary of the Martyrdom of King Charles the First. By William Lord Bishop of Carlile* (London: Printed by Edw. Jones for Tim. Child at the White-Hart at the West-End of St. Paul's Church-yard,1703), 26.

14. Nicolson, *Sermon Preach'd*, 25–26.

15. Nicolson, *Sermon Preach'd*, 26.

16. Leslie Charles, *A Letter from Mr. Lesly to a Member of Parliament in London* (London, 1714), 2. "What has he done?" one tract replies, "He has attempted to invade us with an Army of French Papists; He has hir'd Irishmen with French Money, to take up Arms for him against the Late Queen and His Present Majesty; He is attainted, proscrib'd, and almost every Action of his Life is Treasonable." He has furthermore "harbour'd the most notorious Traytors to this Nation, and Lesley the most notorious of all of 'em; which is of it self sufficient to warrant the driving him about like a Scape-Goat." *Remarks on Lesley's Two Letters from Bar Le Duc; The First, to a High-Flying Member of the Last Parliament. The Second to the Lord Bishop of Salisbury. Remarks also, on Two Papers of the Pretender's, Privately Handed About by the Jacobites* (London: Printed for J. Roberts, near the Oxford-Arms in Warwick-Lane, 1715), 4.

17. Voltaire, *Collection Complette des Oeuvres de Mr. de V****, vol. 13 (Geneva: 1771), 206.

18. The final sentence in this citation appears to have been redacted. *A Letter to a Member of Parliament in the Country, from His Friend in London, Relative to the Case of Admiral Byng: With some Original Papers and Letters which Passed during the Expedition* (London: Printed for J. Cooke, at the King's-Arms, in Great-Turnstile, Holborn, 1756), 6–7.

19. Stentor Telltruth, *The Herald; Or, Patriot Proclaimer. being a Collection of Periodical Essays; on Government, Commerce, Publick Credit, Publick Debts, Publick Virtue, Publick Honour, on our National Disposition and Dangers, on Theatrical Management, and Other Interesting Subjects* (London: Printed for J. Wilkie, behind the Chapter-House, in St. Paul's Church-Yard, 1757), 38.

20. Richard Grenville and George Grenville *The Grenville Papers: Being the Correspondence of*

Richard Grenville, Earl Temple, K.G., and the Right Hon: George Grenville, their Friends and Contemporaries. Now First Published from the Original Mss, ed. William James Smith, vol.1 (London: J. Murray, 1852), 176.

21. Grenville and Grenville, *The Grenville Papers,* 176.

22. Tobias Smollett, *The History of England: From the Revolution to the Death of George the Second. (Designed as a Continuation of Mr. Hume's History.) in Five Volumes,* a new ed., vol. 3 (London: Printed for T. Cadell, and R. Baldwin, 1790), 504.

23. Tobias Smollett, *The History and Adventures of an Atom.* in Two Volumes, vol. 1 (Dublin: 1769), 63.

24. In the category of intuited "evidence" for unconscious origins we might consider the following citation from Proust: "Almost without exception, the faithful burst out laughing, looking like a group of cannibals in whom the sight of a wounded white man has aroused the thirst for blood. For the instinct of imitation and absence of courage govern society and the mob alike. And we all of us laugh at a person whom we see being made fun of, though it does not prevent us from venerating him ten years later in a circle where he is admired. It is in the same fashion that the populace banishes or acclaims its kings." Marcel Proust, *In Search of Lost Time,* rev. ed., trans. C. K Scott-Moncrieff, Terence Kilmartin, D. J. Enright, and Andreas Mayor, vol. 4 (New York: Modern Library, 1993), 452.

25. *The Museum, Or, the Literary and Historical Register. Volume the First* (London: Printed for R. Dodsley, 1746), 332.

26. Sarah Fyge Egerton, *The Female Advocate, Or, an Ansvver to a Late Satyr Against the Pride, Lust and Inconstancy, &c. of Woman Written by a Lady in Vindication of Her Sex* (London: Printed by H.C. for Iohn Taylor, at the Globe in St. Paul's Church-Yard, 1686), 22–24.

Conclusion. The Plowbeam and the Loom

1. Desiderius Erasmus, *An Exhortation to the Diligent Studye of Scripture, made by Erasmus Roterodamus. and Tra[n]Slated in to Inglissh. an Exposition in to the Seventh Chaptre of the First Pistle to the Corinthians* (At Malborow [i.e. Antwerp]: In the londe of Hesse. By my Hans Luft [i.e. J. Hoochstraten], 1529), 5–6.

2. Simon Schama, *A History of Britain: At the Edge of the World: 3000 B.C.–A.D. 1603* (New York: Hyperion, 2000), 284.

3. Schama, *A History of Britain,* 285.

4. Tyndale, *The Pentateuch,* 3.

5. David Norton, *A History of the English Bible as Literature* (New York: Cambridge University Press, 2000), 165.

6. Girard, *The Scapegoat,* 200.

Appendix. *Katharma* and *Peripsēma* Testimonia

For this list I drew heavily on Todd Compton's *The Pharmakos Ritual: Testimonia,* an exhaustive compilation of references assembled as background for his book *Victim of the Muses: Poet as Scapegoat, Warrior and Hero in Greco-Roman and Indo-European Myth and History* (Washington, DC: Center for Hellenic Studies, 2006). Made generously available at http://toddmcompton.com/pharmakos.htm.

1. Rudolf Kassel and Colin Austin, *Poetae Comici Graeci* (*PCG*) (Berolini Berlin; Novi Eboraci New York: W. de Gruyter, 1983), 5, 509.

2. J. M. Edmonds, August Meineke, Theodor Bergk, Theodor Kock, *The Fragments of Attic Comedy After Meineke, Bergk, and Kock,* Augment, ed. (Leiden, Netherlands: E. J. Brill, 1961), 1:347.

3. W. J. W. Koster, et al., *Scholia in Aristophanem III 1ᵇ—Scholia Recentiora in Aristophanis Ranas*, ed. by M. Chantry (Groningen, Netherlands: Egbert Forsten, 2001), 135.

4. Todd Compton, *The Pharmakos Ritual: Testimonia* at http://www.geocities.com/Athens/Oracle/7207/pharmakos.htm

5. Aristophanes. Aristophanes Comoediae, ed. F.W. Hall and W.M. Geldart, vol. 2. F.W. Hall and W.M. Geldart. Oxford. Clarendon Press, Oxford. 1907. At *Perseus:* http://www.perseus.tufts.edu/hopper/text?doc=Perseus%3Atext%3A1999.01.0039%3Acard%3D418.

6. Eugene O'Neill and Whitney Jennings Oates, *The Complete Greek Drama: All the Extant Tragedies of Aeschylus, Sophocles and Euripides, and the Comedies of Aristophanes and Menander, in a Variety of Translations* (New York: Random House, 1938). At *Perseus:* http://www.perseus.tufts.edu/hopper/text?doc=Perseus:text:1999.01.0040:card=418.

7. W. J. W. Koster, et al., *Scholia in Aristophanem III 4ᵇ—Scholia Recentiora in Plutum*, ed. by M. Chantry (Groningen, Netherlands: Egbert Forsten, 1996), 122.

8. Compton, *The Pharmakos Ritual.*

9. Aristophanes, *Aristophanes Comoediae*, eds. F. W. Hall and W. M. Geldart, 2nd ed. (Oxford: Clarendon Press, 1906).

10. O'Neill and Oates, *The Complete Greek Drama: All the Extant Tragedies of Aeschylus, Sophocles and Euripides, and the Comedies of Aristophanes and Menander, in a Variety of Translations.* At *Perseus:* http://www.perseus.tufts.edu/hopper/text?doc=Perseus:text:1999.01.0034:card=1111.

11. W. J. W. Koster, et al., *Scholia in Aristophanem 1.2 In Equites*, ed. D. M. Jones (Groningen: Woltors Noordhoff, 1969), 243.

12. Compton, *The Pharmakos Ritual.*

13. Demosthenes and S. H. Butcher, *Demosthenis Orationes* [Works.] (Oxonii; Londini et Novi Eboraci: E. Typographeo Clarendoniano; apud H. Frowde, 1907). At *Perseus:* http://www.perseus.tufts.edu/hopper/text?doc=Perseus%3Atext%3A1999.01.0073%3Aspeech%3D21%3Asection%3D185.

14. Demosthenes and A. T. Murray, *Private Orations* [Selections.] (Cambridge, MA; London: Harvard University Press; W. Heinemann, ltd., 1939).

15. Demosthenes and S. H. Butcher, *Demosthenis Orationes* [Works.] (Oxonii; Londini et Novi Eboraci: E. Typographeo Clarendoniano; apud H. Frowde, 1907). At *Perseus:* http://www.perseus.tufts.edu/hopper/text?doc=Perseus%3Atext%3A1999.01.0073%3Aspeech%3D21%3Asection%3D198.

16. Demosthenes, *Demosthenes III: Against Meidias, Androtion, Aristocrates. Timocrates, Aristogeiton XXI–XXVI*, ed. J. H. Vince (Cambridge, MA: Harvard University Press, 1935).

17. Lucian, *Lucian. Vol 7*, ed. MacLeod (Cambridge, MA: Harvard University Press, 1969).

18. Plutarch and Bernadotte Perrin, *Plutarch's Lives. with an English Translation by Bernadotte Perrin*, ed. Bernadotte Perrin (Cambridge, MA: Harvard University Press, 1914), vol. 7, 432.

19. Plutarch and Perrin, *Plutarch's Lives*, 432.

20. John Tzetzes and Pietro Luigi Leone, *Ioannis Tzetzae Historiae*, vol. 1 (Naples, Italy: Libreria scientifica editrice, 1968), 725.

21. Todd Compton, *The Pharmakos Ritual: Testimonia.*

22. Photius and S. A. Naber, *Photii Patriarchae Lexicon* (Amsterdam: A. M. Hakkert, 1864).

23. Dennis D. Hughes, *Human Sacrifice in Ancient Greece* (New York: Routledge, 1991), 162.

Bibliography

Abbot, George. *An Exposition Vpon the Prophet Ionah Contained in Certaine Sermons, Preached in S. Maries Church in Oxford. by George Abbot Professor of Diuinitie, and Maister of Vniuersitie Colledge.* London: Imprinted by Richard Field, and are to be sold by Richard Garbrand [Oxford], 1600.

Ackerman, Robert. "Frazer on Myth and Ritual." *Journal of the History of Ideas* 36, no. 1 (1975): 115–134.

———. *J. G. Frazer: His Life and Work.* New York: Cambridge University Press, 1987.

Adams, Rebecca, and René Girard. "Violence, Difference, Sacrifice: A Conversation with René Girard." In "Violence, Difference, Sacrifice: Conversations on Myth and Culture in Theology and Literature," special issue, *Religion & Literature* 25, no. 2 (1993): 9–33.

Ambrose. *A Library of Fathers of the Holy Catholic Church Anterior to the Division of the East and West.* Oxford: John Henry Parker, 1881.

Anderson, Gary A. *Sin: A History.* New Haven, CT: Yale University Press, 2009.

Anselm of Canterbury. *Why God Became Man, and the Virign Conception and Original Sin.* Translated by Joseph M. Colleran. Albany, NY: Magi Books, 1969.

———. *The Major Works.* Oxford World's Classics. Edited by Brian Davies and G. R. Evans. New York: Oxford University Press, 1998.

Aquinas, Thomas. *Summa Theologica.* Translated by the Fathers of the English Dominican Province. 1st complete American ed. New York: Benziger, 1948.

Aquinas, Thomas, and John Henry Newman. *Catena Aurea: Commentary on the Four Gospels Collected Out of the Works of the Fathers by Saint Thomas Aquinas.* New York: Cosimo Classics, 2007.

Atterbury, Francis. *The Epistolary Correspondence, Visitation Charges, Speeches, and Miscellanies, of the Right Reverend Francis Atterbury, D.D. Lord Bishop of Rochester.* Vol. 2. London, 1783–87.

Auerbach, Erich. *Scenes from the Drama of European Literature.* Translated by Ralph Manheim and Catherine Garvin. Gloucester, MA: Peter Smith, 1984.

Aulén, Gustaf. *Christus Victor: An Historical Study of the Three Main Types of the Idea of Atonement.* Translated by A. G. Hebert. New York: Macmillan, 1951.

Baker, Richard. *Meditations and Disquisitions upon the One and Fiftieth Psalme of Dauid Miserere Mei Deus. by Sr. Richard Baker, Knight.* London: Printed by Edward Griffin, for Anne Bouler, and are to be sold at the Marigold, in Pauls Church-yard, 1638.

Barrin, Jean. *The Monk Unvail'd: Or, A Facetious Dialogue, Discovering the Several Intrigues, and Subtil Practises, Together with the Lewd and Scandalous Lives of Monks, Fryers, and Other Pretended Religious Votaries of the Church of Rome. Written by an Eminent Papist in French. Faithfully Translated by C. V. Gent.* London: Printed for Jonathan Edwin, at the Three Roses in Ludgate-street, 1678.

Baumgarten, Albert I. *Sacrifice in Religious Experience.* Numen Book Series, Studies in the History of Religions 93. Boston: Brill, 2002.

Bertonneau, Thomas F. "The Logic of the Undecideable: An Interview with René Girard," *Paroles Gelées* 5 (1987): 1–23.

Besse, Joseph. *A Collection of the Sufferings of the People Called Quakers, for the Testimony of a Good Conscience, from the Time of their Being First Distinguished by that Name in the Year 1650, to the Time of the Act, Commonly Called the Act of Toleration, Granted to Protestant Dissenters in the First Year of the Reign of King William the Third and Queen Mary, in the Year 1689. Taken from Original Record and Other Authentick Accounts, by Joseph Besse. . . .* Vol. 2. London, 1753.

Bettenson, Henry Scowcroft. *The Later Christian Fathers: A Selection from the Writings of the Fathers from St. Cyril of Jerusalem to St. Leo the Great.* New York: Oxford University Press, 1970.

Bilson, Thomas. *The Effect of Certaine Sermons Touching the Full Redemption of Mankind by the Death and Bloud of Christ Iesus Wherein Besides the Merite of Christs Suffering, the Manner of His Offering, the Power of His Death, the Comfort of His Crosse, the Glorie of His Resurrection, are Handled, What Paines Christ Suffered in His Soule on the Crosse: Together, with the Place and Purpose of His Descent to Hel After Death: Preached at Paules Crosse and Else Where in London, by the Right Reuerend Father Thomas Bilson Bishop of Winchester. With a Conclusion to the Reader for the Cleering of Certaine Obiections Made Against Said Doctrine.* London: Imprinted by Peter Short for Walter Burre, and are to be sold in Paules Churchyard at the signe of the Flower deluce, 1599.

———. *The Suruey of Christs Sufferings for Mans Redemption and of His Descent to Hades Or Hel for our Deliuerance: By Thomas Bilson Bishop of Winchester. The Contents Whereof may be Seene in Certaine Resolutions before the Booke, in the Titles Ouer the Pages, and in a Table made to that End. Perused and Allowed by Publike Authoritie.* London: Printed by Melchisedech Bradwood for Iohn Bill, 1604.

Bishop, George. *New England Judged, Not by Man's, but the Spirit of the Lord: And the Summe Sealed Up of New-England's Persecutions being a Brief Relation of the Sufferings of the People Called Quakers in those Parts of America from the Beginning of the Fifth Moneth 1656 (the Time of their First Arrival at Boston from England) to the Later End of the Tenth Moneth, 1660 . . . / by George Bishope.* London: Printed for Robert Wilson, 1661.

Black, Matthew. *The Book of Enoch, Or, I Enoch: A New English Edition with Commentary and Textual Notes.* Leiden, Netherlands: E. J. Brill, 1985.

Boda, Mark J., and Gordon T. Smith. *Repentance in Christian Theology.* Collegeville, MN: Liturgical Press, 2006.

Box, G. H., and J. I. Landsman. *The Apocalypse of Abraham.* New York: Macmillan, 1919.

Bremmer, Jan N. *Greek Religion and Culture, the Bible, and the Ancient Near East.* Jerusalem Studies in Religion and Culture 8. Boston: Brill, 2008.

Browne, Thomas. *Pseudodoxia Epidemica, Or, Enquiries into Very Many Received Tenents and Commonly Presumed Truths by Thomas Browne.* London: Printed by T. H. for E. Dod, 1646.

Bullinger, Heinrich. *Fiftie Godlie and Learned Sermons Diuided into Fiue Decades, Conteyning the Chiefe and Principall Pointes of Christian Religion, Written in Three Seuerall Tomes Or Sections, by Henrie Bullinger Minister of the Churche of Tigure in Swicerlande. Whereunto is Adioyned a Triple Or Three-Folde Table Verie Fruitefull and Necessarie. Translated Out of Latine into English by H. I. Student in Diuinitie.* London: Imprinted By [Henry Middleton for] Ralphe Newberrie, dwelling in Fleet-streate a little aboue the Conduite, Anno. Gratiae, 1577.

Bulstrode, Richard. *Memoirs and Reflections upon the Reign and Government of King Charles the Ist. and K. Charles the IId. Containing an Account of several Remarkable Facts Not Mentioned by Other Historians of those Times: Wherein the Character of the Royal Martyr, and of King Charles II. are Vindicated from Fanatical Aspersions. Written by Sir Richard Bulstrode, Resident at Brussels to the Court of Spain, from King Charles II. and Envoy from King James II. Till the Revolution 1688. Now First Published from His Original Manuscript.* London, 1721.

Burgess, Anthony. *CXLV Expository Sermons upon the Whole 17th Chapter of the Gospel According to St. John, Or, Christs Prayer before His Passion Explicated, and both Practically and Polemically Improved by Anthony Burgess.* London: Printed by Abraham Miller for Thomas Underhill, 1656.

Burkert, Walter, René Girard, Jonathan Z. Smith, and Robert Hamerton-Kelly. *Violent Origins.* Stanford, CA: Stanford University Press, 1987.

Burroughs, Jeremiah. *The Eighth Book of Mr Jeremiah Burroughs. Being a Treatise of the Evil of Evils, Or the Exceeding Sinfulness of Sin. Wherein is Shewed, 1 there is More Evil in the Least Sin, than there is in the Greatest Affliction. 2 Sin is Most Opposite to God. 3 Sin is Most Opposite to Mans Good. 4 Sin is Opposite to all Good in General. 5 Sin is the Poyson, Or Evil of all Other Evils. 6 Sin Hath a Kind of Infiniteness in it. 7 Sin Makes a Man Conformable to the Devil. All these Several Heads are Branched Out into very Many Particulars. / Published by Thomas Goodwyn, William Bridge, Sydrach Sympson, William Adderly, [Double Brace] William Greenhil, Philip Nye, John Yates.* Edited by Thomas Goodwin. London: Printed by Peter Cole in Leaden-Hall, and are to be sold at his shop at the sign of the Printing-Press in Cornhil, neer the Royal Exchange, 1654.

Burton, Henry. *The Christians Bulvvarke, Against Satans Battery. Or, the Doctrine of Iustification so Plainely and Pithily Layd Out in the Severall Maine Branches of it as the Fruits Thereof may be to the Faithfull, as so Many Preservatives Against the Poysonous Heresies and Prevailing Iniquities of these Last Times. By H. B. Pastor of S. Mathevvs Friday-Street.* London: [By R. Young] for Henry Taunton, and are to be sold at his shop in Saint Dunstans Church-yard, 1632.

———. *Truth's Triumph Ouer Trent: Or, the Great Gulfe Betweene Sion and Babylon that is, the Vnreconcileable Opposition Betweene the Apostolicke Church of Christ, and the Apostate Synagogue of Antichrist, in the Maine and Fundamentall Doctrine of Iustification, for which the Church of England Christs Spouse, Hath Iustly, through Gods Mercie, for these Manie Yeares, According to Christs Voyce, Separated Her Selfe from Babylon, with Whom from Henceforth She must Hold no Communion. by H. B. Rector of S. Mathews Friday-Street.* London: Printed [by Robert Young] for Mich. Sparke, 1629.

Calamy, Edmund. *Englands Looking-Glasse Presented in a Sermon Preached before the Honorable House of Commons at their Late Solemne Fast, December 22, 1641 / by Edmund Calamy.* London: Printed by I. Raworth for Chr. Meredith, 1642.

Calef, Robert. *More Wonders of the Invisible World, Or, the Wonders of the Invisible World Display'd in Five Parts . . . : To which is Added a Postscript Relating to a Book Intitled, the Life of Sir William Phips / Collected by Robert Calef, Merchant of Boston in New England.* London: Printed for Nath. Hillar . . . and Joseph Collyer, 1700.

Calvin, Jean. *Commentaries on the Four Last Books of Moses: Arranged in the Form of a Harmony.* Vol. 2. Edinburgh: Printed for the Calvin Translation Society, 1855.

Calvin, Jean. *Tracts and Treatises.* Translated by Henry Beveridge. Grand Rapids, MI: Eerdmans, 1958.

Calvin, Jean. *Commentaries on the Four Last Books of Moses: Arranged in the Form of a Harmony.* Translated by Charles William Bingham. Calvin's Commentaries. Edinburgh: Printed for the Calvin Translation Society by T. Constable, 1852.

Calvin, Jean. *Commentaries.* Vol. 20. Translated by John King. Grand Rapids, MI: Baker Book House, 1984.

Calvin, Jean. *Commentaires de M. Jean Calvin, sur les cinq livres de Moyse. Genese est mis à part, les autres quatre livres sont disposez en forme d'Harmonie: avec cinq indices, dont les deux contenans les passages alleguez et exposez par læautheur, sont adjoustez de nouveau en ceste traduction.* Geneve: Imprimé par François Estienne, 1564.

Calvin, Jean. *Mosis libri V : cum Iohannis Caluini commentariis ; Genesis seorsum, reliqui quatuor in formam harmoniae digesti.* Geneva: Excud. Henr. Stephanus, 1563.

Calvin, John. *Calvin: Institutes of the Christian Religion.* Edited by John Thomas McNeill. Translated by Ford Lewis Battles. Library of Christian Classics 20–21. Philadelphia: Westminster Press, 1960.

Charles, Leslie. *A Letter from Mr. Lesly to a Member of Parliament in London.* London, 1714.

A Choice Collection of Papers Relating to State Affairs; During the Late Revolution. Some Whereof were Never before Printed. Vol. 1. London, 1703.

Church of England, Province of Canterbury. *Brief Remarks on the Late Representation of the Lower House of Convocation; As the Same Respects the Quakers Only.* London, 1711.

Clapham, Henoch. *The Discription of a True Visible Christian Right Confortable & Profitable for all such as are Distressed in Sowle about Present Controversies in the Churche. Dravven by He. Cl. but Published by Occasion (as Will Appeare in the Epistle) by Io. I.* Edited by John Joope. [Amsterdam?], 1599.

Clarke, Samuel. *Medulla Theologiae, Or, the Marrow of Divinity Contained in Sundry Questions and Cases of Conscience, both Speculative and Practical: The Greatest Part of them Collected Out of the Works of our most Judicious, Experienced and Orthodox English Divines, the Rest are Supplied by the Authour / by Sa. Clarke.* . . . London: Printed by Thomas Ratcliff for Thomas Underhill, 1659.

Coppin, Richard. *A Blow at the Serpent; Or a Gentle Answer from Madiston Prison to Appease Wrath Advancing it Self Against Truth and Peace at Rochester. Together with the Work of Four Daies Disputes, in the Cathedral of Rochester, in the Countie of Kent, Betweene Several Ministers, and Richard Coppin, Preacher there, to Whom Very Many People Frequentlie Came to Hear, and Much Rejoyced at the Way of Truth and Peace He Preached, at the Same Whereof the Ministers in those Parts Began to Ring in their Pulpits, Saying, this Man Blasphemeth,* . . . *Whereupon Arose the Disputes, at which were Some Magistrates, Some Officers, and Souldiers, Peaceable and Well-Minded, and Very Many People from all Parts Adjacent, before Whom the Truth was Confirm'd and Maintained. The Whole Matter Written by the Hearers, on Both Sides. Published for the Confirmation and Comfort of all such as Receive the Truth in the Love of it. By Richard Coppin, Now in Maidston Prison for the Witness of Jesus. Twenty Five Articles since Brought Against Him by the Ministers, as Blasphemie, and His Answers to them, How He Was.* London: Printed by Philip Wattleworth, and are to be sold by William Larnar at the Black-moor neer Fleet-Bridge, 1656.

Cragg, Gerald R. *Puritanism in the Period of the Great Persecution, 1660–1688.* Cambridge: University Press, 1957.

Craig, Edward, ed. *Routledge Encyclopedia of Philosophy.* New York: Routledge, 1998.

Culverwell, Nathanael. *An Elegant and Learned Discourse of the Light of Nature, with Several Other*

Treatises. . . . Edited by William Dillingham. London: Printed by T. R. and E. M. for John Rothwell, 1652.

Cyril. *St. Cyril of Alexandria: Letters.* The Fathers of the Church 76–77. Translated by John I. McEnerney. Washington, DC: Catholic University of America Press, 1987.

Danby, Herbert, trans. *The Mishnah.* Oxford: Clarendon Press, 1933.

Demosthenes. *Demosthenes III: Against Meidias, Androtion, Aristocrates. Timocrates, Aristogeiton XXI–XXVI.* Edited by J. H. Vince. Cambridge: Harvard University Press, 1935.

Demosthenes. *Demosthenis Orationes.* Edited by S. H. Butcher and W. Rennie. New York: E. Typographeo Clarendoniano, 1907. At *Perseus*: http://www.perseus.tufts.edu/hopper/text?doc=P erseus%3Atext%3A1999.01.0073%3Aspeech%3D21%3Asection%3D185.

———. *Private Orations.* Translated by A. T. Murray. Cambridge: Harvard University Press; London: W. Heinemann, 1939.

The Dispensary Transvers'd: Or, the Consult of Physicians. A Poem. In Six Canto's. Occasion'd by the Death of His Late H. the D. of G-r. London: Printed for John Nutt, near Stationers-Hall, 1701.

Downname, George. *A Treatise of Iustification by George Dovvname, Doctor of Divinity and Bishop of Dery.* London: Printed by Felix Kyngston for Nicolas Bourne, and are to be sold at his shop, at the south entrance of the Royall Exchange, 1633.

Edmonds, J. M., ed. and trans. *The Fragments of Attic Comedy After Meineke, Bergk, and Kock.* Augmented ed. Leiden, Netherlands: E. J. Brill, 1961.

Egerton, Sarah Fyge. *The Female Advocate, Or, an Ansvver to a Late Satyr Against the Pride, Lust and Inconstancy, &c. of Woman Written by a Lady in Vindication of Her Sex.* London: Printed by H. C. for Iohn Taylor, at the Globe in St. Paul's Church-Yard, 1686.

Erasmus, Desiderius. *An Exhortation to the Diligent Studye of Scripture, made by Erasmus Roterodamus. And Tra[n]Slated in to Inglissh. An Exposition in to the Seventh Chaptre of the First Pistle to the Corinthians.* Malborow [Antwerp] in the londe of Hesse: By my Hans Luft [i.e., J. Hoochstraten], 1529.

Erikson, Kai. *Wayward Puritans: A Study in the Sociology of Deviance.* New York: Wiley, 1966.

The Examiners for the Year 1711. To which is Prefix'd, A Letter to the Examiner. Vol. 2. London, 1712.

Feenstra, Ronald Jay, and Cornelius Plantinga, eds. *Trinity, Incarnation, and Atonement: Philosophical and Theological Essays.* Library of Religious Philosophy 1. Notre Dame, IN: University of Notre Dame Press, 1989.

Fraser, Robert. *The Making of "The Golden Bough": The Origins and Growth of an Argument.* Basingstoke, Hampshire, UK: Macmillan, 1990.

Frazer, James George. *The Golden Bough: A Study in Magic and Religion.* 3rd ed. London: Macmillan, 1913.

Fuess, Claude Moore. "Witches at Andover." *Proceedings of the Massachusetts Historical Society* 70 (1953): 8–20.

Fulton, Rachel. *From Judgment to Passion: Devotion to Christ and the Virgin Mary, 800–1200.* New York: Columbia University Press, 2002.

Gerstenberger, Erhard. *Leviticus: A Commentary.* The Old Testament Library. 1st American ed. Louisville, KY: Westminster John Knox Press, 1996.

Ginther, James R. *The Westminster Handbook to Medieval Theology.* Westminster Handbooks to Christian Theology. 1st ed. Louisville, KY: Westminster John Knox Press, 2009.

Girard, René. *Battling to the End.* East Lansing: Michigan State University Press, 2010.

———. *Deceit, Desire, and the Novel: Self and Other in Literary Structure.* Baltimore: Johns Hopkins University Press, 1976.

———. *The Girard Reader.* Edited by James G. Williams. New York: Crossroad, 1996.

———. *The Scapegoat.* Baltimore: Johns Hopkins University Press, 1986.

———. *Violence and the Sacred.* Translated by Patrick Gregory. Baltimore: Johns Hopkins University Press, 1977.

Girard, René, and Michael Hardin. *Reading the Bible with René Girard: Conversations with Steven E. Berry.* 2011. Unpublished interview transcript.

Girard, René, Jean-Michel Oughourlian, Guy Lefort, Stephen Bann, and Michael Leigh Metteer. *Things Hidden since the Foundation of the World.* Stanford, CA: Stanford University Press, 1987.

Godbeer, Richard. *The Devil's Dominion: Magic and Religion in Early New England.* New York: Cambridge University Press, 1992.

Golsan, Richard Joseph. *René Girard and Myth: An Introduction.* Theorists of Myth 1194. New York: Garland, 1993.

Gouge, William. *A Learned and Very Useful Commentary on the Whole Epistle to the Hebrews Wherein Every Word and Particle in the Original is Explained . . . : Being the Substance of Thirty Years Wednesdayes Lectures at Black-Fryers, London / by that Holy and Learned Divine Wiliam Gouge . . . : Before which is Prefixed a Narrative of His Life and Death: Whereunto is Added Two Alphabeticall Tables. . . .* Edited by Thomas Gouge. London: Printed by A. M., T. W. and S. G. for Joshua Kirton, 1655.

Gove, Richard. *The Saints Hony-Comb, Full of Divine Truths, Touching both Christian Belief, and a Christians Life, in Two Centuries. by Richard Gove.* London: Printed for Richard Royston at the Angel in Ivy-lane, 1652.

Grabbe, Lester L. "The Scapegoat Tradition: A Study in Early Jewish Interpretation." *Journal for the Study of Judaism in the Persian, Hellenistic and Roman Period* 18, no. 2 (1987): 153–167.

Greig, Martin. "Heresy Hunt: Gilbert Burnet and the Convocation Controversy of 1701." *Historical Journal* 37, no. 3 (1994): 569–592.

Grenville, Richard, and George Grenville. *The Grenville Papers: Being the Correspondence of Richard Grenville, Earl Temple, K. G., and the Right Hon: George Grenville, their Friends and Contemporaries. Now First Published from the Original Mss.* Edited by William James Smith. London: J. Murray, 1852.

Guild, William. *Moses Vnuailed: Or those Figures which Serued Vnto the Patterne and Shaddow of Heauenly Things, Pointing Out the Messiah Christ Iesus, Briefly Explained Wherevnto is Added the Harmony of all the Prophets, Breathing with One Mouth the Mysterie of His Comming, and of that Redemption which by His Death He was to Accomplish . . . by William Guild, Minister of Gods Word at King-Edward in Scotland.* London: Printed by G[eorge] P[urslowe] for Iohn Budge: and are to be sold at his shop in Pauls Churchyard, at the signe of the Greene Dragon, 1620.

Hall, David D., John M. Murrin, and Thad W. Tate. *Saints and Revolutionaries: Essays on Early American History.* New York: Norton, 1984.

Hammond, Henry. *A Paraphrase and Annotations upon all the Books of the New Testament Briefly Explaining all the Difficult Places Thereof / by H. Hammond.* London: Printed by J. Flesher for Richard Davis, 1659.

Heylyn, Peter. *Cyprianus Anglicus, Or, the History of the Life and Death of the Most Reverend and Renowned Prelate William, by Divine Providence Lord Archbishop of Canterbury . . . Containing also the Ecclesiastical History of the Three Kingdoms of England, Scotland, and Ireland from His First Rising Till His Death / by P. Heylyn.* London: Printed for A. Seile, 1668.

Hill, Frances. *The Salem Witch Trials Reader*. Cambridge, MA: Da Capo, 2000.

Hobbes, Thomas. *Leviathan, Or, the Matter, Forme, and Power of a Common Wealth, Ecclesiasticall and Civil by Thomas Hobbes. . . .* London: Printed for Andrew Crooke, 1651.

Hornby, Charles. *A Third Part of the Caveat Against the Whiggs, in a Short Historical Account of their Transactions since the Revolution*. London, 1712.

Ishodad of Merv. *Commentaire d'Ishodad de Merv sur l'Ancien Testament*. Vol. 2, *Exode-Deutéronome*. Edited by Ceslas van den Eynde. Louvain, Belgium: Secrétariat du Corpus SCO, 1958.

J. S. *City and Country Recreation: Or, Wit and Merriment Rightly Calculated, for the Pleasure and Advantage of Either Sex. In Two Parts. Part I. Containing the Pleasures of Courtship and Address; Or, the Whole Art of Making Love. Directions for Making a Suitable Choice. A Description of True Love in all its Changes. How to Express Love's Silent Language. To Know if a Party be in Love. Instructions for Courting a Maid Or Widow: And How the Female Sex May Make Love Known, Without Any Injury to a Modest and Vertuous Behaviour; And How to Dive into the Secret Thoughts of their Lovers. The Comforts of Marriage in All its Circumstances; and How a Good Wife May Reclaim a Bad Husband, and the Like of a Husband by a Wife. The Whole Art of Fortune-Telling, Shewing what Good Or Bad Fortune is Assigned You in Affairs of Love, Business, &c. A Collection of Choice Poems, by the Most Celebrated Wits of the Age. Part II. Containing all the Cunning Intreagues of the Beaus, Sharpers, Bullies, and Female-Decoys, to Deceive and Ruin Gentlemen, Tradesmen, &c. with their Lively Characters, and a Plain Discription of their Several Practices, to Prevent their Future Designs. The Town Miss; Or, London Jilt, in all Her Humours, Shifts, and Intreagues; Set Forth, as a Looking-Glass, for the Unthinking Beaus; Keeping Squires, Foolish Tradesmen, and Others, to See their Folly in. To which is Added, the Misery of Gaming: Or, the Art of Keeping Ready Money in One's Pocket at all Times: With Other Useful Matters, Never before Made Publick*. London: Printed by W.O. for P. Parker, at the Leg and Star in Cornhil, 1705.

Jackson, John. *Ecclesiastes the Worthy Church-Man, Or the Faithfull Minister of Iesvs Christ. Described by Polishing the Twelve Stones in the High-Priests Pectorall, as they were First Glossed and Scholyed on in a Synod-Sermon; And After Enlarged by Way of Discourse, to His Two Brethren. By Iohn Iackson Parson of Marske in Richmond-Shire*. London: Printed [by M. Flesher] for Richard More, and are to be sold at his shop in Saint Dunstanes Church-yard in Fleetstreet, 1628.

Jacob, Henry. *A Defence of a Treatise Touching the Sufferings and Victorie of Christ in the Worke of our Redemption*. Middelburg, Netherlands: R. Schilders, 1600.

——— . *A Treatise of the Sufferings and Victory of Christ, in the Work of our Redemption*. Middelburg, Netherlands: Printed by Richard Schilders, 1598.

Jeffrey, David L. *A Dictionary of Biblical Tradition in English Literature*. Grand Rapids, MI: Eerdmans, 1992.

Jensen, Gary F. *The Path of the Devil: Early Modern Witch Hunts*. Lanham, MD: Rowman & Littlefield, 2007.

Jerome. *Homilies of Saint Jerome*. Fathers of the Church, a New Translation 48, 57. Translated by Marie Liguori Ewald. Washington, DC: Catholic University of America Press, 1966.

Jessey, Henry. *The Exceeding Riches of Grace Advanced by the Spirit of Grace, in an Empty Nothing Creature, Viz. Mris. Sarah Wight Lately Hopeles and Restles, Her Soule Dwelling Far from Peace Or Hopes Thereof: Now Hopefull, and Joyfull in the Lord, that Hath Caused Light to Shine Out of Darknes . . . / Published for the Refreshing of Poor Souls, by an Eye and Ear-Witness of a Good Part Thereof, Henry Jesse*. London: Printed by Matthew Simmons for Henry Overton, and Hannah Allen, and are to be sold at their shops, 1647.

John of Salisbury. *Policraticus: Of the Frivolities of Courtiers and the Footprints of Philosophers*.

Cambridge Texts in the History of Political Thought. Translated by Cary J. Nederman. New York: Cambridge University Press, 1990.

Johnson, Edward. *Johnson's Wonder-Working Providence, 1628–1651*. Edited by J. Franklin Jameson. Original Narratives of Early American History. New York: C. Scribner's Sons, 1910.

Jones, Rufus Matthew, Isaac Sharpless, and Amelia M. Gummere. *The Quakers in the American Colonies*. London: Macmillan, 1923.

Julian. *The Works of the Emperor Julian*. Translated by Wilmer Cave Wright. The Loeb Classical Library 13, 29, 157. Cambridge: Harvard University Press, 1954.

Karlsen, Carol F. *The Devil in the Shape of a Woman: Witchcraft in Colonial New England*. New York: Norton, 1987.

Kassel, Rudolf, and Colin Austin. *Poetae Comici Graecii*. New York: W. de Gruyter, 1983.

Kelly, J. N. D. *Early Christian Doctrines*. 5th ed. San Francisco: Harper & Row, 1978.

Kettlewell, John. *A Compleat Collection of the Works of the Reverend and Learned John Kettlewell, B. D. Formerly Vicar of Coles-Hill in Warwick-Shire. In Two Volumes. The Several Treatises Printed from Copies Revis'd and Improv'd by the Author, a Little before His Death. . . . to which is Prefix'd, the Life of the Author. Wherein are Contained Many Remarkable Transactions of His Time; Compiled from the Collections of George Hickes, D. D. and Robert Nelson, Esq; and Compleated by a Friend of the Author at the Desire both of Dr. Hickes and Mr. Nelson. With an Appendix of Several Original Papers*. Vol. 1. London: Printed for D. Browne, A. Churchhill, J. Knapton, T. Horn, R. Knaplock, 1719.

Koehler, Lyle. "The Case of the American Jezebels: Anne Hutchinson and Female Agitation during the Years of Antinomian Turmoil, 1636–1640." *William and Mary Quarterly* 31, no. 1 (1974): 55–78.Koster, W. J. W. et al., eds. *Scholia in Aristophanem*, part I 1b, *Scholia vetera in Aristophanis Equites*. Edited by D. M. Jones. Groningen, Netherlands: Woltors Noordhoff, 1969.

Koster, W. J. W. et al., eds. *Scholia in Aristophanem*. Part III 1b, *Scholia Recentiora in Aristophanis Ranas*. Edited by M. Chantry. Groningen, Netherlands: Egbert Forsten, 2001.

Koster, W. J. W. et al., eds. *Scholia in Aristophanem*, part III 4b, *Scholia Recentiora in Plutum*. Edited by M. Chantry. Groningen, Netherlands: Egbert Forsten, 1996.

Lane Fox, Robin. *Pagans and Christians*. London: Viking, 1986.

Lawson, Deodat. *Christ's Fidelity the Only Shield Against Satans Malignity. Asserted in a Sermon Delivered at Salem-Village, the 24th of March, 1692. Being Lecture-Day There, and a Time of Public Examination, of Some Suspected for Witchcraft. By Deodat Lawson, Formerly Preacher of the Gospel There. [Six Lines of Scripture Texts]*. Printed by Benjamin Harris, bookseller Nicholas Buttolph, 1693.

Leigh, Edward. *A Systeme Or Body of Divinity Consisting of Ten Books: Wherein the Fundamentals and Main Grounds of Religion are Opened, the Contrary Errours Refuted, Most of the Controversies between Us, the Papists, Arminians, and Socinians Discussed and Handled, Several Scriptures Explained and Vindicated from Corrupt Glosses: A Work Seasonable for these Times, Wherein so Many Articles of our Faith are Questioned, and so Many Gross Errours Daily Published / by Edward Leigh*. London: Printed by A. M. for William Lee, 1654.

A Letter to a Member of Parliament in the Country, from His Friend in London, Relative to the Case of Admiral Byng: With some Original Papers and Letters which Passed during the Expedition. . . . London: J. Cooke, at the King's-Arms in Great-Turnstile, Holborn, 1756.

Love, Christopher. *The Penitent Pardoned a Treatise Wherein is Handled the Duty of Confession of Sin and the Priviledge of the Pardon of Sin: Together with a Discourse of Christs Ascension into Heaven and of His Coming again from Heaven: Wherein the Opinion of the Chiliasts is Considered and*

Solidly Confuted / being the Sum and Substance of Several Sermons Preached by that Faithful Servant of Christ, Mr. Christopher Love. . . . London: Printed for John Rothwell . . . and for Nathanael Brooks, 1657.

Lucian. *Lucian.* Vol. 7. Translated by M. D. MacLeod. Cambridge: Harvard University Press, 1969.

Luo, Zhufeng. "Han yu da ci dian bian ji wei yuan hui" and "Han yu da ci dian bian zuan chu." In *Hanyu Da Cidian.* 1st ban ed. Shanghai: Han yu da ci dian chu ban she, 1990.

Lyonnet, Stanislas, and Leopold Sabourin. *Sin, Redemption, and Sacrifice: A Biblical and Patristic Study.* Analecta Biblica 48. Rome: Biblical Institute, 1970.

Maclean, Jennifer K. Berenson. "Barabbas, the Scapegoat Ritual, and the Development of the Passion Narrative." *Harvard Theological Review* 100, no. 3 (2007): 309.

Mall, Thomas. *Truth Held Forth and Maintained According to the Testimony of the Holy Prophets, Christ and His Apostles Recorded in the Holy Scriptures with Some Account of the Judgments of the Lord Lately Inflicted upon New-England by Witchcraft: To which is Added, Something Concerning the Fall of Adam, His State in the Fall, and Way of Restoration to God again, with Many Other Weighty Things . . . / Written in True Love to the Souls of My Neighbours and all Men, which Includeth that Love to them and Myself, by Thomas Maule.* [New York]: Printed [by William Bradford], 1695.

Marseilles, Chambre du Conseil de l'Hôtel de Ville. *An Historical Account of the Plague at Marseilles. Giving a Particular Relation of all the Different Occurrences that Happen'd during the Visitation in that City. Publish'd by Authority at Paris, and Faithfully Translated from the Original French. By a Physician. To which is Added, a Letter from Monsier Pons, Physician of the Faculty of Montpelier, Wrote from Marseilles (while He Resided there by Order of the Regent) to Monsieur De Bon Chevalier, First President of the Court of Aids and Finances of Montpelier; Discovering the Nature and Cause of the Pestilence, its Symptoms, and the Methods and Medicines used for the Recovery of the Infected.* London: Printed for M. Billingsley under the Royal-Exchange; A. Dodd, without Temple-Bar, and J. Fox in Westminster-Hall, 1721.

Mather, Cotton. *Decennium Luctuosum an History of Remarkable Occurrences, in the Long War, which New-England Hath had with the Indian Salvages, from the Year, 1688. To the Year 1698. Faithfully Composed and Improved.* Boston: Printed by B. Green and J. Allen, for Samuel Phillips, at the brick shop near the Old-Meeting-House, 1699.

———. *Diary of Cotton Mather, 1681–1724.* Vols. 7–8. Boston: The Society, 1911.

———. *Magnalia Christi Americana: Or, the Ecclesiastical History of New-England, from its First Planting, in the Year 1620, Unto the Year of our Lord 1698.* . . . Hartford: S. Andrus & Son, 1853.

———. *Memorable Providences Relating to Witchcrafts and Possessions a Faithful Account of Many Wonderful and Surprising Things that have Befallen Several Bewitched and Possesed Person in New-England, Particularly a Narrative of the Marvellous Trouble and Releef Experienced by a Pious Family in Boston, Very Lately and Sadly Molested with Evil Spirits: Whereunto is Added a Discourse Delivered Unto a Congregation in Boston on the Occasion of that Illustrious Providence: As Also a Discourse Delivered Unto the Same Congregation on the Occasion of an Horrible Self-Murder Committed in the Town: With an Appendix in Vindication of a Chapter in a Late Book of Remarkable Providences from the Calumnies of a Quaker at Pen-Silvania / Written by Cotton Mather . . . and Recommended by the Ministers of Boston and Charleston.* Boston: by R. P., sold by Joseph Brunning at his Shop at the Corner of the Prison-Lane next the Exchange, 1689.

———. *The Wonders of the Invisible World Observations as Well Historical as Theological upon the Nature, the Number and the Operations of the Devils: Accompany'd with I. Some Accounts of the Greievous [sic] Molestations by Daemons and Witchcrafts . . . and the Trials of some Eminent Malefactors . . . II. Some Councils Directing a Due Improvement of the Terrible Things Lately Done by the Unusual and Amazing Range of Evil Spirits . . . III. Some Conjectures upon the Great Events*

Likely to Befall the World in General and New England in Particular . . . IV. A Short Narrative of a Late Outrage Committed by a Knot of Witches in Swedeland . . . V. The Devil Discovered, in a Brief Discourse upon those Temptations which are the More Ordinary Devices of the Wicked One / by Cotton Mather. Boston: Printed and sold by Benjamin Harris, 1693.

Maule, Thomas. *Nevv-England Pesecutors [sic] Mauled VVith their Own VVeapons Giving some Account of the Bloody Laws Made at Boston Against the Kings Subjects that Dissented from their Way of Worship: Together with a Brief Account of the Imprisonment and Tryal of Thomas Maule of Salem, for Publishing a Book Entituled Truth Held Forth and Maintained, &c. / by Tho. Philathes.* [New York: William Bradford, 1697].

———. *Truth Held Forth and Maintained According to the Testimony of the Holy Prophets, Christ and His Apostles Recorded in the Holy Scriptures with some Account of the Judgments of the Lord Lately Inflicted upon New-England by Witchcraft: To which is Added, Something Concerning the Fall of Adam, His State in the Fall, and Way of Restoration to God again, with Many Other Weighty Things . . . / Written in True Love to the Souls of My Neighbours and all Men, which Includeth that Love to them and Myself, by Thomas Maule.* [New York]: Printed [by William Bradford], 1695.

McLean, B. Hudson. "The Cursed Christ: Mediterranean Expulsion Rituals and Pauline Soteriology," supplement, *Journal for the Study of the New Testament* 126. Sheffield, England: Sheffield Academic Press, 1996.

McLean, Bradley. "On the Revision of Scapegoat Terminology." *Numen* 37, no. 2 (1990): 168–173.

McNeill, John Thomas, and Helena M. Gamer. *Medieval Handbooks of Penance: A Translation of the Principal "Libri Poenitentiales" and Selections from Related Documents.* Records of Western Civilization. New York: Columbia University Press, 1990.

Memoirs of the Lord Viscount Dundee, the Highland-Clans, and the Massacre of Glenco: With an Account of Dundee's Officers, After they Went to France. By an Officer of the Army. London, 1711.

Milgrom, Jacob. *Leviticus: A Book of Ritual and Ethics; A Continental Commentary.* Continental Commentaries. Minneapolis: Fortress Press, 2004.

———. *Leviticus 1–16: A New Translation with Introduction and Commentary.* The Anchor Bible. Vol. 3. New York: Doubleday, 1991.

Miller, Perry. *The New England Mind: The Seventeenth Century.* Cambridge: Harvard University Press, 1963.

The Museum, Or, the Literary and Historical Register, vol. 1. London: Printed for R. Dodsley, 1746.

Myles, Anne G. "From Monster to Martyr: Re-presenting Mary Dyer." *Early American Literature* 36, no. 1 (2001): 1–30.

Neusner, Jacob. *The Mishnah: A New Translation.* New Haven, CT: Yale University Press, 1988.

Nicolson, William. *A Sermon Preach'd before the Rt Honble the Lords . . . in the Collegiate Church of Westminster, on Saturday, the Thirtieth Day of January, MDCCII. Being The Anniversary of the Martyrdom of King Charles the First. by William Lord Bishop of Carlile.* London: Printed by Edw. Jones for Tim. Child at the White-Hart at the West-End of St. Paul's Church-yard, 1703.

Norden, John. *A Christian Familiar Comfort and Incouragement Vnto all English Subiects, Not to Dismaie at the Spanish Threats Whereunto is Added an Admonition to all English Papists, Who Openly Or Couertly Couet a Change. With Requisite Praiers to Almightie God for the Preseruation of our Queene and Countrie. by the most Vnworthie I. N.* London: [Printed by T. Scarlet and J. Orwin] for J. B[rome], 1596.

Norton, David. *A History of the English Bible as Literature.* New York: Cambridge University Press, 2000.

Norton, Humphrey, John Copeland, and John Rous. *New-England's Ensigne it being the Account of*

Cruelty, the Professors Pride, and the Articles of their Faith, Signified in Characters Written in Blood, Wickedly Begun, Barbarously Continued, and Inhumanly Finished (so Far as they have Gone) by the Present Power of Darkness Possest in the Priests and Rulers in New-England . . . : This being an Account of the Sufferings Sustained by us in New-England (with the Dutch) the Most Part of it in these Two Last Yeers, 1657, 1658: With a Letter to Iohn Indicot, Iohn Norton, Governor, and Chief Priest of Boston, and Another to the Town of Boston: Also, the Several Late Conditions of a Friend upon the Road-Iland, before, in, and After Distraction: With Some Quaeries Unto all Sorts of People, Who Want that which we have, &c. / VVritten at Sea, by Us Whom the VVicked in Scorn Calls Quakers, in the Second Month of the Yeer 1659; This being a Confirmation of so Much as Francis Howgill Truly Published in His Book Titled, the Popish Inquisition Newly Erected in New-England, &c. London: Printed by T. L. for G. Calvert at the Black-Spread Eagle neer the West-end of Pauls, 1659.

Norton, John. *The Heart of New-England Rent at the Blasphemies of the Present Generation. Or a Brief Tractate, Concerning the Doctrine of the Quakers, Demonstrating the Destructive Nature Thereof, to Religion, the Churches, and the State; with Consideration of the Remedy Against it. Occasional Satisfaction to Objections, and Confirmation of the Contrary Truth. / by John Norton, Teacher of the Church [of] Christ at Boston. Who was Appointed Thereunto, by the Order of the General Court.* London: Printed by John Allen at the Rising-Sunne in St. Pauls Church-yard, 1660.

Oates, Whitney Jennings, and Eugene O'Neill Jr., eds. *The Complete Greek Drama: All the Extant Tragedies of Aeschylus, Sophocles and Euripides, and the Comedies of Aristophanes and Menander, in a Variety of Translations.* New York: Random House, 1938.

Origen. *Homilies on Joshua.* Edited by Cynthia White. Translated by Barbara J. Bruce. The Fathers of the Church: A New Translation 105. Washington, DC: Catholic University of America Press, 2002.

———. *Homilies on Leviticus: 1–16.* Translated by Gary Wayne Barkley. The Fathers of the Church: A New Translation 83. Washington, DC: Catholic University of America Press, 1990.

Oughourlian, Jean-Michel, and Guy Lefort. "Psychotic Structure and Girard's Doubles." *Diacritics* 8, no. 1 (1978): 72–74.

Owen, John. *Of Communion with God the Father, Sonne, and Holy Ghost, each Person Distinctly in Love, Grace, and Consolation, Or, the Saints Fellowship with the Father, Sonne, and Holy Ghost, Unfolded by John Owen.* Oxford: Printed by A. Lichfield . . . for Tho. Robinson, 1657.

Paget, James Carleton. "The Epistle of Barnabas." *Expository Times* 117, no. 11 (2006): 441.

Patrologia Cursus Completus. Series Graeca. 161 vols. Paris, 1857–1866.

Patrologia Cursus Completus. Series Latina. 221 vols. Paris, 1841–1864.

Pelikan, Jaroslav. *The Christian Tradition: A History of the Development of Doctrine.* 5 vols. Chicago: University of Chicago Press, 1971–1989.

Pestana, Carla Gardina. "The Quaker Executions as Myth and History." *Journal of American History* 80, no. 2 (1993): 441–469.

Pinker, Aron. "A Goat to Go to Azazel." *Journal of Hebrew Scriptures* 7 (2007): 6–12.

Plutarch. *Plutarch's Lives. with an English Translation by Bernadotte Perrin.* Translated by Bernadotte Perrin. Cambridge, MA: Harvard University Press, 1914.

Pownall, Nathaniel, and Giles Fletcher. *The Young Divines Apologie for His Continuance in the Vniuersitie with Certaine Meditations, Ritten by Nathaniel Povvnoll, Late Student of Christ-Church in Oxford.* [London]: Printed by Cantrell Legge printer to the Vniuersitie of Cambridge, and are to be sold in Pauls Churchyard by Matthevv Lovvnes at the signe of the Bishops head, 1612.

Preston, John. *The Golden Scepter Held Forth to the Humble VVith the Churches Dignitie by Her Marriage. And the Churches Dutie in Her Carriage. In Three Treatises. The Former Delivered in*

Sundry Sermons in Cambridge, for the Weekely Fasts, 1625. The Two Latter in Lincolnes Inne. By the Late Learned and Reverend Divine, Iohn Preston, Dr. in Divinity, Chaplaine in Ordinary to His Maiesty, Mr. of Emanuel Colledge in Cambridge, and Somtime Preacher at Lincolnes Inne. With Thomas Goodwin and George Glover. London: Printed by R. Badger for N. Bourne at the Royall Exchange, and R. Harford at the gilt Bible in Queenes-head Alley in Pater-noster Row, and by F. Eglesfield at the Marigold in Pauls Church-yard, 1638.

The Prophecies, and Predictions, for London's Deliverance with the Conjunction, Effects, and Influences of the Superiour Planets, the Causes Thereof, and the Probability of the Happy Abatement of the Present Dismal Pestilence, (According to Natural Causes the Ti[m]e when, and the We[e]ks and Moneths Fore-Told, when the City of Iondon [sic] *Wil[l] be Freed and Acquitted from the Violent Raging of this Destructive Enemy. The Appearance of which Great Pest was Predicted by the Learned Mr. Lilly. Mr. Booker, Mr. Gadbury, Mr. Trigge, and Mr. Andrews.* [London]: Printed for Tho. Brooks, and are to be sold near the Royal Exchange, 1665.

Proust, Marcel, . *In Search of Lost Time.* Rev. ed. Translated by C. K. Scott-Moncrieff, Terence Kilmartin, D. J. Enright, and Joanna Kilmartin. New York: Modern Library, 1993.

Purchas, Samuel. *Purchas His Pilgrimage. Or Relations of the Vvorld and the Religions Obserued in all Ages and Places Discouered, from the Creation Vnto this Present in Foure Partes. This First Containeth a Theologicall and Geographicall Historie of Asia, Africa, and America, with the Ilands Adiacent. Declaring the Ancient Religions before the Floud . . . with Briefe Descriptions of the Countries, Nations, States, Discoueries, Priuate and Publike Customes, and the Most Remarkable Rarities of Nature, Or Humane Industrie, in the Same. By Samuel Purchas, Minister at Estwood in Essex.* London: Printed by William Stansby for Henrie Fetherstone, and are to be sold at his shoppe in Pauls Church-yard at the signe of the Rose, 1613.

Quinn, Philip L. "Aquinas on Atonement." In *Trinity, Incarnation, and Atonement: Philosophocal and Theological Essays,* vol. 1, edited by Ronald Jay Feenstra and Cornelius Plantinga. Notre Dame, IN: University of Notre Dame Press, 1989.

Raleigh, Walter. *Reliquiae Raleighanae being Discourses and Sermons on several Subjects / by the Reverend Dr. Walter Raleigh.* London: Printed by J. Macock for Joseph Hindmarsh, 1679.

Raynal, Abbe. *A Philosophical and Political History of the Settlements and Trade of the Europeans in the East and West Indies. Revised, Augmented, and Published, in Ten Volumes, by the Abbé Raynal. Newly Translated from the French, by J. O. Justamond, F.R.S. with a New Set of Maps Adapted to the Work, an a Copious Index. in Eight Volumes. . . .* Vol. 1. London, 1783.

Remarks on Lesley's Two Letters from Bar Le Duc; The First, to a High-Flying Member of the Last Parliament. The Second to the Lord Bishop of Salisbury. Remarks also, on Two Papers of the Pretender's, Privately Handed About by the Jacobites. London: Printed for J. Roberts, near the Oxford-Arms in Warwick-Lane, 1715.

Rendtorff, Rolf, Robert A. Kugler, and Sarah Smith Bartel. *The Book of Leviticus: Composition and Reception.* Formation and Interpretation of Old Testament Literature 3. Boston: Brill, 2003.

Reynolds, Edward. *Israels Prayer in Time of Trouble with Gods Gracious Answer Thereunto, Or, an Explication of the 14th Chapter of the Prophet Hosea in Seven Sermons Preached upon so Many Days of Solemn Humiliation / by Edward Reynolds.* London: Printed by Thomas Newcomb for Robert Bostock, 1645 [1649].

Rivers, Christopher. "Safe Sex: The Prophylactic Walls of the Cloister in the French Libertine Convent Novel of the Eighteenth Century." *Journal of the History of Sexuality* 5, no. 3 (1995): 381–402.

Roberts, Alexander, James Donaldson, and A. Cleveland Coxe. *The Ante-Nicene Fathers: Translations of the Writings of the Fathers Down to A.D. 325.* Reprint of the Edinburgh ed. Vol. 4. Grand Rapids, MI: Eerdmanns, 1978.

Roberts, Alexander, James Donaldson, A. Cleveland Coxe, Allan Menzies, Ernest Cushing Richardson, and Bernhard Pick. *The Ante-Nicene Fathers: Translations of the Writings of the Fathers Down to A.D. 325.* Reprint of the Edinburgh ed. Vol. 1. Grand Rapids, MI: Eerdmanns, 1986.

Roberts, Francis. *Mysterium & Medulla Bibliorum the Mysterie and Marrow of the Bible, Viz. God's Covenant with Man in the First Adam before the Fall, and in the Last Adam, Iesvs Christ, After the Fall, from the Beginning to the End of the World: Unfolded & Illustrated in Positive Aphorisms & their Explanation . . . / by Francis Roberts.* London: Printed by R. W. for George Calvert, 1657.

Schaff, Philip. *A Select Library of the Nicene and Post-Nicene Fathers of the Christian Church: First Series.* Grand Rapids, MI: Eerdmanns, 1978.

Schaff, Philip, and Henry Wace. *A Select Library of Nicene and Post-Nicene Fathers of the Christian Church: Second Series.* Grand Rapids, MI: Eerdmanns, 1978.

Schama, Simon. *A History of Britain: The British Wars 1603–1776.* London: BBC, 2001.

———. *A History of Britain: At the Edge of the World? 3000 B.C.–A.D. 1603.* New York: Hyperion, 2000.

A Secret History of One Year. London: Sold by A. Dodd at the Peacock, without Temple-Bar, 1714.

A Sermon Preached Towards the Latter End of the Last Century, on the Anniversary Thanksgiving Day for Putting an End to the Grreat [Sic] Rebellion, by the Restitution of the King and Royal Family, and the Restoration of the Government, in the Church and State, After Many Years Interruption. Strangers have Devoured You. Cambridge, 1715.

Silverman, Kenneth. *The Life and Times of Cotton Mather.* New York: Harper & Row, 1984.

Skarsaune, Oskar, ed. *The Proof from Prophecy: A Study in Justin Martyr's Proof-Text Tradition; Text-Type, Provenance, Theological Profile.* Supplements to Novum Testamentum 56. Leiden, Netherlands: E. J. Brill, 1987.

Smollett, Tobias. *The History and Adventures of an Atom. in Two Volumes. . . .* Vol. 1. Dublin, 1769.

———. *The History of England: From the Revolution to the Death of George the Second. (Designed as a Continuation of Mr. Hume's History.) In Five Volumes.* A new ed. London: Printed for T. Cadell, and R. Baldwin, 1790.

Southey, Robert. *Southey's Common-Place Book,* series 2. Edited by John Wood Warter. London: Longman, Brown, Green and Longmans, 1850.

Sperling, Harry, Maurice Simon, and Paul P. Levertoff. *The Zohar.* 2nd ed. New York: Soncino Press, 1984.

Staniforth, Maxwell, trans. *Early Christian Writings: The Apostolic Fathers.* New York: Dorset Press, 1986.

Steward, Richard. *Catholique Divinity: Or, the Most Solid and Sententious Expressions of the Primitive Doctors of the Church. With Other Ecclesiastical, and Civil Authors: Dilated upon, and Fitted to the Explication of the Most Doctrinal Texts of Scripture, in a Choice Way Both for the Matter, and the Language; And Very Useful for the Pulpit, and these Times. / by Dr. Stuart, Dean of St. Pauls, Afterwards Dean of Westminster, and Clerk of the Closet to the Late K. Charles.* Edited by H. M. London: Printed for H. M. and are to bee sold by Timo. Smart at his shop in the Great Old-Bayly near the Sessions-house, 1657.

Stökl Ben Ezra, Daniel. *The Impact of Yom Kippur on Early Christianity: The Day of Atonement from Second Temple Judaism to the Fifth Century.* Wissenschaftliche Untersuchungen Zum Neuen Testament 163. Tübingen, Germany: Mohr Siebeck, 2003.

Stoughton, John. *XI. Choice Sermons Preached upon Selected Occasions, in Cambridge. Viz. I. The Preachers Dignity, and Duty: In Five Sermons, upon 2. Corinth. 5. 20. II. Christ Crucified, the Tree of Life: In Six Sermons, on 1. Corinth. 2. 2. by John Stoughton, Doctor in Divinity, Sometimes Fellow of Immanuel Colledge in Cambridge, Late Preacher of Aldermanburie, London. According to the Originall Copie, which was Left Perfected by the Authour before His Death.* Edited by Anthony Burgess. London: Printed by R. B[adger] for Iohn Bellamie, Henry Overton, Iohn Rothwell, and Ralph Smith, 1640.

Stradling, George. *Sermons and Discourses upon several Occasions by G. Stradling . . . ; Together with an Account of the Author.* With James Harrington. London: Printed by J. H. for Thomas Bennet, 1692.

Stump, Eleonore. *Aquinas.* Arguments of the Philosophers. New York: Routledge, 2003.

Taylor, Thomas. *Iaphets First Publique Perswasion into Sems Tents, Or, Peters Sermon which was the First Generall Calling of the Gentiles Preached before Cornelius / Expounded in Cambridge by Thomas Taylor, and Now Published for the Further Use of the Church of God.* [Cambridge?]: Printed by Cantrell Legge, printer to the Vniversitie of Cambridge, and are to be sold by Raph Mab at the signe of the Angel in Pauls Churchyard, 1612.

Telltruth, Stentor. *The Herald; Or, Patriot Proclaimer. being a Collection of Periodical Essays; on Government, Commerce, Publick Credit, Publick Debts, Publick Virtue, Publick Honour, on our National Disposition and Dangers, on Theatrical Management, and Other Interesting Subjects.* London: Printed for J. Wilkie, behind the Chapter-House, in St. Paul's Church-Yard, 1757.

Tertullian. *Treatises on Penance: On Penitence and on Purity.* Translated by William P. Le Saint. Ancient Christian Writers: The Works of the Fathers in Translation 28. Westminster, MD: Newman Press, 1959.

Theodoret. *Eranistes.* Translated by Gérard H. Ettlinger. Fathers of the Church 106. Washington, DC: Catholic University of America Press, 2003.

Tolles, Frederick B. "A Quaker's Curse: Humphrey Norton to John Endecott, 1658." *Huntington Library Quarterly* 14, no. 4 (1951): 415–421.

Trapp, John. *A Commentary Or Exposition upon the Four Evangelists, and the Acts of the Apostles: Wherein the Text is Explained, some Controversies are Discussed, Divers Common Places are Handled, and Many Remarkable Matters Hinted, that had by Former Interpreters been Pretermitted. Besides, Divers Other Texts of Scripture which Occasionally Occur are Fully Opened, and the Whole so Intermixed with Pertinent Histories, as Will Yeeld both Pleasure and Profit to the Judicious Reader. / by John Trapp M. A. Pastour of Weston upon Avon in Gloucestershire.* London: Printed by A. M. for John Bellamie, at the sign of the three golden-Lions near the Royall-Exchange, 1647.

Trenchard, John. *Cato's Letters: Or, Essays on Liberty, Civil and Religious, and Other Important Subjects. In Four Volumes.* 6th ed. Vol. 1. London: Printed for W. Wilkins, T. Woodward, J. Walthoe, and J. Peele, 1755.

Tucker, Bruce. "The Reinvention of New England, 1691–1770." *New England Quarterly* 59, no. 3 (1986): 315–340.

Tutchin, John. *A New Martyrology, Or, the Bloody Assizes Now Exactly Methodizing in One Volume Comprehending a Compleat History of the Lives, Actions, Trials, Sufferings, Dying Speeches, Letters, and Prayers of all those Eminent Protestants Who Fell in the West of England and Elsewhere from the Year 1678 . . . : With an Alphabetical Table . . . / Written by Thomas Pitts.* London: Printed (according to the original copies) for John Dunton, 1693.

Tyndale, William. *The Pentateuch.* Malborow in the lande of Hesse [i.e. Antwerp]: By me Hans Luft [i.e. Johan Hoochstraten], 1530.

van Herwaarden, J. *Between Saint James and Erasmus: Studies in Late-Medieval Religious Life; Devotion and Pilgrimage in the Netherlands.* Studies in Medieval and Reformation Thought 97. Boston: Brill, 2003.

Voltaire, *Collection Complette des Oeuvres de Mr. de V****. Vol. 13. Geneva, 1771.

Voltaire. *Philosophical Letters: Letters Concerning the English Nation.* Translated by Ernest Dilworth. Mineola, NY: Dover, 2003.

Walkington, Thomas. *Rabboni Mary Magdalens Teares, of Sorrow, Solace. The One for Her Lord being Lost. The Other for Him being Found. In Way of Questioning. Wondring. Reioycing. . . . Preached at S. Pauls Crosse, After the Rehearsall, and Newly Reuised and Enlarged: By Thomas Walkington, Doctor in Diuinity, and Minister of the Word at Fulham.* London: Printed by Edw. Griffin, for Richard Whitakers, and are to bee sold in Pauls Church-yard at the signe of the Kings Head, 1620.

Wallace, Dewey D., Jr. "Puritan and Anglican: The Interpretation of Christ's Descent into Hell in Elizabethan Theology." *Archiv Für Reformationsgeschichte* 69 (1978): 248–286.

Ward, Edward. *The Pleasures of Matrimony, Intermix'd with Variety of Merry and Delightful Stories. Containing the Charms and Contentments of Wooing and Wedlock, in All its Enjoyments, Recreations, and Divertisements.* London: Printed for H. Rhodes at the Star, the corner of Bride-lane, in Fleetstreet, 1703.

Weld, Thomas. Preface to *A Short Story of the Rise, Reign, and Ruin of the Antinomians Familists & Libertines that Infected the Churches of Nevv-England and How They Were Confuted by the Assembly of Ministers There, as also of the Magistrates Proceedings in Court Against Them: Together with Gods Strange and Remarkable Judgements from Heaven upon Some of the Chief Fomenters of These Opinions, and the Lamentable Death of Ms. Hutchison: Very Fit for these Times, Here Being the Same Errours Amongst Us and Acted by the Same Spirit / Published at the Instant Request of Sundry, by One That Was an Eye and Eare-Witnesse of the Carriage of Matters There*, by John Winthrop. London: Printed for Ralph Smith . . . , 1644.

Wenham, Gordon J. *The Book of Leviticus.* The New International Commentary on the Old Testament 3. Grand Rapids, MI: Eerdmans, 1979.

Wheelwright, John. *Mercurius Americanus, Mr. Welds His Antitype, Or, Massachusetts Great Apologie Examined, Being Observations upon a Paper Styled, A Short Story of the Rise, Reign, and Ruine of the Familists, Libertines, &c. which Infected the Churches of New-England, &c. Wherein Some Parties Therein Concerned are Vindicated, and the Truth Generally Cleared. By John Wheelvvright Junior. Philalethes.* London: Printed, and are to be sold at the Bull near the Castle-Tavern in Cornhill, 1645.

Wilken, Robert L. "The Jews and Christian Apologetics After Theodosius I Cunctos Populos." *Harvard Theological Review* 73, nos. 3–4 (1980): 451–471.

William of Auvergne. *Guilielmi Alverni Episcopi Parisiensis, Mathematici Perfectissimi, Eximii Philosophi, Ac Theologi Praestantissimi, Opera Omnia, Quae Hactenus Reperiri Potuerunt, Reconditissimam Rerum Humanarum, Ac Divinarum Doctrinam Abundè Complectentia, Ac Proinde Bonarum Artium Ac Scientiarum Studiosis, Maximè Verò Theologis, Ac Divini Verbi Concionatoribus Apprimè Necessaria: Nunc Demùm in Hac Novissima Editione Ab Innumeris Errorum Chiliadibus Expurgata, Instaurata, Elucidata, Atque Sermonibus & Variis Tractatibus Aucta Ex m.Ss. Codd. Ut Et Praefationibus Ad Lectorem Apertius Intelligetur: Quorum Catalogum Proxima Post Praefationes Pagina Indicabit Cum Indicibus Locupletissimis Rerum Notabilium.* Orléans: ex typographia F. Hotot; London: apud Robertum Scott, bibliopolam, 1674.

Winthrop, John. *A Short Story of the Rise, Reign, and Ruin of the Antinomians, Familists, and Libertines that Infected the Churches of New-England and How They Were Confuted by the Assembly of Ministers There as also of the Magistrates Proceedings in Court Against Them: Together with God's Strange Remarkable Judgements from Heaven upon Some of the Chief Fomenters of These Opinions:*

And the Lamentable Death of Mrs. Hutchison: Very Fit for These Times, Here Being the Same Errors Amongst Us, and Acted by the Same Spirit: Published at the Instant Request of Sundry, by One That Was an Eye and Ear-Witness of the Carriage of Matters There. London: Printed for Ralph Smith, 1644.

Winthrop, John. *The Journal of John Winthrop, 1630–1649.* Edited by Richard S. Dunn, James Savage, and Laetitia Yeandle. The John Harvard Library. Cambridge: Harvard University Press, 1996.

Winthrop, John. *Winthrop's Journal: "History of New England," 1630–1649.* Edited by James Kendall Hosmer. Original Narratives of Early American History. New York: C. Scribner's Sons, 1908.

Wright, David P. *The Disposal of Impurity: Elimination Rites in the Bible and in Hittite and Mesopotamian Literature.* Society of Biblical Literature Dissertation Series 101. Atlanta, GA: Scholars Press, 1987.

———. "The Gesture of Hand Placement in the Hebrew Bible and in Hittite Literature." *Journal of the American Oriental Society* 106 (1986): 433–446.

Zatelli, Ida. "The Origin of the Biblical Scapegoat Ritual: The Evidence of Two Eblaite Texts." *Vetus Testamentum* 48, no. 2 (1998): 254–263.

Zodhiates, Spiros. *The Hebrew-Greek Key Study Bible: King James Version, the Old Testament, the New Testament; Zodhiates' Original and Complete System of Bible Study.* Chattanooga, TN: AMG Publishers, 1984.